Referential and Relational Discourse Coherence in Adults and Children

Studies on Language Acquisition

―――
Editor
Peter Jordens

Volume 53

Referential and Relational Discourse Coherence in Adults and Children

Edited by
Natalia Gagarina, Renate Musan

DE GRUYTER
MOUTON

ISBN 978-1-5015-2706-7
e-ISBN (PDF) 978-1-5015-1015-1
e-ISBN (EPUB) 978-1-5015-0999-5
ISSN 1861-4248

Library of Congress Control Number: 2020931603

Bibliographic information published by the Deutsche Nationalbibliothek
The Deutsche Nationalbibliothek lists this publication in the Deutsche Nationalbibliografie;
detailed bibliographic data are available on the Internet at http://dnb.dnb.de.

© 2021 De Gruyter Inc., Boston/Berlin
This volume is text- and page-identical with the hardback published in 2020.
Typesetting: Amelie Lohmann
Printing and binding: CPI books GmbH, Leck

www.degruyter.com

Contents

Natalia Gagarina and Renate Musan
Introduction —— 1

Part 1: Relational coherence

Angelika Becker, Valentina Cristante and Renate Musan
The comprehension of coherence relations in expository texts at the age of 10 and 12 —— 11

Jacqueline Evers-Vermeul
Short sentences, easy to read? Effects of connectives and layout on text comprehension by beginning readers —— 41

Henning Czech
Explicit coherence relations in children's and adults' spoken narratives: the importance of *und* for the acquisition of German connectives —— 57

Part 2: Referential coherence

Natalia Gagarina, Julia Lomako, Elizabeth Stadtmiller and Katrin Lindner
Text organization in typically developing bilinguals and bilinguals at risk of DLD: what is different and how language independent is it? —— 85

Johannes Gerwien and Hana Klages
Referential coherence: Children's understanding of pronoun anaphora. Insights from mono- and bilingual language acquisition —— 105

Sarah Schimke, Saveria Colonna and Maya Hickmann
Reference in French and German: a developmental perspective —— 139

Maria Voeikova and Sofia Krasnoshchkova
The use of pronouns as a developmental factor in early Russian language acquisition —— 171

Index —— 207

Natalia Gagarina and Renate Musan
Introduction

This volume unites contributions dealing with different aspects of text or, in a wider sense – discourse – coherence. Text or discourse coherence is a debated notion which is treated differently not only by various domains of linguistics, such as text linguistics or psycholinguistics, but also within the individual domains of linguistics. Generally, coherence captures the observation that all parts of a sequence of sentences must be connected among each other contentwise in order to be a text intuitively, whereby a text may be long or short, spoken or written.

Coherence exists on various levels. A coherent text has, for instance, a theme which ties the parts of the text together, but beyond this there are other aspects of coherence that have to do with connectedness of parts of texts. For the work presented in this volume, the distinction between connectedness on the relational level and connectedness on the referential level is important.

Relational coherence deals with the observation that individual sentences and larger parts of a coherent text are related to each other by so-called coherence relations. Depending on theoretical frameworks, inventories and categorizations of coherence, relations differ (see, for instance, Lascarides and Asher's Segmented Discourse Representation Theory 2007; Mann and Thompson's Rhetorical Structure Theory 1988; or Sanders, Spooren and Noordman's and Sanders and Spooren's Cognitive Approach 1992, 2010). A certain set of coherence relations, however, appears consistently across relevant publications. Among them are the relations of additive combination, temporal sequence, cause, and contrast. Consequently, these relations are especially often the topic of empirical research studies on text coherence. Coherence relations may be explicitly marked by connectives in a text, but they can also remain implicit and then must be worked out by a text recipient. Text producers should be aware of this if they want their intentions to be captured correctly.

Note: The work on the volume and this paper by Natalia Gagarina was supported by the German Federal Ministry of Education and Research (BMBF) Grant No. 01UG1411.

Natalia Gagarina, Leibniz Zentrum Allgemeine Sprachwissenschaft (ZAS), Schützenstraße 18, 10117 Berlin, email: gagarina@leibniz-zas.de
Renate Musan, University of Osnabrück, Neuer Graben 40, 49074 Osnabrück, email: rmusan@uni-osnabrueck.de

https://doi.org/10.1515/9781501510151-001

Referential coherence deals with the fact that people, things, situations or times are often referred to in several sentences of a text. Such re-appearances create a network of referential relationships across the text. There are specific linguistic means of constructing repeated reference to a single discourse referent or a chain. One such device, for instance, is repeating an expression, but substitutions by other expressions can also be used. A systematic means of expressing repeated reference to a certain discourse referent is the use of pronouns.[1]

Although relational and referential coherence function quite differently, ultimately, they are partners. As has often been observed, for instance, clauses related by causality influence the choice of referents for subject pronouns in these constructions.

Both relational and referential coherence have been investigated in various contexts under various perspectives: in written and in spoken discourse, on a local text, or the microstructure level, and on a global text, or macrostructural level, in comprehension and in production, in first languages and in second languages, under a systematic perspective and under a developmental perspective and with regard to didactic or diagnostic purposes, theoretically and experimentally with various methodological designs.

Given the large amount of questions and contexts, text coherence can be investigated with, it is not surprising that there has been much research in the field. Relational and referential coherence have also been viewed together. For example, Kehler (2002) looks at both types of coherence in connection with syntactic phenomena; the volume edited by Sanders et al. (2001) connects relational and referential coherence by presenting studies on text coherence in different contexts; and work on implicit causality directly combines them by investigating how causal coherence relations trigger reference preferences for subject pronouns in causal constructions (Bott and Solstad 2014). The present volume follows this line; it aims to combine different perspectives and show the breadth of the field as well as interconnections. The contributions focus, however, on very recent studies concerning developmental issues; ultimately these issues are not only of theoretical but also of particular practical importance.

The ability to produce and comprehend coherent texts (i.e. narrative ability or narrative skills), whether they are oral or written, is essential for human communication from early childhood through adulthood and indispensable for adequate functioning in society at all ages. The understanding of how texts, or, specifically, narrative texts and their episodic structure are organized and how the components within an episode are connected can be said to be of more universal

---

[1] For more information on text coherence see, for instance, Sanders and Spooren (2010).

nature and to partially reflect our cognitive skills. Generally, if a bilingual narrator knows how to tell a story s/he will be able to do it in both languages. Of course, a certain amount of language (proficiency) is necessary thereby. It is still unknown, however, exactly how much language proficiency is necessary to produce or comprehend a well-formed comprehensive oral or written text.

In typically developing children, oral narrative skills start to develop in early childhood, starting from age 3 to 4 (e.g. Berman and Slobin 1994; Peterson and McCabe 1991; Trabasso and Rodkin 1994; Gagarina et al. 2015), when the basics of grammar have already been acquired. These early oral narrative skills are the first predictors of later literacy, e.g., reading comprehension skills (Bliss, McCabe and Miranda 1998; McCabe 1996) and they build the fundament for later aptitude to produce and comprehend more complex written texts. Thus, the knowledge of their early development is fundamental for forecasting school achievements as well as for the diagnosis of developmental language disorders or specific language impairment (DLD or SLI; e.g. Altman, Armon-Lotem, Fichman and Walters 2016; Boerma, Leseman, Timmermeister, Wijnen and Blom 2016; Tsimpli, Peristeri and Andreou 2016).

In school, comprehension and production of written texts is a part of the curriculum from first grade onwards. Children deal with the comprehension of written texts through their school career in all subjects, including languages, mathematics, physics, biology, etc. Thus, the ability to comprehend texts is fundamental for achievements in these subjects. There have been few studies investigating how children comprehend school texts and how/whether they rely on coherence cues in the texts. Also, little is known on the development of children's ability to rely on these coherence cues. Which role, generally, do coherence cues play in the comprehension of texts and how one can improve/optimize children's comprehension of texts' content? How could the texts in school curricula – as far as the relational and referential cues are concerned – be optimized for better comprehension? How can oral text production be used to better differentiate children with developmental language disorders (DLD), in order to offer them more suitable support? And, finally, to what extent is the macrostructure of well-formed comprehensible oral texts language-(in)dependent?

As two intertwined partners creating well-formed comprehensive texts, referential and relational coherence are discussed from various perspectives in the papers selected for this volume. They go back to two workshops on "Text coherence und text comprehension of children and adults" at the Annual Conference of the German Linguistic Society, 23.-25.02.2011, at the University of Göttingen, and on "Cohesion and coherence in text comprehension and text production", 26.-27.09.2013, at the University of Osnabrück. The main aim of these conferences was to provide a forum for researchers studying competence related and acquisition related aspects of text coherence. Given these perspectives on text coherence, the studies in this volume discuss theoretical issues on the basis of various empirical findings. They come from different experimental designs, make use of various methods of investigation and present recent research in the field.

As pointed out above, it is important to investigate how these competences develop. Becker et al. (this volume) follow this question with regard to the comprehension of relational coherence in written texts, while Czech (this volume) investigates the development with regard to spoken language.

As Schimke et al. (this volume) and Voiekova and Krasnoshchekova (this volume) show, there seem to be cross-linguistic differences with regard to the development of text constructions. There may, moreover, be crucial differences between the use and comprehension in a second language in contrast to first language. How does this ability develop in bilingual children and does child second language acquisition differ from first language acquisition (in monolinguals and bilinguals)? Gerwien and Klages (this volume) pursue similar questions. More specifically, Gagarina et al. (this volume) are concerned with the question of how language-(in)dependent narrative skills in children are and whether the association between oral narratives and language proficiency is manifested differently in a telling vs. retelling task. They also address the question of differentiation within a bilingual population between typically developing bilingual children and those at risk of DLD, using narrative production tasks.

Having to do with developmental questions, it is not surprising that results in the field of study may apply to the improvement of school text books (Evers-Vermeul, this volume), as well as to the support of comprehension with regard to coherence relations in second language acquisition. Thus, the theoretical issues and empirical findings discussed in this volume are of importance not only for theoretical linguistics, but also have broad potential for practical implications.

The volume is organized as follows: The first part introduces four contributions dealing with relational coherence and the second part contains four chapters on referential coherence. A more detailed description of the contributions is given below.

Part 1: Relational coherence

The volume starts with three contributions on comprehension and production of connectives in German. The first contribution is by Becker et al. on the comprehension of coherence relations in primary school children. In particular, they investigate how children construct additive, causal, contrastive, and temporal relations and ask whether the children's comprehension of texts is positively influenced by the explicit use of connectives. The skills Becker et al. examine are crucial for the comprehension of texts. Thus, they are fundamental for school success and in the long term for lifelong achievements in society, since comprehension of texts is a basis for successful performance in all school subjects and generally for effective communication. The authors propose a developmental path starting with the acquisition of causal relations, followed by adversative relations. During this period, the comprehension of additive and temporal anteriority relations remains low. They are presumably acquired properly later. The authors also observe that weak readers do not profit from the presence of connectives in school texts, only fluent readers make an advantage thereof.

The second study, by Jacqueline Evers-Vermeul, examines the effects of connective use and of layout on text comprehension by beginning readers, i.e. seven- and eight-year-old children. The author focuses on *because* and *but* and shows children's ability to already profit from the use of these connectives at an early age. The layout, which presents sentences with line breaks, seems not to have an impact on text comprehension, but is perceived by children as easier. This finding is explained from two perspectives: first, children are still in the process of acquiring reading techniques and the line break is neither facilitating nor impeding text comprehension; second, children might not understand the *'visual message'* of the extra line break.

The third contribution, by Henning Czech, scrutinizes the production of connectives in three age groups of children aged three, five and nine and in young adults aged 20 with the polysemous German connective *und* 'and' compared with its English equivalent. The author targets the distribution of connectives in terms of their syntactic classes and analyses the coherence relations these connectives express. Czech shows that for the acquisition of connectives a combination of both aspects – syntactic and semantic – plays a crucial role. The conjunction *and* is analysed in more detail. The author finds that with increasing age the distribution of meanings of *and* changes; this finding differs from the previous study by Peterson and McCabe (1987).

Part 2: Referential coherence

This part contains four contributions on L1 and L2 acquisition of referential relations (on macro- and microstructural text levels) in different languages.

The section begins with a study by Gagarina et al., which deals with the more general level of story organisation and macrostructure, and investigates how components of episodes and episodes themselves are comprehensively produced in typically developing children and children at risk of DLD. By doing this, the study compares macro- and microstructure of elicited narratives in both languages by Russian-German bilingual four-year-olds with and without risk of DLD. By considering story structure, story complexity and internal state terms (as constituents of macrostructure), the authors attempt to disentangle the two groups. They find evidence that story structure and story complexity (in telling and retelling mode) differentiate the groups significantly. The theoretical component of this study taps into the discussion of universality, i.e. language independence, of macrostructural story organization. They found the multifactorial associations between language and narrative skills, with the qualitative component – story complexity – being more independent of language proficiency than the quantitative component – story structure.

Gerwien and Klages investigate children's understanding of referential coherence in first and second language acquisition of German. In a *visual world* paradigm experiment, they examined the pronoun resolution in monolingual and bilingual speakers of German between five and ten years and manipulated the two variables: *gender* and *referent type*. The results show that all children first rely on gender and only later on the referent type. The former cue is acquired differently by monolinguals and bilinguals: while the youngest group of monolinguals already processes gender and starts with the pre-pronominal position, bilinguals use the gender cue only starting from age seven and only in the post-pronominal position.

Schimke et al. examine the introduction and maintenance of discourse referents of French and German speakers who are seven and ten years old and of adults. The subjects in the study were asked to retell video clips that introduce a protagonist and refer back to them. The resulting data can be used for comparing language use in French and German and for investigating the development of speakers in both languages. One of the noticeable differences as compared to adults is that children often produce definite forms for referent introduction. Also, they use fewer reduced forms like pronouns for reference maintenance than adults. An adult-like discourse organization is not fully acquired by the age of ten in either language. However, adult-like complex clauses, e.g. containing presentational constructions or relative clauses, are used earlier by French-speaking than by German-speaking children.

Voiekova and Krasnoshchekova scrutinize the use of pronouns interacting with other developmental factors in early child Russian. For this purpose, they use spontaneous longitudinal corpora of four children. The results show that in all children the occurrence of pronouns is associated with the mean length of utterance and vocabulary diversity. Once the pronouns appear in children's speech, the strategies of their acquisition differ. While two children begin with the balanced use of personal and demonstrative pronouns, the two other children demonstrate a bias for the early demonstratives. The authors explain this finding via children's different acquisitional strategies, which might be connected with the physiological age of the onset of first words. The early speakers start with the demonstrative pronouns, which express the meaning of locality and are more transparent by nature, and do not put a high demand on the children's cognitive system, while children who start speech production at a later age, e.g. after twenty-four months, produce both personal and demonstrative pronouns.

References

Altman, C., Armon-Lotem, S., Fichman, S., & Walters, J. 2016. Macrostructure, microstructure, and mental state terms in the narratives of English-Hebrew bilingual preschool children with and without specific language impairment. *Applied Psycholinguistics* 37 (1), 165–193.

Berman, R. A. and Slobin, D. I. (eds.). 1994. *Relating events in narrative: A crosslinguistic developmental study*. Mahwah, NJ: Erlbaum.

Boerma, T.D., Leseman, P.P.M., Timmermeister, M., Wijnen, F.N.K. & Blom, W.B.T. 2016. Narrative abilities of monolingual and bilingual children with and without language impairment: implications for clinical practice. *International Journal of Language and Communication Disorders* 51 (6) ,626–638.

Bliss, L. S., McCabe, A., & Miranda, E. A. 1998. Narrative assessment profile: Discourse analysis for school-age children. *Journal of Communication Disorders* 31, 347–363.

Bott, O. and Solstad, T. 2014. From verbs to discourse: A novel account of implicit causality. In *Psycholinguistic approaches to meaning and understanding across languages*, eds. B. Hemforth, B. Mertins and C. Fabricius-Hansen, 213–251. Chicago: Springer International Publishing.

Gagarina, N., Klop, D., Kunnari, S., Tantele, K., Välimaa, T., Balčiūnienė, I., et al. 2015. Assessment of narrative abilities in bilingual children. In S. Armon-Lotem, J. de Jong, & N. Meir (Eds.), Language impairment testing in multilingual settings (pp. 241–274). Amsterdam: Benjamins.

Kehler, A. 2002. Coherence, reference, and the theory of grammar Stanford: CSLI.

Lascarides, A. and N. Asher. 2007. Segmented Discourse Representation Theory: Dynamic Semantics with Discourse Structure, in eds. H. Bunt and R. Muskens, *Computing Meaning: Volume 3*, 87–124. New York: Springer.

McCabe, A. 1996. Evaluating narrative discourse skills. In K. Cole, P. Dale, & D. Thal (Eds.), Assessment of communication and language (pp. 121–141). Baltimore, MD: Paul H. Brooks.

Mann, W. C. and S. A. Thompson. 1988. Rhetorical Structure Theory: Toward a functional theory of text organization. *Text* 8, 243–281.

Peterson, C., and McCabe, A. 1991. Developmental psycholinguistics: Three ways of looking at a child's narrative. New York: Plenum Press.

Sanders, T., Spooren, W. and Noordman, L. 1993. Coherence relations in a cognitive theory of discourse representation. *Cognitive Linguistics* 4, 93–133.

Sanders, Ted, Joost Schilperoord and Wilbert Spooren (eds.) 2001. *Text representation: Linguistic and psycholinguistic aspects.* Amsterdam/Philadelphia: Benjamins.

Sanders, Ted and Spooren, Wilbert. 2010. Discourse and Text Structure. In *The Oxford Handbook of Cognitive Linguistics*, eds. Dirk Geeraerts and Hubert Cuyckens, 916–943. Oxford: Oxford University Press.

Trabasso, T., and Rodkin, P. C. 1994. Knowledge of goals/plans: A conceptual basis for narrating Frog, where are you? In *Relating events in narrative: A cross-linguistic developmental study*, eds. R. Berman and D. Slobin, 85–106. Hillsdale, NJ: Erlbaum.

Tsimpli, I. M., Peristeri, E., & Andreou, M. 2016. Narrative production in monolingual and bilingual children with specific language impairment. *Applied Psycholinguistics* 37 (1), 195-216.

Part 1: **Relational coherence**

Angelika Becker, Valentina Cristante and Renate Musan
The comprehension of coherence relations in expository texts at the age of 10 and 12

Abstract: The ability to understand coherence relations like cause/result between parts of texts is crucial for the comprehension of texts. The present study investigates how well students of grade 4 and grade 6 manage the construction of coherence in expository texts. Performance differences in comprehending additive, causal, contrastive, and temporal anteriority relations suggest a specific line of development: After an early phase which does not show significant differences in dealing with the four relations, there is first progress in constructing causal relations and, after a short delay, in constructing adversative relations. The performance concerning additive and temporal anteriority relations remains on a comparatively low level. What seems to be crucial for the developmental progress is the relevance of relations for the meaning of the text and – especially for temporal anteriority relations – the sequence of propositions. Not all text recipients profit from the presence of connectives to the same degree, least of all weak readers.

1 Text comprehension and coherence relations

Comprehending texts implies being able to construe content-related connections and a coherent mental representation of the facts conveyed by the text. Coherence relations – i.e. relations like cause/result, problem/solution or contrast – are a particularly crucial aspect of coherence. Texts may contain signals for construing coherence relations, i.e. connectives like *because*, *but* or *before*, in variable degrees. When such explicit signals are lacking, recipients have to imply them. The present study deals with the question of how well 4th grade and 6th grade children

---

Note: This paper presents results of the project DFG MU3056/1-1 that was supported by Deutsche Forschungsgemeinschaft 2011-2013.

Angelika Becker
Renate Musan, University of Osnabrück, Neuer Graben 40, 49074 Osnabrück, email: rmusan@uni-osnabrueck.de
Valentina Cristante, Goethe-University Frankfurt, Norbert-Wollheim-Platz 1, 60323 Frankfurt, email: cristante@em.uni-frankfurt.de

https://doi.org/10.1515/9781501510151-002

manage to mentally construe certain coherence relations in expository texts, how their ability to do this develops, and what kind of role explicit marking of coherence relations by connectives plays.

Researchers have suggested various inventories of coherence relations (cf. Asher and Lascarides 2003; Mann and Thompson 1988; Martin 1992). The present study investigates four specific relations that belong to a generally assumed core of relations: additive, adversative, causal, and temporal anteriority relations.

One may safely assume that these relations constitute differing challenges for text processing. Sanders, Spooren and Noordman (1992, 1993) present an account of cognitive complexity of coherence relations. They classify coherence relations using four basic cognitive concepts:
– A relation is either "causal" or "additive". This corresponds to the intuition that a relation is either "weakly connective" (additive) or "strongly connective" (causal). Temporal relations are classified as additive.
– A relation is either "positive" or "negative".
– A relation is either "semantic" or "pragmatic".[1]
– The sequence of text segments combined by a coherence relation is either iconic (e.g. cause/result) or non-iconic (result/cause).

Based on this classification, Spooren and Sanders (2008) developed assumptions concerning the complexity of coherence relations, among them the following ones:
– Additive relations are less complex than causal ones.
– Negative relations are more complex than positive ones.
– Iconic sequences are less complex than non-iconic ones.

Regarding the complexity of processing the relations investigated in this study, one may hence arrive at the assumption that, according to some criteria, additive relations may be viewed as cognitively most simple among the four relations of the present study.

---

[1] The differentiation goes back to Sweetser's (1990) three level theory according to which a relation can be interpreted on three levels of meaning: the situation level (e.g. Fritz stays at home because he expects a phone call), the epistemic level of assumptions of the speaker (e.g. Fritz is at home because the light is switched on) and the speech act level (e.g. Will you be at home in a bit? – because I would like to give you the books). Sanders et al. (1992) capture the situation level under the notion "semantic" and the other two levels under "pragmatic". In more recent work (e.g. Spooren and Sanders 2008), they have also used the three level distinction of Sweetser.

Additive relations are prototypically marked by *und* ('and'). However, not every occurrence of *und* corresponds to an additive relation (Czech, this volume). But when expressing an additive relation, *und* presupposes that the combined propositions are compatible and that they can be bundled by superordinate criteria (Lang 1991). For the following example, for instance, the superordinate criterion may be "outer appearance":

(1)　*The moose is 2.5 to 3.2m long and its antlers are formed like shovels.*

Adversative or contrastive relations establish a contrast between two states of affair. Contrast is prototypically expressed by *aber* ('but'). As it is the case with additive relations, the combined propositions are compatible, but the feature of bundling, which is positively specified with additive relations, is negative in the case of adversative relations (Breindl 2004; Brauße 1998): the propositions cannot be bundled with respect to a superordinate criterion (Breindl 2004). According to the criteria of complexity of Spooren and Sanders (2008), adversative relations are more complex than additive relations because of this negative feature. Moreover, the relation is even more complex, because contrast can be established in many different ways. Stede (2004: 282) lists eight of possibly more subtypes of contrastive relations, among them the following two (examples after Stede):

(2)　a.　Information about an unexpected correlation:
　　　　In July we went to the Canaries, but we were freezing as if at the South Pole.

　　　b.　Neutral comparison of two facts:
　　　　Munich has a great soccer club. In Berlin the baseball players are better.

Some authors doubt that contrastive relations exist on the level of true states of affairs, e.g. Breindl (2004), Brauße (1998) and Stede (2004). Stede (2004: 281) argues as follows: If contrast in the relevant sense existed 'in the world', then the notion would have little content, because diversity exists everywhere; rather, text producers present diversity of objects or situations relative to the text and its purpose. As Brauße (1998) shows, this is also the reason why one cannot always derive from the meaning of context-free propositions whether they are additively or adversatively related to each other. Hence it seems likely that the mental construction of adversative relations presupposes deeper text comprehension than that found with additive relations.

　　Causal relations include according to recent proposals all relations that can be derived from conditional relationships (Duden Grammatik 2005; Waßner

2004). The most important markers of causality in German are *weil, denn* and *da* ('because'). Causal relations connect propositions with different roles, e.g. cause/reason vs. result/effect. According to Spooren and Sanders (2008), causal relations are 'strongly connecting' and more complex than additive relations. A causal relation always implies an additive relation, because in both cases the respective pairs of propositions are asserted.

However, there are also indicators that causal relations can be processed very well: Researchers often assume that text comprehension is primarily oriented at the construction of causal relationships (van den Broek 1990, 1994; Trabasso and Suh 1993). Causality can generally be viewed as a crucial cognitive category structuring human perception and experience (Noordman and de Blijzer 2000). The representation of causal relations is directly anchored in experiencing the world, in observing the repeated sequencing of events. Even children are already constantly confronted with such experiences: When grabbing something hot, it hurts. This early orientation towards causal relationships may still be of influence in the comprehension of expository texts, even if the relationships are not directly accessible to immediate perception. Hence, one can imagine that the construction of causal coherence – at least in deep text processing – already takes priority over additive and adversative relations in childhood. But the ease of processing a causal relation also depends on factors like the complexity of the text topic and the relevant knowledge of the recipient. Noordman, Vonk and Kempff (1992) investigated the processing of causal relations in challenging expository texts indicated by *because*. The following sentence from their study is frequently cited:

(3) *Chlorine compounds make good propellants because they react with almost no other substances.* (Noordman, Vonk and Kempff 1992: 573).

The causal relation here requires inferences and the activation of subject-specific knowledge. The subjects, who were not chemistry specialists, were not able to construct the connection despite its explicit marking.

Temporal coherence is in a certain sense more basic than additive, adversative and causal coherence. Temporal connections and time structure are largely obligatorily expressed in every clause, especially by the use of tenses. Temporal relations – simultaneity, anteriority, and posteriority – can be marked by connectives. The relation of anteriority (terminology according to Blühdorn 2004), which is investigated in the present study, can be expressed by *bevor* and *zuvor* ('before'). A connective like *bevor* indicates that the situation of the matrix clause is located anterior and proximal to the situation expressed by the *bevor*-clause. When anteriority is not indicated by a connective, it can often be inferred from the tenses used in the sentence, e.g. past perfect combined with present perfect. Such combinations of tenses also often occur in sentences containing *bevor*; hence, the relation will be indicated twice. Following Spooren and Sanders (2008), the processing complexity crucially depends on the sequence of the clauses: iconic sequences as in (4a) (first situation < second situation) can be processed more easily than non-iconic sequences as in (4b) (second situation < first situation).

(4) a. *The animals look for sheltered places before hibernation begins.*

    b. *Before hibernation begins, the animals look for sheltered places.*

2 Processing of coherence relations: investigations

While several empirical studies investigate the acquisition order of connectives and coherence relations with regard to language production, few compare the processing complexity of different coherence relations or their acquisition in expository texts. However, investigations by Meyer and Freedle (1984) and Sanders and Noordman (2000) suggest that adults process causal and adversative relations more easily than additive ones. To our knowledge, comparable studies on children do not exist. Hence, it is an open question whether children at certain stages of their cognitive development construct certain coherence relations more easily than others.

In language production, relations are marked at different developmental points. Bloom et al. (1980) investigated the occurrence of connectives in the data of four English speaking children during the second and third year. Coherence relations were explicitly marked in the sequence additive < temporal (*and then*) < causal < adversative (cf. the summary in Tomasello 2003: 258f). Similar developments were demonstrated in Diessel's (2004) study on the acquisition of connectives. Diessel also showed that *after* and *before* are productively used only relatively late, namely at the age of three. Clark (1971) investigated the comprehension of *before* (and *after*) by three to five year olds. The children consistently presupposed that events took place according to the sequence in which they were mentioned in the text. With iconic sequences, they interpreted the texts correctly, with non-iconic sequences they achieved only false interpretations (cf. the summary in Clark 2003). However, it is not possible to draw conclusions from the development of spoken language production for the development of text comprehension in school: the children are more advanced in their cognitive development and text comprehension does not concern spoken and contextually anchored communication.

The role of explicit marking of coherence relations is treated in a number of studies. The subjects in these studies are mostly practiced adult readers, typically university students. The general method is the following one: Subjects read texts of at least two versions, an 'explicit' version (containing explicit coherence markers) and an implicit version (without coherence markers). Several methods were used in order to measure in which way the reading process or the resulting text representations are influenced by the text differences.

It seems plausible that the mental construction of coherence is simplified to the degree of explicit marking of coherence relations. Connectives, for the reader, first signal that a content connection is intended, and second which type of relation is to be constructed. However, the results of the studies are controversial.

To be sure, the results show consistently that explicit marking of coherence relations accelerates the on-line processing; especially the text segment following the connective is processed faster (Sanders und Noordman 2000; Bestgen and Vonk 1995; Haberlandt 1982).

But studies that measure the effect of explicit marking on the resulting text representation after reading, i.e. off-line, have contradictory outcomes. Some studies using different off-line methods show a positive effect of marking on text comprehension. For instance, text reproduction was improved (Lorch and Lorch 1986; Loman and Mayer 1983; Meyer, Brandt and Bluth 1980), assertions could be verified more quickly (Sanders and Noordman 2000) and questions concerning the text could be answered better (Degand, Lefèvre and Bestgen 1999; Degand and Sanders 2002).

Other studies were not able to show any effect improving the comprehension of coherence marking. They neither had effects on the amount of information that could be recalled during text reproduction (Meyer 1975; Sanders and Noordman 2000), nor were questions concerning the text answered more adequately (Spyridakis and Standal 1987). The study of Millis, Graesser and Haberlandt (1993) even showed better memorizing performance when coherence relations were not marked in the text.

Further studies investigated how coherence marking interacts with other text properties. They looked, for instance, at text genre (Kamalski et al. 2008), the level of difficulty (Linderholm et al. 2000) and the comprehension ability of readers (O'Reilly and McNamara 2007). McNamara and Kintsch (1996) investigated the effect of the pre-knowledge of readers. The study showed that students with little previous knowledge profited from a maximally coherent and explicit text version, whereas students with much pre-knowledge profited from the less coherent version. The less coherent text stimulated more active and deeper processing, because the coherence gaps in the text had to be bridged by knowledge based inferences. The interaction effect of pre-knowledge and text coherence could be replicated for adult readers in McNamara and Kintsch (1996). In the study of McKeown et al. (1992) with children, however, the subjects profited from an augmented text version regardless of whether they had little or much pre-knowledge. The contradictory results of these studies can perhaps be explained by intervention of additional factors. Linderholm et al. (2000) were able to show that highly coherent texts also helped university students with much pre-knowledge with text comprehension when the texts were of a high level of difficulty.

There are also some studies investigating the comprehension of expository texts which work with younger subjects. Sanders, Land and Mulder (2007, experiment 2) conducted a study with 561 second year students in Dutch pre-vocational secondary education (13 to 14 years old) who are described as poor readers by the authors. In the explicit version, relations of various types were marked by connectives or functionally similar expressions like *as a consequence*. Text comprehension was measured by three written tasks: answering multiple choice questions about the text content, ordering events according to their temporal sequence, and inserting prepared sentences into a given schema that represented content connections from the text. The students who had read the explicit version clearly performed better than the other group. Recent research by van Silfhout (2014) and Evers-Vermeul (this volume) attained similar results with students of class 8 and class 2, respectively.

A group investigated by Zinar (1990) consisted of 5th grade students of varying reading competence levels. The students were grouped into two classes by using standardized reading tests, one with a relatively high reading competence level, the other one with a relatively low reading competence level. The subjects read short expository texts in which cause-result relations were either explicitly marked or not. Reading comprehension was measured by oral text replication. While students of low reading competence very rarely replicated the causal relations under both conditions, the high level readers showed a better replication performance after reading the explicit text version. But the performance of the better group was restricted, too: Under the implicit condition, they hardly ever replicated the causal relations, and under the explicit condition 48% of the students did not construct a causal condition from the text.

Zinar's interpretation of these results takes up considerations of Johnston and Pearson (1982), who also found in a study with 8th graders that better readers

profited from the presence of connectives. Johnston and Pearson compared their results with a study of Marshall and Glock (1978) that was performed with college students. This latter group showed the reverse effect: low-level readers performed better when the relations were explicitly marked. Based on this, Johnston and Pearson formulated a hypothesis according to which one can distinguish three developmental stages:
1. Younger children and older children with low level reading performance process a text word after word or proposition after proposition and focus little on the combination of text parts.
2. More advanced younger readers and low-level adult readers are sensitive to connectives and make use of them when construing text coherence. Their performance depends to a higher degree on the presence of connectives.
3. Experienced adult readers are relatively independent of the support by connectives.

According to Zinar's supposition, the 5th graders are between the first and the second developmental stage. The group of low-level readers and some of the better readers focus on single propositions, disregarding coherence relations. Some children of the better group started to develop relation related interpretation strategies whereby they make use of connectives.

To summarize, previous research does not sketch a clear picture, neither with regard to adults nor with regard to children as text recipients. It is not possible to derive what kind of developmental process the children of the two groups follow. However, it seems likely that the relevance of connectives changes with age and that it depends on additional factors, too (For a summary of such factors, see Czech, this volume).

3 The present study

Research questions

Given these research results, the present study adresses three research questions.
1. Does the ability to construe coherence change between 4th graders and 6th graders and according to the school attended by the children? – We started with the hypothesis that the performance improves with age, i.e. from the 9 to 10 year olds to the 11 to 12 year olds, because the older group consists of more experienced readers, possesses broader world knowledge, and their ability to infer should be more developed. Moreover, we assumed that students of

higher level education (school type "Gymnasium") in class 6 perform better than students of medium and lower level education (school types "Realschule" and "Hauptschule", respectively) in class 6.
2. How does the ability of the children to construe additive, adversative, causal, and temporal anteriority coherence relations in expository texts develop? – The hypothesis was that additive and causal relations are candidates for less complex processing, whereas adversative and temporal anteriority relations are candidates for more complex processing.
3. What is the effect of explicit marking of the four relations by a connective on the construction of the relation compared to non-marking of the relation? – This hypothesis is less grounded in the previous findings due to their scarcity and controversy, but it was just conjectured that the effect of connectives could differ depending on the age of the subjects.

Participants

Participants were 72 German-speaking children, i.e. 36 4th graders of primary school and 36 6th graders of the German secondary school system, aged 9 to 10 years (mean age = 10.25, sd 0.59) and 11 to 12 years (mean age 11.96, sd 0.69), respectively. Of the 36 4th graders, 12 children had a recommendation for lower level (Hauptschule HAU), 12 for middle level (Realschule REA) and 12 for higher level (Gymnasium GYM) secondary schools. Of the 6th graders, 12 children belonged to each of the respective secondary school types.

Materials

Eight expository texts about various themes were presented to the children: roller coaster, cotton, the conquest of the North pole, lions, popcorn, Nikolaus Kopernikus, migration birds, and water. The variety of themes aimed at neutralizing individual pre-knowledge. Each text was presented in an explicit and in an implicit version, respectively, i.e. in a version in which coherence relations were marked by connectives and in a version in which the same coherence relations were not marked by connectives. The explicit text versions consisted of 160 words on average, the implicit versions of 153 words. The texts had been checked and evaluated informally by teachers in order to make sure that the difficulty of the texts was appropriate especially for the younger children. The teachers evaluated the texts as not easy, but also not as overstraining. It was intended not to have a very low degree of text difficulty in order to avoid passive text processing. The two text versions of the text on lions may serve as an illustration:

(5) Explizit version: *Der Löwe ist neben dem Tiger die größte Raubkatze der Erde. Der Körper eines Löwenmännchens ist – ohne Schwanz – fast zwei Meter lang und seine Schulterhöhe beträgt etwa einen Meter. Die große Löwenmähne hat praktischen Nutzen, denn sie schützt den Löwen vor Bissen und Prankenhieben von Rivalen. Die Weibchen sind kleiner und ihnen fehlt die Mähne. Als einzige Raubkatze lebt der Löwe in Rudeln. Die Weibchen gehen auf die Jagd, die Männchen verteidigen dagegen das Revier des Rudels. Die führenden Männchen bleiben nur wenige Jahre beim Rudel, weil sie von jüngeren, stärkeren Männchen vertrieben werden. Bei der Jagd können Löwen bis zu 50 Kilometer pro Stunde schnell laufen, aber dieses Tempo können die Tiere nur kurz durchhalten. Bevor sie sich mit langen Sprüngen auf ihre Beute stürzen, haben sie sich geduckt bis auf dreißig Meter an ihr Opfer herangeschlichen. Das erlegte Wild wird von dem ganzen Rudel gefressen. Zuvor haben die Tiere die Beute auf einen ruhigen und schattigen Platz gezogen.*[2]

(6) Implicit version: *Der Löwe ist neben dem Tiger die größte Raubkatze der Erde. Der Körper eines Löwenmännchens ist – ohne Schwanz – fast zwei Meter lang. Seine Schulterhöhe beträgt etwa einen Meter. Die große Löwenmähne hat praktischen Nutzen. Sie schützt den Löwen vor Bissen und Prankenhieben von Rivalen. Die Weibchen sind kleiner. Ihnen fehlt die Mähne. Als einzige Raubkatze lebt der Löwe in Rudeln. Die Weibchen gehen auf die Jagd. Die Männchen verteidigen das Revier des Rudels. Die führenden Männchen bleiben nur wenige Jahre beim Rudel. Sie werden von jüngeren, stärkeren Männchen vertrieben. Bei der Jagd können Löwen bis zu 50 Kilometer pro Stunde schnell laufen. Dieses Tempo können die Tiere nur kurz durchhalten. Sie stürzen sich mit langen*

---

2 Translation: "Aside from the tiger, the lion is the largest feline predator on earth. The body of a male lion measures – without the tail – almost two meters **and** the shoulder height is about one meter. The huge lion's mane is of practical use, **because** it protects the lion from bites and paw swipes of rivals. Female lions are smaller **and** they do not have a mane. The lion is the only feline predator living in prides. Female lions hunt for food, male lions, **on the other hand** protect the territory of the pride. The leading male lions stay with their pride only for a few years **because** they are expelled by younger, stronger males. When hunting, lions reach a speed of about 50 km/h, **but** the animals can keep this speed only for a short while. **Before** they dart for the prey, they sidle up to the prey up to a distance of thirty meters. The prey is eaten by the whole pride. **Before that**, the animals have dragged the prey to a quiet and shady location."

Sprüngen auf ihre Beute. Sie haben sich geduckt bis auf dreißig Meter an ihr Opfer herangeschlichen. Das erlegte Wild wird von dem ganzen Rudel gefressen. Die Tiere haben die Beute auf einen ruhigen und schattigen Platz gezogen.

Every explicit text contained eight connectives: two additive (*und* ('and')), two adversative (*aber/dagegen* ('but', 'however')), two causal (*weil/denn* ('because')) and two temporal anteriority connectives (*bevor/zuvor* ('before')). These connectives were chosen because they occur frequently and are typical for the respective coherence relation. Differences with regard to the degree of their interpretability were neutralized insofar as the content of the connected clauses and the context given by the text material optimally supported a certain interpretation with regard to kind as well as level of connection.

Implicit and explicit text versions were supposed to be – except for the presence or absence of connectives – identical to each other as far as possible. Certain deviations concerning word order, however, could not be avoided, e.g. raising the finite verb in the absence of subjunctions such as *weil* or *bevor* in the implicit version. Connectives with various position options were consistently located in one position, e.g. *dagegen* in the 'Mittelfeld' and *zuvor* in the 'Vorfeld'. Furthermore, the sequence of clauses was fixed: Embedded clauses beginning with *weil* or *bevor* can be located in front of or after the matrix clause; in the text material they occurred consistently as second clause. Hence, all causal connections appeared in the non-iconic sequence "consequence/result < cause". Similarly, all temporal connections appeared in the sequence "second event < first event", i.e. in the non-iconic sequence.

Procedure

To each child, eight texts were presented, four explicit and four implicit ones in a random order. Which text was presented in the implicit or explicit version was also randomized across participants.

The data was collected with each child individually in the schools. In a first step, the children heard the text read from a tape. The children were supposed to read the text while hearing it. Hearing the text was supposed to guarantee that the text was pursued completely. Afterwards, the children were to read the text again without hearing it simultaneously. The second reading was not restricted by a time limit.

Then the children listened to eight questions and were instructed to answer them orally. The questions referred to the manipulated passages in the text and were randomized across participants in order to avoid effects of sequencing. The sequence of the questions did not correspond at all to the sequence of the respective contents in the text. The oral answering was chosen in order to prevent that factors like different degrees of alacrity or formulation problems might affect the quality of the answers. The interviews were taped.

Data coding

The interviews were transcribed, and the answers evaluated. 1 point was assigned when the coherence relation was recognized and the propositions were correctly recalled. The recognition of a coherence relation was not only accepted, when expressed by an appropriate connective; with temporal relations, for example, the anteriority could also be expressed by the use of certain tenses. 0.5 points were assigned when the coherence relation was recognized and the propositions were at least partially correctly recalled. 0 points were assigned when the coherence relation was not recognized or the propositions were not or incorrectly recalled; e.g. in the case of two additively connected propositions in the text, 0 points were assigned when a child recalled only one of the propositions, when the child gave a false answer or when it could not answer the question at all.

4 Results and discussion

Statistical analysis

The data was submitted to analyses of variance (ANOVA) with participants' ability to construe coherent relations (measured by the scores 1, 0.5 and 0) as dependent variable. In the by-subject analyses, the models included the between-subject factors, "age/school grade" (9 to 10 years-old/4th graders and 10 to 11 years-old/6th graders) and "school type" (Gymnasium, Realschule and Hauptschule) and the within-subject factors, "coherence relation" (additive, adversative, causal and temporal anteriority) and "text version" (implicit and explicit). In the by-item analyses, the between-item factors were "coherence relation" and "text version" and the within-item factors were "age/school grade" and "school type". For each research question, we present in the following sections the model and the effects we found.

4.1 Development of the ability to construct coherence

The general performance of the six groups is as follows:

Tab. 1: Mean score of subjects and mean score for all questions

Age	School type	Mean score of subjects (max. 60 P.)	Mean score for all questions
9–10	GR-GYM	30.06	0.50
	GR-REA	28.5	0.47
	GR-HAU	23.6	0.39
11–12	GYM	41.23	0.69
	REA	36.58	0.61
	HAU	25.35	0.42

The students of the 'Gymnasium' perform best, followed by the students of the 'Realschule'. The next best scores were reached by two of the younger groups, GR-GYM and GR-REA, whose scores are close to each other. The students of the group GR-HAU and the only marginally better students of the 'Hauptschule' were at the lowest range. The best score at all was reached by a student of the 'Gymnasium' with 48.5 points, the lowest by a student of the 'Hauptschule' with 8.5 points.

The differences with regard to the performance of the three younger groups is smaller than the one between the three older groups. The mean scores of GR-GYM and GR-HAU differ only by 0.11 points, the mean scores of GYM and HAU by 0.27 points. The difference has more than doubled.

The by-subject ANOVA with the independent variables of "age/school grade", "school type" and their interaction revealed a main effect of "age/school grade" and "school type" and no significant interaction between the two factors.

The main effect of "age/school grade" and inspections of the data indicate that all three groups perform better when the children were older, thus attending the 6th grade. The main effect of "school type" signals that those children belonging to a specific school revealed overall a better performance. Inspections of the data show that in both age groups the GYM and the REA children were better than the HAU children.

Subsequent t-test comparisons revealed that within the 6th graders, there were no significant differences between the GYM and the REA children but only between the GYM and the HAU children and between the REA and the HAU children. Within the 4th graders the differences between the groups did not reach statistical significance.

The by-item ANOVA displayed the same significant main effects. However, differently to the previous by-subject analysis, the interaction reached statistical significance.

Post-hoc t-test analyses revealed the same significant differences for the 6th graders as in the subject-analysis. As for the 4th graders, we found significant differences between the GYM and the HAU children and between the REA and the HAU children but not between the GYM and the REA children. These effects explain the significant interaction as they show that while the GYM and the REA children, at both age levels, did not significantly differ in their performance, the GR-HAU and the HAU children at both age levels differ from the GYM and the REA age-matched children.

These results suggest, firstly, that performance improves between 4th graders and 6th graders. Even if improvement of the HAU children was descriptively minimal, the fact that the interaction was not significant in the subject analysis and only in the item analysis, indicates that this group experienced a development as well. Secondly, belonging to a school type was shown to affect children's performance. The GYM and the REA children in both age groups performed better than the HAU children without differing significantly from each other. Thirdly, stronger differences in performance between the groups were found for the 6th graders whereas for the 4th graders they only reached significance in the by-item analysis. This suggests that differences with regard to performance between the school types increase more robustly after leaving primary school.

4.2 Developmental stages of coherence relations

The second research aim dealt with the development of the ability to construct additive, adversative, causal and temporal anteriority coherence relations. The following table presents the mean scores of the 4th graders and 6th graders differentiated for school type and coherence relations:

Tab. 2: Mean scores of the six groups for individual relations

Age	School type	additive	advers.	causal	temp.-ant.	Average
9–10	GR-GYM	0.44	0.52	0.57	0.47	0.50
	GR-REA	0.46	0.44	0.56	0.43	0.47
	GR-HAU	0.34	0.37	0.45	0.42	0.39
11–12	GYM	0.61	0.77	0.74	0.62	0.69
	REA	0.56	0.63	0.71	0.52	0.61

Age	School type	additive	advers.	causal	temp.-ant.	Average
	HAU	0.33	0.41	0.53	0.43	0.42
Average		0.46	0.52	0.59	0.48	

Comparing descriptively the within-group mean scores for every relation (Tab. 2, last line), causal relations are mastered best. The second best result is observed with the construction of adversative relations. The performance with additive and temporal anteriority relations is less good, whereby these differ only minimally from each other.

The following graph shows how the group-specific differences regarding the construction of the four coherence relations look:

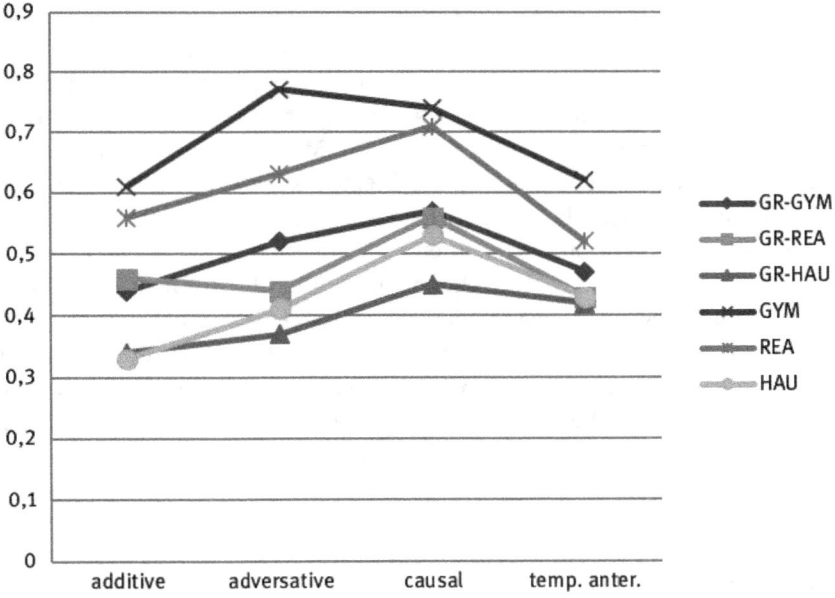

Fig. 1: Mean scores of the groups in constructing the relations

Relatively high, in five of the six groups even the best scores, were reached with causal relations, relatively lower scores – with additive and temporal anteriority relations. In the case of adversative relations, the scores vary among the age groups. Two of the younger groups, GR-REA und GR-HAU, show a similarly bad performance with adversative relations as with additive relations, which the performance with causal relations contrasts favourably with. In the GR-GYM group, however, there is a constant progress from additive to adversative and further to causal relations. Comparing GR-GYM to GYM, there is a huge progress regarding adversative relations: Adversative relations are mastered as well as causal relations by the GYM group, even slightly better, whereas the performance with additive relations remains comparatively low.

Since we found in section 4.1. that the factor "age/school grade" was statistically significant, we conducted the following analyses separately for the 4th and 6th graders.

4th graders

The by-subject ANOVA showed a main effect of "coherence relation", a significant interaction between "school type" and "coherence relation" and no significant effect of "school type". To investigate the origin of this interaction, we tested in each school group, whether performance with a specific coherence relation differed significantly from another. We found that the GR-GYM children mastered causal relations significantly better than additive and temporal relations. The GR-REA children performed significantly better with causal than with adversative and temporal relations. In both groups, the difference between additive and temporal relations was not significant. On the other hand, for the GR-HAU no significant differences between the coherence relations were detected. This absence of significant differences explains the significant interaction between "school type" and "coherence relation". The by-item ANOVA displayed a main effect of "school type" and no further effects. The main effect of "school type" mirrors the significant overall better performance of the GR-GYM and the GR-REA in comparison to the GR-HAU.

6th graders

The by-subject ANOVA revealed a main effect of "school type" and of "coherence relation" without significant interaction. Subsequent t-test comparisons per "school type" showed a significant better performance of the GYM and the REA children than of the HAU children and no significant difference between the GYM and the REA children. Post hoc t-test analyses per "coherence relation" showed an overall significant better performance of the three groups with causal than adversative, causal than temporal and finally, causal than additive relations. The latter were mastered worst by all three groups. Furthermore, adversative relations were also shown to be constructed significantly better than temporal and additive relations, whereas the difference between additive and temporal relations was not significant. Importantly, the absence of a significant interaction suggests that the 6th graders performed qualitatively similar, thus revealing the same comprehension pattern, and only differed quantitatively.

The by-item ANOVA displayed as well a main effect of "school type" and of "coherence relation". Subsequent analyses per "school type" revealed significant differences between the three groups, as in the subject analysis. As for the "coherence relation", causal relations were mastered significantly better than additive and temporal, whereas the other pairwise comparisons were not significant.

We started out with the hypothesis that additive and causal relations can be processed easier, whereas the two other relations, adversative and temporal anteriority ones, challenge processing to a relatively higher extent. This hypothesis, however, was only confirmed in part. The results presented above show another differentiation: Causal and adversative relations are mastered better than additive and temporal anteriority relations. In the following, we will first take a closer look at the development of additive, adversative and causal relations.

Statistical analysis documents that the best of the younger groups, GR-GYM, already performs significantly better with regard to causal relations than with regard to additive relations, and such a significant performance difference later shows in all three older groups. An analogous performance difference was shown by Sanders and Noordman (2000) and by Meyer and Freedle (1984) for adults. Hence, the children have in this respect reached a performance differentiation that can also be assumed for adult, experienced readers.

Notably, causal relations are also significantly better constructed by the HAU group than additive relations, whereas the younger GR-HAU group does not yet show any significant differences with regard to the specific relations. That is, there is also an improvement between the weakest younger group and the weakest older group with regard to the construction of relations; it concerns causal relations. With the advantage of causal relations as compared to additive ones, the HAU group shows a developmental stage that is reached by children with a better performance at an earlier age. This suggests a decelerated developmental pace in the weaker group. Hence, the development of stronger and weaker groups does not seem to differ qualitatively, but the weaker groups go through the development with a certain delay.

The advantage of causal relations as compared to additive relations shows that the difference in complexity between them that was proposed by Spooren and Sanders (2008) apparently does not play a crucial role in the development of relation processing: if it did, then causal relations would be more complex than additive ones and hence should be developed later. It seems to be more important that – as was proposed by Spooren and Sanders (2008), too – that additive relations are only weakly connecting, whereas causal relations are strongly connecting.

Several answers of the children show effects that lead into the same direction. E.g. with additive relations in the text a certain proportion of the children recalled only one of the two connected propositions; on average, this was the case with 16 children per question. Additive connections that were especially vivid or surprising were recalled better.

For instance, one of the questions concerning the text on popcorn was: "How did the indigenous people of America use popcorn?" The respective part of the text is as follows: "Sie haben Popcorn gegessen (und) Sie/sie haben es als Schmuck getragen." ('They ate popcorn (and) T/they wore it as jewellery.') The majority of the subjects, i.e. 67 children, constructed the additive relation. The other extreme showed with a question concerning the North pole text: "Wie lässt sich das Klima am Nordpol beschreiben?" ('How can one describe the climate at the North pole?') The text says: "Dort wehen eisige Stürme (und) Die/die Temperatur fällt auf minus 50 Grad." ('There are icy storms (and) T/the temperature can be as low as minus 50 degrees.'). In this case only 36 children, i.e. half of the subjects, were able to construct the additive relation. The rather weak combination of additive connections also showed with other phenomena: some children were able to construct an additive relation but combined one of the relevant propositions with some other proposition from the text or with facts from background knowledge. On average, this reaction was shown by eight children per question.

Another relation that shows a clear development is the adversative one. However, the development of adversative relations happens after the development of causal relations. In earlier phases of the development, weaker performance with additive and adversative relations contrast with better performance with causal relations. Statistically, we found that the GR-REA children performed significantly better with causal than with adversative relations and this difference was almost significant for the GR-HAU children. The strongest young group, the GYM children, did not reveal significant differences in the construction of causal and adversative performance, although their performance was descriptively better with the former.

Over development, all three 6th grader groups improved their performance with adversative and causal and not with additive. We found the same qualitative pattern, that is no significant difference between causal and adversative relations and only between adversative and additive ones.

Again, cognitive complexity in the sense of Spooren and Sanders (2008) cannot explain the differences regarding the performance with different relations, here adversative and additive ones: adversative relations are cognitively more complex than additive ones because of their inherent negation. But again the 'strength of connectivity' of the relation can be the crucial factor. Adversative relations are, like causal relations, highly connecting and highly relevant for text meaning (Meyer and Freedle 1984).

Based on the differences regarding the performance with specific relations among the six groups, one can postulate developmental stages for additive, adversative and causal relations. We assume that all children run through the same developmental stages, but with different speed, even though it is not yet clear how the development proceeds with older children. Hence, we transfer one of the central assumptions of first language acquisition theory to coherence construction in text comprehension. The aim of this development is presumably the performance differentiation observed with adults that was shown in studies of Sanders and Noordman (2000) and Meyer and Freedle (1984): causal and adversative relations can be managed better than additive relations.

Based on these assumptions, one can derive a developmental sequence with an initial state, a final state and states in between. The initial state is represented by the weakest group, GR-HAU. In this group there are no significant performance differences concerning the construction of the individual relations. In a second stage, first causal relations and later, with some delay, adversative relations are developed while the performance regarding additive relations remains on a relatively low level. Children go through this development with different paces. An early stage can only be observed with the 'slowest' younger group, the GR-HAU group, a late developmental stage can only be seen with the older group whose development was the quickest, the GYM group. Whether this developmental sequence can be confirmed or not is a matter of future research, preferably of longitudinal studies.

Developmental progress is demonstrated in two ways: On the one hand, performance concerning individual relations improves, on the other hand, performance differences among the relations are established as they can also be assumed for adult and experienced readers. For the HAU group, the fact that causal relations are processed better than additive ones can be assessed as progress. Hence, the subjects of this group get closer to the developmental aim. However, the scores for both relations are significantly lower than for the GYM group. Hence, there is considerable developmental need in this group. In the GYM group, however, there is a performance differentiation among the relations as it is also documented for adults. But whether the children of this group are already as good as adults with respect to the construction of individual relations is still an open question. Comparative studies with adults and children would be desirable in future research.

4.3 Development of temporal anteriority relations

To our knowledge, there are no studies that compare temporal anteriority relations to additive, adversative or causal relations, neither for children nor for adults. In the present study, temporal anteriority relations behave largely like additive relations. In the two younger groups, GR-GYM, GR-REA, the mean scores of the two relations are close to each other. Towards GYM and REA, they improve to the same degree and are also on the same level in these two older groups. Moreover, statistically, there were no significant differences between the two coherence relations in both age groups.

The advantage of causal relations as compared to temporal anteriority ones is very clear: All three 6th grader groups were shown to construct causal relations significantly better than temporal anteriority ones. Within the 4th graders, this better performance was detected in the GR-GYM and in the GR-REA group but not in the GR-HAU group. This last finding fits well to our assumption, as it shows that the less advanced group, GR-HAU, later shows the tendency that we found in the more advanced groups, according to which causal relations are already better constructed than temporal ones.

Concerning temporal and adversative relations, in the older groups significant differences were found between the two. Moreover, as the main effect of "school type" was significant, it indicates that although this difference was present in all three groups, the groups differed quantitatively in their overall performance, with the HAU group scoring significantly worse than the REA and the GYM group.

Crucially, whether the scores achieved by the GYM children are already the final stage of the development or whether there may be further improvements leading to more performance differentiations between the relations is not clear.

But which property of temporal anteriority relations is responsible for the fact that the performance is rather weak and does not show improvement? One can assume that it is not the relation as such that is problematic but the non-iconic sequence of the propositions in the study. It is non-iconic since it does not correspond to the 'principle of natural or chronological order' (Clark 1970, 1971): the sequence of mentioning the situations in the text usually corresponds to their temporal sequence if nothing else is signalled (see, for instance, Klein 1994: 45).

This principle becomes manifest in narratives in particular, especially when they are presented orally (Labov 1972). A comprehension strategy following the principle is most likely to be developed early by children. As was shown in several studies, seven to eight year olds are already able to construct a mental model of narratives (Oakhill 1982; Nieding 2006) as far as the appropriate construction of temporal relations is concerned. On the other hand, deviations from the principle of natural order lead to comprehension problems, especially with younger children: in Clarks (1971) investigation of the interpretation of *before* (and *after*) by three to five year olds, the children consistently assumed that the events occurred in the sequence in which they were mentioned in the text. With iconic sequences, they achieved correct interpretations, with non-iconic sequences a wrong interpretation (cf. the summary in Clark 2003).

Unsurprisingly, in our data we observed effects of sequencing, too – under the explicit as well as under the implicit condition. They are, however, relatively rare, i.e. they show in 39 out of 1008 answers to 14 questions. One of the questions conerning the lion-text, for instance, was: "Was passiert mit der erlegten Beute?" ('What happens to the killed prey?') The question was related to the following part of the text: "Das erlegte Wild wird von dem ganzen Rudel gefressen. Zuvor haben die Tiere die Beute auf einen ruhigen und schattigen Platz gezogen/Die Tiere haben die Beute auf einen ruhigen und schattigen Platz gezogen" ('The prey is eaten by the whole pride. (Before that,) the animals have dragged the prey to a quiet and shady location.'). Ten children recalled the sequence of events wrongly, a REA-student for instance in the following way: "Das ganze Rudel frisst die Beute und sie ziehen es dann auf einen sicheren und schattigen Platz." ('The whole pride eats the prey and then drags it to a safe and shady location.') The compliance with the sequence of propositions in the text is strong enough to override content-related logical considerations as well as signals by connectives *bevor* and *zuvor* ('before').

Most of the children in our study, however, are already relatively independent of the principle of natural order, as can be concluded from the small number of sequences that were misunderstood. However, they do not deal confidently with deviations from the principle of natural order: in about one quarter of the answers no temporal relations were recalled at all, and, moreover, the content was often recalled only incorrectly or incomplete. Interestingly, such obvious problems with the non-iconic order of clauses occurred only with the temporal coherence relations, not with the causal ones.

4.4 Implicit and explicit text versions

Let us now consider the last research question: What kind of effect on the construction of a relation does the explicit marking by connectives have? Regarding this question we formulated – due to the vague results of former research – only a weak hypothesis, namely that the role of explicit marking may change with age. Table 3 shows the mean scores of the six groups concerning the factor "text version".

Tab. 3: Mean scores (all relations) of the six groups after reading explicit vs. implicit text versions

text version	GR-GYM	GR-RE	GR-HAU	GYM	REA	HAU	Ø
Implicit	0.47	0.4	0.40	0.66	0.58	0.42	0.49
explicit	0.53	0.5	0.39	0.72	0.64	0.42	0.53

One can see that there is a division into two types of groups: stronger groups (GR-GYM, GR-REA, GYM, REA) and weaker groups (GR-HAU and HAU). The four strongest groups achieve better scores after reading the explicit text version than after reading the implicit text version, whereas the scores of the two weaker groups do not differ or differ hardly at all under the two conditions. Hence, these two groups are supported less by connectives than the stronger groups.

The lack of utilization of connectives as supportive means by the two weaker groups gets even clearer when looking at the mean scores of the four relations individually. In some cases, the implicit condition triggered even better scores than the explicit condition. This is the case in the GR-HAU group with causal and temporal anteriority relations and in the HAU group with additive and adversative relations.

Tab. 4: Mean scores of the groups for additive, adversative, causal and temporal anteriority relations after reception of implicit vs. explicit text versions

	additive		adversative		causal		temporal anter.	
	impl.	expl.	impl.	expl.	impl.	expl.	impl.	expl.
GR-GYM	0.42	0.46	0.48	0.56	0.55	0.6	0.44	0.49
GR-REA	0.42	0.51	0.4	0.48	0.55	0.57	0.39	0.48
GR-HAU	0.34	0.34	0.36	0.37	0.46	0.43	0.44	0.4
GYM	0.61	0.62	0.75	0.79	0.72	0.76	0.55	0.7
REA	0.56	0.56	0.59	0.67	0.72	0.69	0.43	0.63
HAU	0.35	0.3	0.45	0.37	0.46	0.58	0.42	0.43

4th graders

In the by-subject ANOVA we found a significant main effect of the factor "text version" (implicit, explicit) meaning that an explicit text version consistently lead to better text processing than an implicit version. There was, however, no main effect of school type, no interaction effect of "text version" with the variable "age/school type" or with the variable "coherence relation". The lack of significance of the last interaction suggests that the better performance with an explicit text version was not dependent on a particular coherence relation. The by-item analysis revealed a main effect of "school type" only. This indicates that for the younger groups the present items did not lead to a significant better performance in one of the two versions, but rather to an overall better performance of the GYM than the REA and the HAU group.

Noteworthy is the absence of interaction between "text type" and "school type", as descriptively, we see that the GR-HAU did not take advantage from the explicit version and performed similarly in both "text type" conditions.

6th graders

In the analysis of the 6th graders, we found in the subject analysis a main effect of "text version" and "school type" whereas the interaction between "text version" and "school type" was almost significant. However, in the item analysis, the interaction achieved significant degree. This last finding explains the lack of difference for the HAU group while constructing relations in the implicit and explicit text version in comparison to the GYM and the REA group.

These results are – at least to some extent – comparable to those of Zinar (1990), who, however, only investigated causal relations. Zinar showed, as was presented in section 2 above, that among 5th graders, 'good' readers achieved a better performance with explicit text versions. 'Bad' readers on the other hand showed the same weak performance after reading the explicit as well as the implicit version. Although reading ability and the general reading competence was not measured independently in our study, one may assume that these competences are less developed in the GR-HAU group and in the HAU group than in the other four groups. In any case, in agreement with Zinar one can state the following: There are weaker children, who do not profit from the presence of connectives, and there are stronger children, who are able to make use of the presence of connectives when construing coherence relations.

In addition to Zinar (1990), the investigation of Sanders, Land and Mulder (2007, experiment 2) is the second study whose results can be compared to ours.

However, a comparison is somewhat complicated because the students of their study are older, namely 13 to 14 years old, and visited another type of school, i.e. a pre-vocational secondary education school. The subjects were relatively poor readers but showed a better performance after reading the explicit text version – as was the case with the more advanced but younger children of our own study. These facts can be interpreted by making use of the assumptions developed by Johnston and Pearson (1982) on the development of reading comprehension in three stages that was already mentioned above.

In stage 1, younger children and somewhat older children with a low level of reading comprehension process texts word for word or proposition by proposition and do not pay much attention to connections among the propositions. Corresponding to the reading strategy, they hardly use connectives as signals. – According to Zinar (1990), the 5th graders of her study are just about to overcome this stage and are – more or less advanced – on their way to the next stage. This classification also seems appropriate for the weaker 4th graders and 6th graders of our study, GR-HAU and HAU. It is, however, certainly not the case that these groups process texts only "proposition by proposition". But they construe fewer coherence relations than more advanced children and do not pay much attention to connectives.

In stage 2, the more advanced younger readers and weaker adult readers are sensitive for connectives and make use of them for construing coherence relations. Their performance is more dependent on the presence of connectives. – The subjects of Sanders, Land and Mulder (2007) may be in this stage, i.e. older children with low reading comprehension. The two younger, advanced groups may be in this stage, too, at least when considering that they perform better under the explicit condition than under the implicit condition.

A certain problem with this classification results from the fact that specific coherence relations develop differently as was shown above. A good example in this respect is the HAU group, of which we assumed above that they have not yet reached the second stage. This classification seemed justified because the scores under both conditions did either not differ (temporal anteriority relations) or they performed even better under the implicit condition (additive and adversative relations). But another picture arises with regard to causal relations, where the score after reading the explicit text version was better (average for explicit text versions: 0.58; average for implicit text versions: 0.46). The analysis of the text results showed that the HAU-students show first progress with causal relations. The focus on causal relations may correspond to stronger alertness to causal connectives. This amounts to saying that this group has already started stage 2 with regard to causal connectives whereas the development with regard to other relations is still delayed.

In stage 3 experienced adult readers are relatively independent of the support by connectives. – It seems that they are at least not to the same extent dependent or independent of connectives with every type of coherence relation. Additive relations often remain unmarked, adversative and causal ones to a lesser extent. Hence, one may assume that adult and advanced readers make use of connectives to different degrees depending on the relation.

As long as there are no more detailed investigations, it is also hardly possible to match the performance of the most advanced children to one of the stages. The GYM and the REA group achieved about the same scores for additive relations under the explicit and under the implicit condition. One may interpret this in such a way that the support by connectives does not play a crucial role for them anymore. The scores for temporal anteriority relations, however, differ more strongly than with any other group and with any other relation (mean score REA implicit: 0.43 vs. mean score REA explicit: 0.63; mean score GYM implicit: 0.55 vs. mean score GYM explicit: 0.70). One may interpret this in different ways. On the one hand it is possible that the children are still in stage 2 with regard to this relation. But on the other hand it seems equally likely that text recipients with fully developed processing capability also need more support with this relation than it is the case with additive relations.

One may say that as far as future research in this field is concerned, much remains to be done.

5 Conclusions

To conclude, the present study provided results with regard to several aspects of the development of coherence relations:
- Performance differences regarding the construction of coherence relations are triggered less by age than by the developmental speed. Depending on the type of school, the development proceeds faster or slower: The best progress was achieved from GR-GYM to GYM, only minimal progress was shown from GR-HAU to HAU.
- There are group-specific performance differences with regard to the construction of the four relations. They suggest a development as follows: After an early stage with no significant differences in the mastering of the four relations, there is first progress with regard to the construction of causal relations

and, somewhat later, with adversative relations. The performance with additive and temporal anteriority relations remains on a lower level.
– Different degrees of cognitive complexity of coherence relations in the sense of Spooren and Sanders (2008) cannot capture the later developmental stages, they can be attributed only to the onset. Rather, the relevance of relations for the unfolding of meaning of a text and – for temporal anteriority relations – the sequence of the propositions seems to be crucial.
– The results concerning the importance of explicit marking of relations for text comprehension support the assumption that text recipients profit to different degrees from the presence of connectives, depending on their preconditions; the weaker groups profit least.

At the beginning of our study we hoped that the results would be relevant for practical use in school education. And they indeed are – insofar as we found an alarmingly delayed development from GR-HAU-students to HAU-students. But this amounts essentially only to the conclusion that these students crucially need additional assistance – a conclusion that will hardly be surprising for teachers. Reading education programmes have been taken into account in school for some time. Support regarding expository texts, however, has only developed recently (Fix and Jost 2010). According to Gierlich (2010: 25), expository texts for a long while only played a marginal role in school education by doing nothing more than marking key words, by inserting subsections and section titles, or by writing summaries.

Gierlich (2010: 31), however, recognizes the necessity to approach especially expository texts in an analytic way that takes text structure into account – with regard to macro structure as well as with regard to micro structure, e.g. syntax and cohesion. With cohesion, Gierlich addresses text surface features including connectives, i.e. an issue of the present study. Our results, however, suggest a somewhat broader focus, namely coherence relations in general, marked ones as well as unmarked ones.

A second practically relevant aspect of the study concerns the question of whether explicit marking of coherence relations plays a crucial role in text comprehension. Regarding this point, one may at least safely say that marking supports an average reader. But ultimately, texts should always be natural, i.e. mark coherence relations where their construction is hampered by difficulties concerning the relation (like non-iconic temporal anteriority relations), by contentwise complicated connections (like cause-result relations in texts with complicated content) or by lack of pre-knowledge. When connections are less important for text comprehension (as with additive relations), when other text features already support an interpretation (like contrasts expressed by lexical oppositions) or when the text is about well-known connections, marking is unnecessary. The children in our study showed a considerable performance even under the implicit condition. One reason for this may be that the contexts were formulated in such a way that they maximally supported a particular interpretation. This seems to be advisable for texts that are supposed to be appropriate for children: With connections that require a considerable amount of processing energy, the interpretation should not only hinge on taking the connective into account but should be supported by additional text features, too.

References

Asher, N. & Lascarides, A. 2003. Logics of conversation. Cambridge: Cambridge University Press.
Becker, A. & Musan, R. 2014. Leseverstehen von Sachtexten: Wie Schüler Kohärenzrelationen erkennen. In Averintseva-Klisch, Maria & Peschel, Corinna (eds.), Aspekte der Informationsstruktur für die Schule. Baltmannsweiler: Schneider Verlag Hohengehren, 126–154.
Bestgen, Y. & Vonk, W. 1995. The role of temporal segmentation markers in discourse processing. *Discourse Processes* 19, 385–406.
Bloom, L., Lahey, M., Hood, L., Lifter, K. & Fiess, K. 1980. Complex sentences: Acquisition of syntactic connectives and the meaning relations they encode. *Journal of Child Language* 7, 235–261.
Blühdorn, H. 2004. Die Konjunktionen *nachdem* und *bevor*. In Blühdorn, H., Breindl, E. & Waßner, U. H. (eds.), 185–211.
Blühdorn, H., Breindl, E. & Waßner, U. H. (eds.) 2004. Brücken schlagen. Grundlagen der Konnektorensemantik. Berlin/New York: de Gruyter.
Brauße, U. 1998. Was ist Adversativität? Aber oder und? *Deutsche Sprache* 26, 138–159.
Breindl, E. 2004. Relationsbedeutung und Konnektorbedeutung. Additivität, Adversativität und Konzessivität. In: Blühdorn, H., Breindl, E. & Waßner, U. H. (eds.), 225–253.
Clark, E. 1970. How young children describe events in time. In Flores d'Arcais, G. B. & Levelt, W. J. M. (eds.): Advances in Psycholinguistics. Amsterdam: North Holland Publishing, 275–293.
Clark, E. 1971. On the acquisition of *before* and *after*. *Journal of Verbal Learning and Verbal Behavior* 10, 266–275.
Clark, E. 2003. First Language Acquisition. Cambridge: Cambridge University Press.
Czech, H. (this volume): Explicit coherence relations in children's and adults' spoken narratives: the importance of *und* for the acquisition of German connectives. In Gagarina, N. & Musan, R. (eds.): Referential and relational discourse coherence in adults and children: Applied psycholinguistics. Heidelberg: Springer. (Studies in Theoretical Psycholinguistics)
Degand, L. & Sanders, T. 2002. The impact of relational markers on expository text comprehension in L1 and L2. *Reading and Writing* 15, 739–757.
Degand, L., Lefèvre, N. & Bestgen, Y. 1999: The impact of connectives and anaphoric expressions on expository discourse comprehension. *Document Design* 1, 39–51.

Diessel, H. 2004. The acquisition of complex sentences. Cambridge: Cambridge University Press.
Duden. 2005. Die Grammatik [= Duden, vol. 4]. 7., völlig neu erarbeitete und erweiterte Auflage. Mannheim/Leipzig/Wien/Zürich: Dudenverlag.
Evers-Vermeul, J. (this volume): Short sentences easy to read? Effects of connectives and layout on text comprehension by beginning readers. In Gagarina, N. & Musan, R. (eds.): Referential and relational discourse coherence in adults and children: Applied psycholinguistics. Heidelberg: Springer. (Studies in Theoretical Psycholinguistics)
Fix, M. & Jost, R. (eds.) 2010. Sachtexte im Deutschunterricht. 2. edition. Baltmannsweiler: Schneider Verlag Hohengehren.
Gierlich, H. 2010. Sachtexte als Gegenstand des Deutschunterrichts – einige grundsätzliche Überlegungen. In Fix, M. & Jost, R. (eds.), 25–46.
Haberlandt, K. F. 1982. Reader expectations in text comprehension. In Le Ny, J. F. & Kintsch, W. (eds.): Language and comprehension. Amsterdam: North-Holland Publishing, 239–249.
Johnston, P. & Pearson, P. D. 1982. Prior knowledge, connectivity, and the assessment of reading comprehension. Tech. Rep. No. 245. Urbana: University of Illinois (ERIC Document Reproduction Service No. ED 247 525).
Kamalski, J., Lentz, L., Sanders, T. & Zwaan, R. A. 2008. The forewarning effect of coherence markers in persuasive discourse. Evidence from persuasion and processing. *Discourse Processes* 45, 545–579.
Klein, W. 1994. Time in Language. London/New York: Routledge.
Lang, E. 1991. Koordinierende Konjunktionen. In: Stechow, A. von & Wunderlich, D. (eds.): Semantik. Ein internationales Handbuch der zeitgenössischen Forschung. Berlin/New York: de Gruyter, 597–623.
Linderholm, T., Gaddy Everson, M., van den Broek, P., Mischinski, M., Crittenden, A. & Samuels, J. 2000. Effects of causal text revisions on more- and less-skilled readers' comprehension of easy and difficult texts. *Cognition and Instruction* 18, 525–556.
Loman, N. L. & Mayer, R. E. 1983. Signaling techniques that increase the understandability of expository prose. *Journal of Educational Psychology* 75, 402–412.
Lorch, R. F. & Lorch, E. P. 1986. On-line processing of summary and importance signals in reading. *Discourse Processing* 9, 489–496.
Mann, W. C. & Thompson, S. A. 1988. Rhetorical structure theory. Toward a functional theory of text organization. *Text* 8, 243–281.
Marshall, N., & Glock, M. D. 1978. Comprehension of connected discourse: A study into the relationship between the structure of text and information recalled. *Reading Research Quarterly* 14, 10–56.
Martin, J. R. 1992. English text: System and structure. Philadelphia/Amsterdam: John Benjamins.
McKeown, M. G., Beck, I. L., Sinatra, G. M. & Loxterman, J. A. 1992. The contribution of prior knowledge and coherent text to comprehension. *Reading Research Quarterly* 27, 79–93.
McNamara, D. S. & Kintsch, W. 1996. Learning from text. Effects of prior knowledge and text coherence. *Discourse Processes* 22, 247–287.
Meyer, B. J. 1975. The organization of prose and its effect on memory. Amsterdam: North-Holland Publishing.
Meyer, B. & Freedle, R. O. 1984. Effects of discourse type on recall. *American Educational Research Journal* 21, 121–144.

Meyer, B. J., Brandt, D. M. & Bluth, G. J. 1980. Use of top-level structure in text. Key for reading comprehension of ninth-grade students. *Reading Research Quarterly* 16, 72–103.
Millis, K. K., Graesser, A. C. & Haberlandt, K. 1993. The impact of connectives on the memory for expository texts. *Applied Cognitive Psychology* 7, 317–339.
Nieding, G. 2006. Wie verstehen Kinder Texte? Die Entwicklung kognitiver Repräsentationen. Lengerich: Papst.
Noordman, L. G. M., Vonk, W. & Kempff, H. J. 1992. Causal inferences during the reading of expository texts. *Journal of Memory and Language* 31, 573–590.
Noordman, L. G. M. & de Blijzer, F. 2000. On the processing of causal relations. In Kortmann, B. & Closs Traugott, E. (eds.): Cause – Condition – Concession – Contrast. Cognitive and discourse perspectives. Berlin/New York: Mouton de Gruyter, 35–56.
Oakhill, J. V. 1982. Constructive processes in skilled and less-skilled comprehenders. *British Journal of Psychology* 73, 13–20.
O'Reilly, T. & McNamara, D. S. 2007. Reversing the reverse cohesion effect. Good texts can be better for strategic, high-knowledge readers. *Discourse Processes* 43, 121–152.
Sanders, T. & Noordmann, L. 2000. The role of coherence relations and their linguistic markers in text processing. *Discourse Processes* 29, 37–60.
Sanders, T., Land, J. & Mulder, G. 2007. Linguistic markers of coherence improve text comprehension in functional contexts. *Information Design Journal* 15, 219–235.
Sanders, T., Spooren, W. & Noordmann, L. G. M. 1992. Toward a taxonomy of coherence relations. *Discourse Processes* 15, 1–35.
Sanders, T., Spooren W. & Noordman, L.G.M. 1993. Coherence relations in a cognitive theory of discourse representation. *Cognitive Linguistics* 4, 93–133.
Schnotz, W. 2006. Was geschieht im Kopf des Lesers? Mentale Konstruktionsprozesse beim Textverstehen aus der Sicht der Psychologie und der kognitiven Linguistik. In Blühdorn, H., Breindl, E. & Waßner, U. H. (eds.), 223–238.
Spooren, W. & Sanders, T. 2008. The acquisition order of coherence relations: On cognitive complexity in discourse. *Journal of Pragmatics* 40, 2003–2026.
Spyridakis, J. H. & Standal, T. C. 1987. Signals in expository prose. Effects on reading comprehension. *Reading Research Quarterly* 22, 285–298.
Stede, M. 2004. Kontrast im Diskurs. In Blühdorn, H., Breindl, E. & Waßner, U. H. (eds.), 255–285.
Sweetser, E. 1990. From etymology to pragmatics. Metaphorical and cultural aspects of semantic structure. Cambridge: Cambridge University Press.
Tomasello, M. 2003. Constructing a language. Cambridge: Harvard University Press.
Trabasso, T. & Suh, S. 1993. Understanding text. Achieving explanatory coherence through online inferences and mental operations in working memory. *Discourse Processes* 16, 3–34.
van den Broek, P. 1990. The causal inference maker: Towards a process model of inference generation in text comprehension. In Balota, D. A., Flores d'Arcais, G. B. & Rayner, K. (eds.): Comprehension processes in reading. Hillsdale, NJ: Lawrence Erlbaum, 423–445.
van den Broek, P. 1994. Comprehension and memory of narrative texts. Inference and coherence. In Gernsbacher, M. A. (eds.): Handbook of psycholinguistics. San Diego: Academic Press, 539–588.
van Silfhout, G. 2014. Fun to read or easy to understand? Establishing effective text features for educational texts on the basis of processing and comprehension research. Ph. D.

dissertation Utrecht University. Utrecht: LOT. Available at: http://www.lotpublications.nl/Documents/368_fulltext.pdf.

Waßner, U. H. 2004. Einleitung. In Blühdorn, H., Breindl, E. & Waßner, U. H. (eds.), 311–324.

Zinar, S. 1990. Fifth-graders' recall of propositional content and causal relationships from expository prose. *Journal of Reading Behavior* 22, 181–199.

Jacqueline Evers-Vermeul
Short sentences, easy to read? Effects of connectives and layout on text comprehension by beginning readers

Abstract: The use of coherence markers, such as the connectives *because* and *but*, and presenting texts in an integrated layout support the text comprehension of students in secondary education (Land 2009; Van Silfhout 2014). For children in the early years of primary education, however, the picture is less clear. Children show a gradual increase in their ability to benefit from connectives in texts (Irwin and Pulver 1984), and making return sweeps at the end of lines is a relatively new skill. In a reading experiment among children in grade 2, we tested the effects of layout and the presence of connectives on children's text comprehension. It is shown that 7- and 8-year-olds benefit from connectives, but that layout (presenting sentences with or without line breaks) does not affect text comprehension. However, children perceive texts with an integrated layout as easier. A corpus-based study revealed that books designed for children in grades 1-3 often do not show such a layout, and that fragmented layouts are predominant in texts for grades 1 and 2. Possible explanations and implications for the design of educational materials for beginning readers are discussed.

1 Introduction

Children start acquiring markers of relational coherence just after their second birthday. Within a year, they are able to produce a variety of additive, temporal, causal and adversative connectives, such as *and, then, because* and *but* (Bloom et al. 1980; Evers-Vermeul 2005; Evers-Vermeul and Sanders 2009; Van Veen et al. 2009, 2014; see also Czech, *this volume*).

Acknowledgement: The experimental part of this research was conducted in collaboration with Jentine Land and an MA-student from Utrecht University: David-Jan Punt (see Punt 2010). I would like to thank Marleen Pardoel for compiling the corpus of children's books.

Jacqueline Evers-Vermeul, Utrecht Institute of Linguistics OTS, Utrecht University, Trans 10, 3512 JK Utrecht, email: j.evers@uu.nl

Despite children's early proficiency in using connectives, many publishers of Dutch school texts seem to believe that students in the early years of secondary education still have difficulties in interpreting sentences containing explicitly marked coherence relations. Especially in pre-vocational education, the majority of Dutch school texts consist of simplex main clauses with few or no connectives (Land 2009).[1] For example, the translated text in (1) comes from a Geography text book for 14-year-olds.

(1) On February 1, 1953 there was a north-westerly storm.
It raged along the shore with wind-force 10.
The dikes didn't hold it any longer.
Large parts of Zeeland and South-Holland flooded.
Over 1,800 people died and many stocks of cattle drowned.
Thousands of houses were destroyed.
Dikes, dams and sea walls had to be built.
The Delta Works and the Zuiderzee Works now protect the Netherlands against floods.

Fragment (1) consists of short sentences, without subordinating clauses, and only one coordinating clause. Due to the lack of coherence markers, readers have to establish coherence relations themselves, or might end up thinking the text presents a mere list of facts. For example, in order to construct a coherent mental representation of the text (Kintsch 1998, 2013; Kintsch and Van Dijk 1978; Zwaan and Radvansky 1998), a cause-consequence relation should be established between the fourth sentence on the one hand, and the following two sentences on the other: the death of people and cattle and the destruction of the houses are caused by the flood. The fragmented nature of text (1) is strengthened by its layout, as each sentence is presented on a separate line.

In a corpus-based study, Land (2009; Land et al. 2008) has shown that 69% out of 126 school texts on the subjects History, Economics, and Geography used in the second year of pre-vocational education (comparable to grade 8 in the American school system) show such a fragmented layout. Only 22% of the 1,365 sentences in these texts contained coherence markers. Publishers told Land to prefer a fragmented layout with short sentences because it made the texts look simple,

---

[1] Dutch secondary education is divided into three levels ranging from pre-vocational education (*vmbo*) to pre-university education (*vwo*). Dutch *vmbo* is divided into four levels, ranging from mainly vocational to mainly theoretical training. Fragmented text books are typically developed for the vocational levels of *vmbo*.

and because they thought it would make such texts easier to read for students in pre-vocational education.

However, Land (2009; Sanders, Land and Mulder 2007) has shown that such fragmented texts have the opposite effect on text comprehension: 13- and 14-year-old students understand texts with connectives and with an integrated layout better than texts without such coherence markers and with each sentence starting a new line. Similarly, Van Silfhout (2014) and colleagues found that both pre-vocational and pre-university students in grade 8 answer bridging inference questions better after reading texts with connectives than after reading texts without connectives. This held true for History texts (Van Silfhout et al. 2014b), as well as for Economy and Biology texts and narratives (Van Silfhout et al. 2015). Eye-tracking results indicate that connectives speed up students' processing, especially when texts have an integrated layout, and that students' processing slows down when they read texts with a fragmented layout. A significant positive correlation between reading times and scores on bridging inference tasks indicated that explicit texts with an integrated layout place fewer processing demands on students' working memory (Van Silfhout et al. 2014a).

In conclusion, connectives seem to benefit adolescents' text comprehension. However, the picture is less clear for students in primary education (see also Becker et al., *this volume*). Cain and Nash (2011) found that both 8- and 10-year-olds interpret connectives differently according to the type of coherence relations they signal: children were able to select appropriate temporal, adversative, and causal connectives to link two short sentences, although the 10-year-olds outperformed the 8-year-olds in the case of temporal and adversative relations. The fact that children's use of connectives in text comprehension is still developing during primary education is also shown by Irwin and Pulver (1984): they found main effects of adding causal connectives on text comprehension for fifth- and eighth-grade students, but not for students in grade 3. Hence, it remains to be seen how beneficial connectives will be for even younger children in primary education.

Similarly, it is not self-evident that young, less-skilled readers will benefit from an integrated layout, compared to a fragmented layout. Previous studies have shown that it is a complex maneuver to move eyes from the end of one line to the beginning of the next. The first word of a new line usually takes longer to read than other words (Haberlandt and Graesser 1985) and is often skipped, which sometimes requires the reader to make a corrective movement (Rayner 1998). This might suggest that the number of return sweeps should be kept at a minimum for young readers. However, as Van Silfhout et al. (2014a: 1038) have mentioned, an integrated layout may generate other reading problems. Proficient readers automatically segment the sentences of a text into syntactically and semantically appropriate units or phrases (Just and Carpenter 1987; LeVasseur et al. 2006), but for many inexperienced, developing readers, parsing a sentence into phrases and clauses seems to be problematic (Fuchs et al. 2001; LeVasseur et al. 2006). For example, LeVasseur et al. (2006) found that when phrasal constituents were interrupted by a line break, 7- to 9-year-olds obtained lower fluency ratings and made more than twice as many false starts than they did with texts in which the end of a line corresponded to a clause boundary.

These findings raise the following question: what effect do layout and the presence of connectives have on the text comprehension by students in grade 2 in primary education? In this study, the focus is on grade 2, because that is the first grade in which children have mastered technical reading skills (identifying characters and words) to such a degree that they are expected to be able to focus on text comprehension beyond the word and sentence level (see Section 2).

In order to get an impression of children's experience with fragmented and integrated layouts, respectively, a corpus-based analysis was performed of text books developed for children in grades 1, 2 and 3 (see Section 3).

2 Method and results reading experiment

We conducted an off-line reading experiment in which children in grade 2 had to read two texts that were manipulated in two respects: layout and presence of connectives. The following subsections provide details about the participants and design, the materials used in the study, as well as the procedure followed while conducting the experiment.

2.1 Participants and design

Participants in the reading experiment were 213 children (51% boys, 49% girls) from grade 2. Children were recruited from ten classes at seven schools in The Netherlands, and were seven or eight years old (mean age 7.8, SD 0.6).
Each child read two texts, for example an explicit fragmented version of one text, and an implicit integrated version of another text. Text versions and text orders were randomly assigned to students.[2]

---

[2] The original experiment tested five versions of each text, including an explicit version with subordinating connectives. Because this version was only developed in an integrated layout, it

Because text comprehension scores may vary with reading proficiency, we measured children's reading proficiency using a standardized Dutch reading proficiency test for students in grade 2. This resulted in proficiency scores on an ordinal scale ranging from insufficient (1) to good (5). The distribution of proficiency scores was equal across conditions (χ^2 (12) = 6.08, p = .91).

2.2 Materials

The experimental texts were in Dutch, and were based on texts from recent Biology textbooks for children: one about gorillas and one about spiders. Each text was manipulated in two aspects: layout (integrated vs. fragmented) and the presence of connectives (explicit vs. implicit). A fragmented layout was created by presenting each sentence on a separate line. In the versions with an integrated layout, sentences continued on the same line, as far as page width allowed. In both types of layout, the sentences were grouped in subsections of three to seven sentences, without headings.

The presence of connectives was manipulated by adding frequent connectives such as the coordinating conjunctions *want* 'because' and *maar* 'but', and the adverbial *daarom* 'that's why' to the explicit versions. Compare, for example the implicit version in (2a) with its explicit counterpart in (2b). In the latter version, the consequence-cause relation between the running of the spider and his longing for food is made explicit, as well as the contrastive relation between the longing for food and his inability to chew. As (2b) illustrates, the sentences starting with a connective were presented as independent syntactic units, so that both the implicit and the explicit versions of the texts only contained single main clauses, and showed the same word order.[3] Such sentences are very common in books for 7- and 8-year-olds. The spider text consisted of 135 words in the explicit conditions and 121 words in the implicit conditions. The gorilla text consisted of 131 words in the explicit and 119 words in the implicit conditions.

(2) a. *De spin rent naar de vlieg. Hij wil de vlieg opeten. De spin kan niet kauwen.*

---

did not allow for testing effects of layout, and was therefore disregarded in the current study (44 cases for the gorilla text, and 41 for the spider text).

3 In Dutch, the word order in subordinating clauses is different from the one in main clauses, as Dutch main clauses exhibit Verb Second, whereas the subordinating clauses have the finite verb at or near the end of the clause. Because word order might also affect processing, the current study only focused on the role of connectives in main clauses.

'The spider runs to the fly. He wants to eat the fly. The spider cannot chew.'
b. *De spin rent naar de vlieg.* **Want** *hij wil de vlieg opeten.* **Maar** *de spin kan niet kauwen.*
'The spider runs to the fly. Because he wants to eat the fly. But the spider cannot chew.'

The excerpts in (3) show two translated sentences from the four resulting combinations of the Dutch gorilla text.

(3) a. Fragmented, implicit version:
A gorilla has strong arms.
He is good at climbing trees.
b. Fragmented, explicit version:
A gorilla has strong arms.
That's why he is good at climbing trees.
c. Integrated, implicit version:
A gorilla has strong arms. He is good at climbing trees.
d. Integrated, explicit version:
A gorilla has strong arms. That's why he is good at climbing trees.

Children answered two text appreciation questions per text. One question was about the text's attractiveness: *I find the text about gorillas/spiders...*, with a five-point scale, presented in a multiple-choice format, ranging from *not nice at all* to *very nice*. The other question concerned the comprehensibility of the text: *I find the text about gorillas/spiders...*, with answers ranging from *very difficult* to *very easy*.

After each text, participants were also asked to answer eight text comprehension questions that tapped both literal and inferential information. For both texts, two questions addressed students' text base representation (e.g., *What color does a gorilla have?*), asking for facts that had been presented in a single sentence in the text (compare the use of this type of question in Cain et al. 2004; Ozuru et al. 2009). In line with previous research (Kamalski 2007; McNamara et al. 1996; Van Silfhout 2014b, 2015), the comprehension test also contained open-ended bridging inference questions. These six questions per text tested children's understanding of coherence relations in the text, and hence their situation model representation (Kintsch 1998). To answer such questions, children had to combine information from at least two different sentences in the text. For example, students' comprehension of text fragment (4) was tested with question (5).

(4) *Sommige mensen jagen op gorilla's. Zij schieten gorilla's dood. Daardoor leven er nog maar weinig gorilla's.*
'Some people hunt for gorillas. They shoot gorillas to death. As a result only few gorillas remain.'
(5) *Er leven nog maar weinig gorilla's. Hoe komt dat?*
'Only few gorillas remain. How come?'

The maximum possible score per text was eight: two points for the literal questions, and six for the inference questions.

2.3 Procedure

All tests were administered at school, during morning hours. The experiment started with a spoken instruction of approximately five minutes, in which the procedure and task were explained to the group. Then, the first text and accompanying questions were presented in a booklet. The text was followed by a small puzzle (to avoid verbatim recall) and the two appreciation questions. Subsequently, children had to answer the comprehension questions. Participants were not allowed to re-read the text, so they could not look up the answers. This procedure was then repeated for the second text. There was no time limit for reading an individual text and answering the questions. After 30 minutes, all participants had finished the entire task. The experiments were conducted over a period of two weeks.

2.4 Results

Per text, the comprehension questions were moderately reliable (gorilla text: $\alpha = .65$; spider text: $\alpha = .46$). Because the reliability scores did not change as a result of deleting individual questions or grouping questions into literal vs. inference questions, sum scores per student per text were used for further statistical analyses. Table 1 provides the mean scores per version, irrespective of text topic because there were neither main nor interaction effects of text topic (all $ps > .29$).[4]

---

[4] Importantly, the main effect of connective use on comprehension surfaced in both texts (gorilla text: $F(1, 155) = 6.45$, $p = .01$; $\eta_p^2 = .04$; spider text: $F(1, 155) = 5.30$, $p = .01$; $\eta_p^2 = .03$).

Tab. 1: Mean comprehension scores (and standard deviations) per text version (max. = 8, N = 320)

Layout	Explicit	Implicit
Fragmented	6.67 (1.55)	6.15 (1.37)
Integrated	6.86 (1.20)	6.22 (1.42)

An ANOVA with reading proficiency as covariate revealed a main effect of connective use on comprehension ($F(1, 311) = 12.19$, $p = .001$; $\eta_p^2 = .04$). There was no effect of layout on comprehension ($F(1, 311) = 0.18$, $p = .67$), and no interaction effect of layout and connectives ($F(1, 311) = 0.14$, $p = .71$). This means that the texts with connectives resulted in higher comprehension scores, but that layout did not affect the quality of the mental representation children made of text.

The results of the two appreciation questions per topic are provided in Table 2 – again without separating out the scores per text because of a lack of effects of text topic (all $ps > .16$).

Tab. 2: Mean appreciation scores (and standard deviations) for attractiveness and perceived difficulty per text version (min. = 1, max. = 5)

	Attractiveness (N=308)		Perceived difficulty (N=302)	
	Explicit	Implicit	Explicit	Implicit
Fragmented	4.02 (0.95)	3.99 (0.82)	3.99 (1.05)	3.70 (1.01)
Integrated	4.08 (0.92)	3.95 (1.00)	4.32 (0.95)	4.18 (1.08)

An ANOVA with reading proficiency as covariate revealed no significant effects for attractiveness (connective use ($F(1, 303) = 1.00$, $p = .32$; layout: $F(1, 303) = 0.06$, $p = .81$; interaction connective use * layout: $F(1, 303) = 0.28$, $p = .60$). This means that children's appreciation of the attractiveness of the texts did not vary as a result of the layout or the use of connectives in these texts.

A significant effect was found for perceived difficulty: there was a main effect of layout ($F(1, 297) = 7.08$, $p = .008$; $\eta_p^2 = .023$). No effect of connective use ($F(1, 297) = 0.002$, $p = .97$) and no interaction effect of connective use and layout were found ($F(1, 297) = 0.004$, $p = .95$). Children considered texts with an integrated layout easier to read than texts with a fragmented layout, irrespective of the presence of connectives. There was no correlation between children's appreciation of the attractiveness and the perceived difficulty of texts ($r = .15$, $p = .008$).

3 Method and results corpus-based study

In order to get an impression of the layouts children get acquainted with during their first years of primary education, a corpus-analytic study investigated the layouts used in text books for grades 1, 2 and 3. Materials, analytical model and results are discussed in the following subsections.

3.1 Materials

The corpus consisted of 96 books written for children in the first, second or third grade in primary school: 32 per grade. Books were labeled as written for grade 1 if they contained an age indication for 7-year-olds and/or a standardized readability index frequently used in The Netherlands: AVI-M3 of E3.[5] Books with an age indication for 8-year-olds and/or the readability index AVI-M4 or E4 were considered to be written for grade 2. Books were labeled as written for grade 3 if they contained an age indication for 9-year-olds and/or the readability index AVI-M5 of E5.

Per grade, books from two genres were collected: 16 narrative texts, and 16 expository texts. Narrative texts contained stories with speaking and acting characters; expository texts contained information on a subject and/or instructions how to do things.

3.2 Analytical model

For each text, the layout was established. We distinguished texts showing a consistent use of an integrated layout from texts with no clear integrated layout. A text was considered to be integrated if new sentences within the same section started immediately after the previous one as far as page width allowed, as in examples (2), (3c) and (3d). If a text exhibited a fragmented layout – with each sentence starting a new line, as in (3a) and (3b) – or if it did not show a consistent layout, it was classified as having no clear integrated layout.

---

5 See http://www.slo.nl/primair/leergebieden/ned/taalsite/lexicon/00029/ for a Dutch explanation of this readability index.

3.3 Results

Out of 96 texts, 91 texts exhibited a consistent layout. Four expository texts (three for grade 1 and one for grade 3) showed a mixture of sections with a fragmented layout and sections with an integrated layout. Compare fragment (6) from page 14 of an expository text for grade 1, and fragment (7) from page 15 of the same text book about islands.

(6) *Op een nieuw gevormd eiland groeien nog geen planten en
er leven geen dieren. Maar na verloop van tijd vliegen er
vogels naar het eiland. Andere dieren zwemmen er naartoe.*
'On a newly formed island there are no plants and no animals (lit. no plants grow and no animals live). But after some time birds fly to the island. Other animals swim there.'

(7) *Door de wind of door de golven komen zaden op
het eiland terecht.
De zaden ontkiemen en er gaan planten groeien.*
'Through the wind or through the waves seeds end up on the island.
The seeds germinate and plants start to grow.'

For one text, the layout could not be determined because it presented only one sentence per page. This text was disregarded in the statistical analyses. Percentages of texts with a consistent integrated layout are mentioned in Table 3.

Tab. 3: Percentage of integrated texts per grade and genre, with actual number plus total number of texts between brackets (N = 95)

	grade 1	grade 2	grade 3
Narrative	0.0 (0/16)	12.5 (2/16)	43.8 (7/16)
Expository	53.3 (8/15)	37.5 (6/16)	93.8 (15/16)

A Logit analysis showed the distribution over layouts differed with grade (χ^2 (2) = 18.75, $p < .001$), and with genre (χ^2 (1) = 14.19, $p < .001$). There was no interaction effect of grade and genre (χ^2 (2) = 8.72, $p = .19$). See Table A in the Appendix for more statistical details. Overall, the integrated layout occurs less frequently in narrative texts than in expository texts ($z = -4.02, p < .001$). Also, the integrated layout is more frequent in texts for grade 3 than in texts for grade 1 ($z = -3.45, p = .001$) and grade 2 ($z = -3.57, p < .001$). This means that the number of integrated texts increases with age/grade, and that the use of layouts is not consistent across genres.

4 Conclusions

Because children's use of connectives in text comprehension is still developing during primary education (Cain and Nash 2011; Irwin and Pulver 1984), and because making return sweeps at the end of lines is a relatively new skill for beginning readers, this study set out to test the effects of layout and the presence of connectives on the text comprehension and text appreciation of children in grade 2. A reading experiment among 7- and 8-year-olds revealed that informative texts with connectives resulted in higher comprehension scores than their implicit counterparts, but that layout did not affect the quality of the mental representation children made of a text.

The beneficial effect of connectives use on children's text comprehension is in accordance with previous findings among adolescents (Land 2009; Van Silfhout 2014; Van Silfhout et al. 2014b, 2015), and with the relatively high proficiency level of connective use found by Cain and Nash (2011). However, it goes against Irwin and Pulver's (1984) finding that the presence of connectives does not benefit the text comprehension of children in grade 3. First, this difference in findings may be attributed to a difference in task. As Irwin and Pulver (1984) indicate themselves, "the scores on these recall questions were fairly low, indicating that this task was difficult for these students" (p. 403). Second, Irwin and Pulver only examined effects of adding causal connectives, whereas the manipulation in the present study also included other types of connectives (e.g. adversatives). A third explanation comes from a difference in clause orders: the current study only contained connectives in main clauses that followed the corresponding main clause. Irwin and Pulver, however, also used experimental sentences with a reversed clause order, i.e. containing a pre-posed *because*-clause. It is known from processing studies that pre-posed adverbial clauses put a heavier burden on readers' working memory than do post-posed clauses (Gibson 2000). This also shows from Irwin and Pulver's (1984: 403) results: children in grade 3 scored better in the condition with post-posed *because*-clauses than in the condition with pre-posed *because*-clauses. Interpreting the difference in results from a processing perspective implies that beginning readers are able to benefit from connectives as long as these connectives are presented in sentences following their main clause. Additional research needs to be done to test this hypothesis. This might refine the overall developmental trajectory posited in other work: from unawareness of explicit connectives, to awareness of explicit connectives and dependence upon them, to an active reading style in which relationships are inferred and explicit connectives are unnecessary (Becker et al., *this volume*; Johnston and Pearson 1982; Zinar 1990).

In the current study, children's comprehension scores were not significantly affected by layout: comprehension scores after reading a text with an integrated layout were comparable to the ones after reading a text with a fragmented layout. This result can be interpreted from two angles. It means that presenting a line break in the middle of a sentence does not have a negative impact on children's text comprehension, and conversely, that presenting each sentence on a separate line is not beneficial for children in grade 2. This is remarkable, because children in grade 2 are still refining their technical reading skills, including making a return sweep from the end of one line to the beginning of the next. Future studies using eye-tracking techniques will have to indicate whether effects can be found during reading, but the current study has already shown that no effects are present after reading, i.e. once the mental representation of the text is constructed.

The finding that children's text comprehension does not benefit from an integrated layout goes against findings among adolescents (Van Silfhout et al. 2014a). Perhaps children in grade 2 are not aware of the 'visual message' that is provided by presenting sentences without a line break: an integrated layout may trigger readers to infer that the sentences form a coherent whole, and hence may invite readers to look for coherence relations between clauses. An on-line processing study might reveal whether an integrated layout alters children's processing speed or re-reading behavior, and hence give indications of children's sensitiveness to this visual cue.

The present study, however, already provides indications that the current practice in texts for beginning readers is not particularly helpful for children in grade 1 and 2 in finding out what the visual message of layout may be. A corpus-based analysis of 96 text books reveals that the majority of texts for grade 1 and 2 show a fragmented layout, with sentences separated by a line break, whereas only in grade 3 the majority of texts exhibit an integrated layout. Moreover, the use of layouts was found not to be consistent across genres: integrated layouts were predominant in expository texts, while narratives were often presented in a fragmented layout.

A practical implication of these findings is that publishers might reconsider the layout they use in texts for beginning readers. At present, they seem to prefer a fragmented layout for the youngest age groups, even though an integrated layout does not have a negative impact on children's comprehension scores. Selecting an integrated layout, however, might help young readers to discover the visual message provided by layout more easily. An integrated layout would also match children's preferences found in the current experiment: children in grade 2 considered texts with an integrated layout easier to read than texts with a fragmented layout, irrespective of the presence of connectives.

Another practical implication concerns the teaching of text structure. Williams and colleagues (e.g. Williams and Atkins 2009; Williams et al. 2005) have repeatedly found that children in the early grades of primary education are already able to benefit from explicit teaching of text structure (see also Hebert et al. 2016; Pyle et al. 2017). The current study underlines these findings: even 7- and 8-year-olds benefit from connectives in texts. Increasing children's awareness of coherence markers and the role of connectives in explicating text structure, and providing children with texts that exhibit a gradual increase in syntactic complexity (from single main clauses to post-posed adverbial clauses to pre-posed adverbial clauses) are crucial components if we want to help children become proficient readers who are able to construct a coherent mental representation of a text's content.

Appendix: Logit-analysis on layout in children's books

Tab. A: Goodness of fit per model (with the best fitting model in bold)

Model	χ^2 model	df	p model	χ^2 factor	df	p factor
1. constant + layout	36.22	5	<.001	-	-	-
+ 2. layout*genre	22.03	4	<.001	14.19	1	<.001
+ 3. layout*grade	**3.28**	**2**	**.19**	**18.75**	**2**	**<.001**
+ 4. layout*grade*genre	0	0	<.1	3.28	2	.19

References

Bloom, L., Lahey, M., Hood, L., Lifter, K., and Fiess, K. 1980. Complex sentences: Acquisition of syntactic connectives and the semantic relations they encode. *Journal of Child Language* 7, 235–261. Reprinted in L. Bloom (1991), *Language development from two to three* (pp. 261-289). Cambridge: Cambridge University Press.

Cain, K., and Nash, H. M. 2011. The influence of connectives on young reader's processing and comprehension of text. *Journal of Educational Psychology* 103 (2), 429–441. doi: 10.1037/a0022824.

Cain, K., Oakhill, J., and Bryant, P. 2004. Children's reading comprehension ability: Concurrent prediction by working memory, verbal ability and component skills. *Journal of Educational Psychology* 96 (1), 31–42. doi: 10.1037/0022-0663.96.1.31.

Evers-Vermeul, J. 2005. *The development of Dutch connectives: Change and acquisition as windows on form-function relations*. Ph.D. dissertation Utrecht University. Utrecht: LOT. Available at: http://www.lotpublications.nl/Documents/110_fulltext.pdf.

Evers-Vermeul, J., and Sanders, T. 2009. The emergence of Dutch connectives: How cumulative cognitive complexity explains the order of acquisition. *Journal of Child Language* 36 (4), 829–854.

Fuchs, L. S., Fuchs, D., Hosp, M. K., and Jenkins, J. R. 2001. Oral reading fluency as an indicator of reading competence: A theoretical, empirical, and historical analysis. *Scientific Studies of Reading* 5, 239–256. doi: 10.1207/S1532799XSSR0503_3.

Gibson, E. 2000. The dependency locality theory: A distance-based theory of linguistic complexity. In A. Marantz, Y. Miyashita, and W. O'Neil (eds.), *Image, language, brain: Papers from the first mind articulation project symposium* (pp. 95–126). Cambridge, MA: MIT Press.

Haberlandt, K. F., and Graesser, A. C. 1985. Component processes in text comprehension and some of their interactions. *Journal of Experimental Psychology: General* 114, 357–374. doi: 10.1037/0096-3445.114.3.357.

Hebert, M., Bohaty, J. J., Nelson, J. R., and Brown, J. 2016. The effects of text structure instruction on expository reading comprehension: A meta-analysis. *Journal of Educational Psychology* 108, 609–629. doi: 10.1037/edu0000082.

Irwin, J. W., and Pulver, C. J. 1984. Effects of explicitness, clause order, and reversibility on children's comprehension of causal relationships. *Journal of Educational Psychology* 76 (3), 399–407.

Johnston, P., and Pearson, P. D. 1982. *Prior knowledge, connectivity, and the assessment of reading comprehension* (Technical Report No. 245). Urbana: University of Illinois, Center for the Study of Reading. Available at https://eric.ed.gov/?id=ED217402.

Just, M. A., and Carpenter, P. A. 1987. *The psychology of reading and language comprehension*. Boston, MA: Allyn and Bacon.

Kamalski, J. 2007. Coherence marking, comprehension and persuasion: On the processing and representation of discourse. Ph.D. dissertation Utrecht University. Utrecht: LOT. Available at: http://www.lotpublications.nl/Documents/158_fulltext.pdf.

Kintsch, W. 1998. *Comprehension: A paradigm for cognition*. Cambridge: Cambridge University Press.

Kintsch, W. 2013. Revisiting the construction-integration model of text comprehension and its implications for instruction. In D. E. Alvermann, N. J. Unrau, and R. B. Ruddel (eds.), *Theoretical models and processes of reading* (6e ed., pp. 807–839). Newark, DE: International Reading Association.

Kintsch, W., and Van Dijk, T. A. 1978. Towards a model of text comprehension and production. *Psychological Review* 85, 363–394. doi: 10.1037/0033-295X.85.5.363.

Land, J. F. H. 2009. Zwakke lezers, sterke teksten? Effecten van tekst- en lezerskenmerken op het tekstbegrip en de tekstwaardering van vmbo-leerlingen [Less-skilled readers, well-built texts? Effects of text and reader characteristics on text comprehension and text appreciation by students in prevocational secondary education]. Ph.D. dissertation Utrecht University. Delft: Eburon.

Land, J. F. H., Sanders, T., and Van den Bergh, H. 2008. Effectieve tekststructuur voor het vmbo: Een corpus-analytisch en experimenteel onderzoek naar tekstbegrip en tekstwaardering van vmbo-leerlingen voor studieteksten [Effective text structure in prevocational education: A corpus-based and experimental study of students' text comprehension and appreciation]. *Pedagogische Studiën* 85 (2), 76–94.

LeVasseur, V. M., Macaruso, P., Palumbo, L. C., and Shankweiler, D. 2006. Syntactically cued text facilitates oral reading fluency in developing readers. *Applied Psycholinguistics* 27, 423–445.

McNamara, D. S., Kintsch, E., Songer, N. B., and Kintsch, W. 1996. Are good texts always better? Interactions of text coherence, background knowledge, and levels of understanding in learning from text. *Cognition and Instruction* 14 (1), 1–43. doi: 10.1207/s1532690xci1401_1.

Ozuru, Y., Dempsey, K., and McNamara, D. S. 2009. Prior knowledge, reading skill, and text cohesion in the comprehension of science texts. *Learning and Instruction* 19, 228–242. doi: 10.1016/j.learninstruc.2008.04.003.

Pyle, N., Vasquez, A. C., Lignugaris/Kraft, B., Gillam, S. L., Reutzel, D. R., Olszewski, A., et al. 2017. Effects of expository text structure interventions on comprehension: A meta-analysis. *Reading Research Quarterly* 52 (5), 1–33. doi: 10.1002/rrq.179.

Punt, D.-J. 2010. Dáárom dus omdat! Een experimenteel onderzoek naar het effect van structuurkenmerken op het tekstbegrip van beginnende lezers [So that's why because! An experiment on the effect of structural features on the text comprehension of beginning readers]. MA thesis Communication Studies, Utrecht University. Available at: http://dspace.library.uu.nl/handle/1874/242130.

Rayner, K. 1998. Eye movements in reading and information processing: 20 years of research. *Psychological Bulletin* 124, 372–422. doi: 10.1037/0033-2909.124.3.372.

Sanders, T. J. M., Land, J., and Mulder, G. 2007. Linguistic markers of coherence improve text comprehension in functional contexts. *Information Design Journal* 15 (3), 219–235. doi: 10.1075/idj.15.3.04san.

Van Silfhout, G. 2014. Fun to read or easy to understand? Establishing effective text features for educational texts on the basis of processing and comprehension research. Ph. D. dissertation Utrecht University. Utrecht: LOT. Available at: http://www.lotpublications.nl/Documents/368_fulltext.pdf.

Van Silfhout, G., Evers-Vermeul, J., Mak, W.M., and Sanders, T. J. M. 2014a. Connectives and layout as processing signals: How textual features affect students' on-line processing and text representation. *Journal of Educational Psychology* 106 (4), 1036–1048. doi:10.1037/a0036293.

Van Silfhout, G., Evers-Vermeul, J., and Sanders, T. J. M. 2014b. Establishing coherence in school book texts: how connectives and lay-out affect students' text comprehension. *Dutch Journal of Applied Linguistics* 3 (1), 1–29. doi: 10.1075/dujal.3.1.01sil.

Van Silfhout, G., Evers-Vermeul, J., and Sanders, T. 2015. Connectives as processing signals: How students benefit in processing narrative and expository texts. *Discourse Processes* 52 (1), 47–76. doi: 10.1080/0163853X.2014.905237.

Van Veen, R., Evers-Vermeul, J., Sanders. T., and Van den Bergh, H. 2009. Parental input and connective acquisition in German; a growth-curve analysis. *First Language* 29 (3), 267-289. doi:10.1177/0142723708101679.

Van Veen, R., Evers-Vermeul, J., Sanders, T.J.M., and Van den Bergh, H. 2014. "Why? Because I'm talking to you!" Parental input and cognitive complexity as determinants of children's connective acquisition. In H. Gruber, and G. Redeker (eds.), *The pragmatics of discourse coherence: Theories and applications* (pp. 209–242). Amsterdam/Philadelphia: John Benjamins. doi:10.1075/pbns.254.08vee.

Williams, J. P., and Atkins, J. G. 2009. The role of metacognition in teaching reading comprehension to primary students. In D. J. Hacker, J. Dunlosky, and A. C. Graesser (eds.), *Handbook of metacognition in education* (pp. 26–43). Mahwah, NJ: Erlbaum.

Williams, J. P., Hall, K. M., Lauer, K. D., Stafford, K. B., DeSisto, L. A., deCani, J. S. 2005. Expository text comprehension in the primary grade classroom. *Journal of Educational Psychology* 97 (4), 538–550.

Zinar, S. 1990. Fifth-graders' recall of propositional content and causal relationships from expository prose. *Journal of Reading Behavior* 12 (2), 181–199. doi: 10.1080/2F10862969009547703.

Zwaan, R. A., and Radvansky, G. A. 1998. Situation models in language comprehension and memory. *Psychological Bulletin* 123 (2), 162–185. doi: 00006823-199803000-00003.

Henning Czech
Explicit coherence relations in children's and adults' spoken narratives: the importance of *und* for the acquisition of German connectives

Abstract: This study investigates the usage of German connectives in spoken narratives of the so called 'frog stories' by children aged 3, 5 and 9 as well as by young adults. Two aspects are looked at separately: a) the distribution of connectives in terms of their syntactic classes, and b) the distribution of coherence relations marked by these connectives. It is shown that both syntactic and semantic aspects play a crucial role for the acquisition of connectives. Moreover, the coordinating conjunction *und* is analysed in detail because it is the most polysemous German connective. In particular, it is tested whether the usage of *und* can be compared to that of its English equivalent *and*. At first sight, the results indicate that this is not unreservedly the case: As speakers get older, the distribution of coherence relations expressed by *und* does not remain constant in the narratives of the four age groups. Thus, the results reported for *and* by Peterson and McCabe (1987) cannot be replicated for *und*. Furthermore, *und* is not increasingly restricted to additive relations instead. To get a clearer picture of the underlying circumstances, a subsequent analysis of English frog stories is added, which suggests similarities between German *und* and its English equivalent. Since Peterson and McCabe's (1987) data are based on free narratives of personal experiences, the results of the present study illustrate that at least the usage of English *and* is presumably strongly dependent on the respective method of speech elicitation.

1 Introduction

Semantic relations between adjacent clauses or larger segments of a text are referred to as coherence relations. On the one hand, these relations can be implicit. In that case, the relation between the segments is to a high degree underspecified and has to be inferred by the recipient. On the other hand, the speaker can delimit

---

Henning Czech, LearningCenter, University of Applied Sciences Osnabrück, Caprivistraße 30, 49076 Osnabrück, email: h.czech@hs-osnabrueck.de

https://doi.org/10.1515/9781501510151-004

the amount of possible relations by using a connective (cf. Breindl and Waßner 2006) because connectives serve as "lexical markers of coherence relations" (Sanders and Spooren 2009: 198). However, there is no one-to-one mapping between connectives and coherence relations. To begin with, a single relation can be marked by different lexemes. This is illustrated by the German subordinating conjunction *weil* ('because') and the conjunctional adverb *deshalb* ('therefore'), both words being restricted to a causal relation. At the same time, some connectives can indicate different types of relations (cf. Fabricius-Hansen 2011: 6). The coordinating conjunction *und* ('and') is the most polysemous German connective (cf. Breindl and Waßner 2006: 55). While the relation between the segments in (1a) is primarily additive, the second proposition in (1b) is interpreted as the consequence of the first one.

(1) a. [Das Buch hat nur wenige Seiten] **und** [die Schrift ist relativ groß].
The book has only few pages and the font size is quite large.
b. [Sie fiel vom Fahrrad] **und** [brach sich das Bein].
She fell off the bike and broke her leg.

These observations lead to the assumption that children's acquisition of connectives is influenced by at least three factors – the syntactic conditions of their use, their semantic underspecification, and the cognitive complexity of the coherence relations marked by these lexemes. A multitude of empirical studies have been published to examine these aspects of relational coherence in monolingual children's language. While some authors explain the acquisition order of specific connectives mainly with respect to semantic factors (cf. Bloom et al. 1980; Eisenberg 1980; Braunwald 1985 for English; Evers-Vermeul and Sanders 2009 for Dutch), others put great emphasis on the syntactic behaviour of the words acquired (cf. Rothweiler 1993; Diessel 2004). Spooren and Sanders (2008) investigate the acquisition of coherence relations without considering the usage of connectives. Information structural aspects and the notion of iconicity are dealt with by Clark (1970). Some articles focus on specific semantic relations (cf. Clark 1971 and French and Brown 1976 for temporal relations) or other factors influencing the production of connectives, e.g. the non-linguistic context (cf. Kyratzis and Ervin-Tripp 1999). The influence of connectives and of different types of coherence relations on text comprehension by German fourth- and sixth-graders is discussed by Becker et al. (this volume) while Evers-Vermeul (this volume) focuses on the presence of Dutch connectives and its effect on the comprehension and appreciation of informative texts by seven- and eight-year-olds.

As documented in many studies, the semantically underspecified connective *and* is normally the first connective English-speaking children use at the beginning of their third year of life in order to explicitly mark coherence relations (cf. Bloom et al. 1980: 249-254; Eisenberg 1980: 72; Braunwald 1985: 518; Diessel 2004: 172). Other connectives are not acquired until a few months later. These facts may lead one to expect that in the beginning of the acquisition process *and* is used as a connective expressing a larger variety of coherence relations and that with increasing age of the children it becomes more or less restricted to additive relations. However, as is illustrated by Peterson and McCabe (1987), a comparison of free narratives by children aged between four and nine reveals that there is no empirical evidence for this assumption:

> The relative frequencies of each of the meaning categories did not change with age. Thus, the children at all ages were using *and* in the same ways: a simple temporal relationship [...] was present about a third of the time, followed by enabling, causal and co-ordinating relationships which were each present about a fifth of the time. About 10 % of the relationships involved antithesis, and restatement was rare. (Peterson and McCabe: 380)

What is crucial for the current study is that the reported usage of *and* suggests a deeper investigation of the connective *und* and its importance for the acquisition of German connectives. To my knowledge, there are hardly any studies which focus on the acquisition of this specific connective in monolingual German-speaking children. However, using the SIMONE Corpus from the CHILDES database, Hartung-Schaidhammer (2012) presents a single-case study investigating spontaneous speech of the child Simone at the age period of 1;9 to 4;0 years (data collected by Miller 1976). While the author mainly concentrates on the (syntactic) symmetry of the two elements coordinated by *und*, the results also tend to confirm that the acquisition of German *und* is quite similar to that of English *and*: Firstly, *und* is the first connective to be used productively by the child Simone. Secondly, the semantic relations marked by this connective seem to be acquired in the order *additive* < *temporal* < *causal* (see below). These results are in line with the well-known facts presented for English *and* (cf. Bloom et al. 1980).[1]

---

[1] Besides, there is a study by Tribushinina, Valcheva and Gagarina (2017) describing the acquisition of German *und* and *aber* ('but') as well as Russian *i* ('and') and *a* ('and/but') by bilingual and monolingual children aged between four and six years. But as far as the semantic usage of these connectives is concerned, the authors "collapsed the data from different age groups" due to "relatively low frequencies of each function" (cf. Tribushinina, Valcheva and Gagarina 2017: 223).

Before having a closer look at the research objectives, I will present the inventory of coherence relations and connectives considered in this paper. Furthermore, I will shortly summarize in what way the relations and connectives can be classified according to their cognitive and syntactic complexity.

I assume here a closed inventory of ten relations: *additive, alternative, adversative, causal* (volitional or non-volitional, cf. Mann and Thompson 1988), *conditional, consecutive, instrumental, purpose, concessive* and *temporal relations* (including different subtypes, the most important one being *sequence*). Each of these relations is illustrated by a German example below (cf. (1a) for an additive relation; German connectives in bold print).

(2) a. Alternative: Peter ist beim Sport **oder** er ist zu Hause.
Peter is either doing sports or he is at home.
b. Adversative: Hans ist groß, **aber** Fritz ist klein.
Hans is tall whereas Fritz is short.
c. Causal: Sie brach sich das Bein, **weil** sie vom Fahrrad fiel.
She broke her leg because she fell off the bike.
d. Conditional: **Wenn** es morgen regnet, fahre ich nicht mit dem Fahrrad.
If it is raining tomorrow, I won't go by bike.
e. Consecutive: Sie fiel vom Fahrrad, **sodass** sie sich das Bein brach.
She fell off the bike so that she broke her leg.
f. Instrumental: Ich öffne die Tür, **indem** ich den Schlüssel benutze.
I open the door by using the key.
g. Purpose: **Um** Sport zu machen, geht Ramona schwimmen.
In order to do sports, Ramona usually goes swimming.
h. Concessive: **Obwohl** es den ganzen Tag geregnet hat, ist er spazieren gegangen.
Although it has been raining all day, he went for a walk.
i. Sequence: Um 7 Uhr frühstückt Julia. **Dann** füttert sie den Hund.
At 7 a.m. Julia has breakfast. Then she feeds the dog.

Following the Cognitive approach to Coherence Relations (CCR, cf. Sanders, Spooren and Noordman 1992; Spooren and Sanders 2008; Sanders and Spooren 2009), different types of relations can be classified on the basis of four cognitively anchored concepts. Each of these concepts includes at least two alternative values: 1) source of coherence (content vs. epistemic vs. speech act relation), 2) order of segments (basic vs. non-basic, as compared to the logical sequence of the two related segments), 3) basic operation (additive vs. causal[2]), and 4) polarity (positive vs. negative relation). Since this study is predominantly concerned with content relations, the source of coherence will not be discussed further. More information on this topic, which goes back to Sweetser (1990), is provided by Fabricius-Hansen (2011) and Becker et al. (this volume).[3] The cognitive complexity of coherence relations is usually estimated on the basis of the latter two concepts, i.e. basic operation and polarity (cf. Evers-Vermeul and Sanders 2009): In an additive relation, the two related segments "have equal semantic functions and equal semantic weight" (Blühdorn 2008: 70), whereas in a causal relation, one of the related segments is semantically subordinated to the other. Therefore, causal relations are more complex than additive relations. The difference between positive and negative relations can be explained as follows (Sanders, Spooren and Noordman 1992: 10):

> A relation is *positive* if the two discourse segments *S1* and *S2* function in the basic operation as antecedent (*P*) and consequent (*Q*), respectively. A relation is *negative* if not *S1* or *S2* but their negative counterparts, not-*S1* or not-*S2*, function in the basic operation.

Again, the latter type of relation (negative) is more complex than the former (positive). Table 1 illustrates the distribution of the corresponding values for the inventory of relations mentioned above. Temporal relations in the narrow sense are excluded from this taxonomy because temporality is regarded as a secondary notion in CCR (cf. Sanders, Spooren and Noordman 1992: 28). In addition, the various subtypes of temporal relations do not necessarily have the same degree of complexity.

---

2 Notice that the terms *additive* and *causal* are used in a slightly different, broader sense in this context. The same approach is chosen by Tribushinina, Valcheva and Gagarina (2017: 208).
3 One interesting point noted by Hartung-Schaidhammer (2012: 81-122) is the differentiation between *und* (or *and*, respectively) as a discourse marker on the one hand and as a coordinating conjunction on the other hand. Following this idea, which is suggested by, for example, Diessel (2004) and Pafel (2011), one would classify *und* as a discourse marker whenever it is used in an utterance-initial position like *Und was machst du am Wochenende?* ('And what are you planning to do this weekend?'). However, in contrast to Hartung-Schaidhammer (2012), I do not put emphasis on the syntactic behaviour of *und* but rather on its status as a connective. Therefore, its potential classification as a discourse marker would only be a problem for the current study if there was no preceding utterance. For all other instances one could not deny that *und* is used to mark at least an additive relation – in case of doubt, this would be a pragmatic one (speech act relation).

Tab. 1: Cognitive complexity of coherence relations

	Add.	Altern.	Advers.	Causal	Cond.	Consec.	Instrum.	Purp.	Concess.
Causal	–	–	–	+	+	+	+	+	+
Negative	–	–	+	–	–	–	–	–	+

The additive and alternative relations are neither causal nor negative. Consequently, they represent the level of lowest cognitive complexity. In contrast, the concessive relation is the only one which is both causal and negative, hence being the most complex relation. The remaining relations are either additive and negative (adversative relation) or causal and positive. These relations should be classified on an intermediate level of complexity between additive and alternative relations on the one hand and concessive relations on the other hand.

In accordance with Pasch et al. (2003) and Pasch (2004), the connectives dealt with in this study can be classified in terms of their syntactic behaviour. Roughly speaking, the position of each connective in relation to its internal connect, i.e. the clause preceded by or containing the connective (other clause: external connect, cf. Pasch et al. 2003: 8), is used as a criterion to distinguish between two main classes: Connectives which belong to the first class are either *coordinating conjunctions* (e.g. *und* ('and'), *oder* ('or'), *sondern* ('but rather')) or *subordinating conjunctions* (e.g. *weil* ('because'), *wenn* ('when, if'), *sodass* ('so that')). Although all of these lexemes have a fixed position in front of their internal connect, they do not have the same syntactic complexity: while coordinating conjunctions are used to combine clauses of equal syntactic status, subordinating conjunctions introduce subclauses and are therefore more complex. Connectives of the second main class are referred to as *adverbial connectives* (also cf. Blühdorn 2008) because for the most part these lexemes are pronominal and conjunctional adverbs. However, this class also contains few lexemes which would normally be assigned to other word classes, e.g. the coordinating conjunction *aber* ('but') and the particle *auch* ('also') (cf. Pasch et al. 2003). As illustrated by the pronominal adverb *deshalb* ('therefore') in (3a, b), all adverbial connectives have a more or less flexible position in relation to their internal connect.

(3) a. Max möchte ins Ausland gehen. **Deshalb** hat er einen Flug gebucht.
 b. Max möchte ins Ausland gehen. Er hat **deshalb** einen Flug gebucht.
 Max wants to go abroad. Therefore, he booked a flight.

Even if adverbial connectives do not syntactically subordinate the internal connect, they are expected to be more complex than coordinating conjunctions due to their flexible position. Besides, a semantic factor must be considered: As Fabricius-Hansen (2011: 12) points out, most adverbial connectives consist of a referential component and a relational component (e.g. *des-* and *-halb*, respectively in *deshalb*). Hence, the internal argument of a relation marked by one of these words, i.e. the segment the connective is semantically associated with (cf. Pasch et al. 2003: 8), is realized by the external connect. For the examination of the underlying data I will additionally include some *adpositions* (e.g. *wegen* ('because of')) because German PPs can have the status of a proposition (cf. Roch 2018 for further information on this topic). In this case, the PP itself forms the internal connect and is integrated into the other segment of the relation (cf. example (7) below). Therefore, adpositions are also regarded as relatively complex connectives in this study.[4]

As mentioned above, *und* belongs to the class of coordinating conjunctions, which implies that it does not introduce a new subclause level and that it appears in a fixed position in front of its internal connect. Therefore, its syntactic behaviour is maximally simple. In terms of semantics, *und* is maximally simple as well. Its usage is not restricted to a specific coherence relation and (unlike adverbial connectives) it is not composed of a referential and a relational component. The same is true for the English equivalent *and*.

2 Research objectives and hypotheses

Given the background discussed in the previous section, this study serves to shed some light on the distribution of connectives and coherence relations in spoken narratives by German-speaking children of different age groups. More precisely, I will trace:
- the overall distribution of connectives in terms of their syntactic classes,
- the overall distribution of coherence relations marked by these connectives, and
- the distribution of coherence relations marked by the specific connective *und*.

---

[4] Besides, there are some other words in German which do not belong to one of these syntactic classes, but are considered as connectives by Pasch et al. (2003) and Fasch (2004), e.g. the causal connective *denn*.

Particular emphasis will be placed on the following question:
– Does the usage of German *und* resemble that of English *and* as described by Peterson and McCabe (1987)?

Since narratives by children aged five and nine are not only analysed by Peterson and McCabe (1987) but also in the study at hand, the basis for a direct comparison is at least partially provided. Moreover, while the youngest speakers considered by Peterson and McCabe (1987) have already reached the age of four, I will have a look at three-year-old children. This is important, because it gives an impression of how *und* is used in a very early stage of the acquisition of connectives. Finally, narratives by young adults will be considered in order to compare children's usage of connectives to that of proficient speakers.

Though crucial steps in the acquisition of relational coherence have already taken place in the children's third year of life (cf. Bloom et al. 1980; Eisenberg 1980; Braunwald 1985), the acquisition process is not closed at the age of three years. Hence, I expect to observe age-specific differences, especially as far as the connective *und* is concerned. In spite of the results reported by Peterson and McCabe (1987), it seems reasonable to hypothesise on the basis of the theoretical background that with increasing age of the children, *und* is restricted to additive relations. Other relations should be marked by semantically more specific lexemes in order to minimize semantic ambiguity.

3 Data

The data to be analysed is taken from the CHILDES (Child Language Data Exchange System) database (cf. MacWhinney 2000) and is composed of spoken narratives told by 43 monolingual German-speaking children and young adults. These narratives are based on the picture story "Frog, where are you?" (cf. Mayer 1969) and have been collected by Bamberg (cf. Bamberg 1985). Before telling the story, the subjects have a look at the 24 pictures, which are also available while the story is told. As the interviewers are asked not to give much support, the children's narratives are usually not interrupted. The recordings are transcribed with CHAT (Codes for the Human Analysis of Transcripts, cf. MacWhinney 2013). According to their age, participants are divided into the following groups: group A: 12 children aged between 3;3 and 3;11 (labelled 03a to 03l in the database), group B: 11 children aged between 5;0 and 5;11 (05a to 05k), group C: 10 children aged between 9;0 and 9;11 (09a to 09j), group D: 10 adults aged 20 (20a to 20j). Further information is given by Berman and Slobin (1994) and by the database manuals on the CHILDES website.

Because of the surprising results presented in section 5.4, the actual study is expanded by a short explorative analysis of narratives by monolingual English-speaking participants. This subsequent analysis is mainly restricted to the connective *and*; it is needed to review the preliminary interpretation concerning the usage of German *und*. The data (recorded by Renner 1988 and Marchman 1989; cf. Berman and Slobin 1994: 28) are also based on the frog story and are provided by the CHILDES database as well.[5] Originally, the sample consists of 59 participants from California aged three, four, five, nine and 20 years. I chose to exclude the four-year-old children. Thus, in parallel to the German sample, the following groups are compared: group A_e: 12 children aged between 3;1 and 3;11 (labelled 03a to 03l in the database), group B_e: 11 children aged between 5;1 and 5;11 (05a to 05k), group C_e: 12 children aged between 9;1 and 9;11 (09a to 09l), group D_e: 12 adults aged 20 (20a to 20l).

4 Method

The elementary data for each group (average number of words and utterances, MLU) are computed with the aid of CLAN (Computerized Language Analysis, cf. MacWhinney 2014). The MLU values are important to estimate the younger children's level of language acquisition. All remaining aspects are analysed manually: Coherence relations are named after their internal argument, e.g. a cause-consequence relation is classified as a 'causal relation' if the connective is related to the connect representing the cause, but as a 'consecutive relation' if the connective marks the consequence. When a connective is polysemous, the most specific plausible relation is chosen; for example, when *und* is used to combine two causally related segments, it is not only assumed to mark an additive or temporal relation because causal and consecutive relations logically imply an additive relation and a temporal sequence of the related events.

The status of a word as a connective and the coherence relation marked by this connective are assessed on the basis of the picture story and the textual context. Since it was not possible to decide "by consensus" or "proportions of agreement" (Bloom et al. 1980: 239) with other judgements and in order to avoid inaccuracies, no decision is made concerning the intended relation if the usage of a connective

---

[5] Thanks to one of my reviewers who proposed this subsequent analysis.

remains ambiguous even after taking the context into account. Instead, the relation in question is assigned to the category 'not definable' (cf. figures 2, 3 and 4). Besides, some utterances contain combinations of *und* with one or more other connectives.[6] Even in these cases, *und* is not assigned to a specific relation because it is semantically underspecified, i.e. it is not clear whether *und* marks the same relation as one of the combined connectives or whether it marks an additive relation, which is implied by the more specific relation anyway. In order to keep these two cases of semantically 'non-definable' connectives apart, the category '*und* in combination' is created. The more specific connectives combined with *und* are treated as single connectives since their meanings do usually not change in combination with *und*. Connectives which are obviously repeated at one point of speech are only counted once. This is illustrated for the combined connectives *und* and *dann* in the following extract (German speaker 05e, line 35 of the transcript):[7]

(4)   35* CHI: und dann <und dann gehn sie> [/?] dann gehn die ein Stück[8] weiter.
        and then <and then they are moving> [/?] then they are moving on a bit .

For the subsequent analysis of English *and*, the methodological approach is exactly the same as for the German data.

5 Results and discussion

The sections 5.1 to 5.4 serve to present the results for the German data while the subsequent study of English frog stories is discussed in section 5.5.

---

6 The most frequent combinations are *und dann* ('and then', temporal sequence marked by *dann*) and *und auch* ('and also', additive relation marked by *auch*). In addition, there are some other combinations like *und trotzdem* ('and nevertheless') and *und inzwischen* ('and meanwhile').

7 The usage of *und* (be it isolated or immediately followed by *dann*) at the beginning of a sentence or utterance might primarily have the (pragmatic) function of continuing with the narration. In my view, as long as there is some preceding material in the text, this function does not at all preclude the additional interpretation of *und* as a connective (see also fn. 3).

8 I chose to add the specific German umlaut where necessary.

5.1 General remarks

Table 2 displays the elementary data for each of the four German age groups compared in this study. The comparison of the MLUs reveals statistically significant differences between group A und group B (t=3.3455, df=20, p=0.0032, α_1=0.025; Welch's t-test, two-tailed)[9] as well as between group B and group C (t=3.2945, df=18, p=0.0040, α_2=0.05).

Tab. 2: Elementary data for each German age group (mean values)

Group	Number of words	Number of utterances	MLU	Standard deviation MLU
A	315.17	61.9	5.08	0.63
B	348.27	58.8	5.94	0.61
C	563.80	83.3	6.83	0.62
D	873.30	126.2	6.84	0.39

Even if the mean length of the narratives (= number of words) seems to increase with age, it must be considered that the picture story is told twice by some participants, namely 05k, 09e, 09g, 20a and 20e. The first part then functions as the preparation of the actual task, i.e. the pictures of the story are rather described beforehand (cf. the description of data above). However, both versions are analysed here because they do not differ considerably in terms of their textual structure; for example, both versions contain deictic forms like *da* ('there', line 117) and *hier* ('here', line 121) as illustrated by the following extract (speaker 20a). The transition between the two versions is signalled in line 120.

(5) 117 *CHI: und einer sitzt da unten noch so [/?].
 and down there one (of them) is still sitting [/?] .
 118 *CHI: <war es das> [/?].

---

9 Unexceptionally all specific alpha levels α_r in this study are adjusted by using Holm-Bonferroni correction to avoid alpha cumulation (cf. Eid et al. 2013: 400f.). With this method, the specific alpha levels get stricter with decreasing p-values, i.e. the most significant p-value is assigned to the strictest alpha level α_1. As usual, I chose α_{fam}=0.05 as the family-wise error rate. Since the presented group comparisons are more of an explorative character, I do not use the global test of a one-way ANOVA beforehand. Welch's t-test is chosen because of inequality of variances. All t-tests are based on relative frequencies, i.e. on continuous data.

>   <is that all> [/?] .
> 119 @G:01-
> 120 *CHI: <also jetzt ich ich erzähl dir jetzt die Geschichte> [/?] .
>   <ok now I I am going to tell you the story> [/?] .
> 121 *CHI: es geht hier um nen Frosch nen Jungen und nen Hund zunächst .
>   first of all it's about a frog a boy and a dog here .

It is also important to notice that all participants except 09d use the present tense for telling the story – even if there are two versions. This is surprising because according to Klein and Stutterheim (1987: 174), the *quaestio* of a narrative is usually formulated in the past tense. Finally, some children obviously overuse the pictures as an aid for telling the story by frequently choosing deictic forms; this is exemplified by the extract in (6) (speaker 05j). What can also be seen here is that the connective *und* is produced very often by younger children. This will be discussed in section 5.4.[10]

> (6) 45 *CHI: und da ist ein Eichhörnchen .
>   and there is a squirrel .
>   46 *CHI: und da ist der Hund .
>   and there is the dog .
>   47 *CHI: und da ist das Bienenhaus .
>   and there is the bee house .
>   48 *CHI: und da ist der Junge .
>   and there is the boy .

5.2 Inventory and syntactic classes of connectives

The analysis shows that the average number of connectives used per utterance increases at least until the age of nine (group A: 0.42, standard deviation s=0.20; group B: 0.79, s=0.28; group C: 0.88, s=0.31), but while the differences between mean values are statistically significant for the comparison of group A and group

---

[10] One might prefer to look on *und da* as a unit so that it can be analysed just like other combinations of connectives, e.g. *und dann*. However, in most cases observed here, *da* is not interpretable as a temporal element in the sense of 'then' but rather as a local deictic used to refer to the respective pictures of the story. This deictic element does not connect two propositional arguments or larger segments of the text. Consequently, *da* used in passages similar to (6) cannot be regarded as a connective, wherefore *und* should be treated as a single connective.

B (t=3.6071, df=18, p=0.0020, $α_1$=0.017), the results for group B and group C are quite similar in this respect (t=0.7492, df=18, p=0.4634, $α_3$=0.05). Furthermore, the adults seem to use less connectives (0.64, s=0.12) than the nine-year-old children. Even though this difference is not statistically significant on the adjusted specific alpha level (t=2.3259, df=11, p=0.0402, $α_2$=0.025), the results at least indicate that the process is even inverted later on. However, adults use more different lexemes of connectives than children do (total numbers: group A: 10, group B: 12, group C: 22, group D: 37).[11]

I will now turn to the first of the three core issues mentioned above. The distribution of connectives in terms of their syntactic classes is illustrated in figure 1.

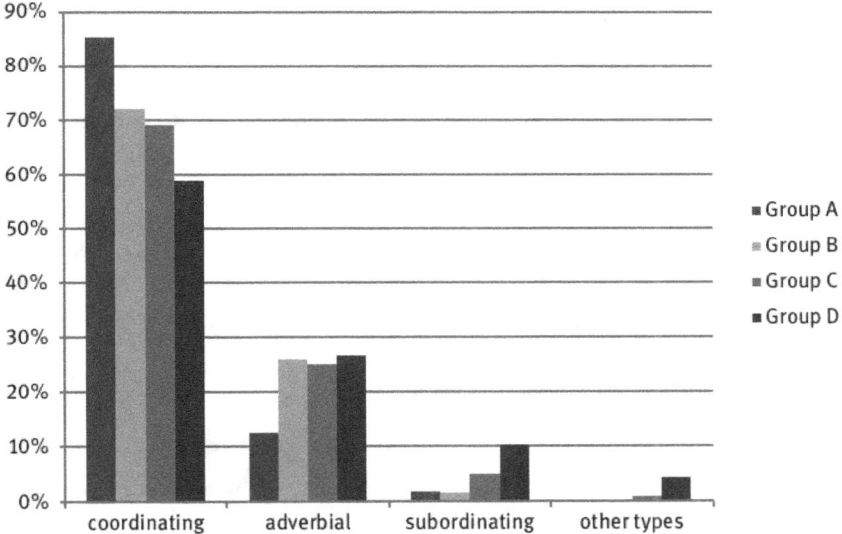

Fig. 1: Specific classes of connectives out of all connectives produced by each group

First of all, the percentage of coordinating conjunctions is rather high for all of the four groups, but continuously decreases as the children get older (85.4 % for group A as compared to 58.9 % for the adults). The greatest difference is observed

---

11 Since one of the youngest children (03i) does not use any connective appropriately, these data are excluded from the calculations above. This child even has the lowest MLU of 3.71 words per utterance.

between group A and group B, where the proportion of coordinating conjunctions decreases by 13.4 %. At the same time, the proportion of adverbial connectives increases by 13.2 % between these two age groups and remains on a constant level of 25-27 % afterwards. Subordinating conjunctions are hardly produced at all by group A and group B. In the stories told by the nine-year-old children and the adults, 5 and 10 %, respectively, of the lexemes belong to this syntactic class of connectives. These findings suggest that subordinating conjunctions are generally and in all age groups produced very rarely in spoken narratives. Besides, the adults use some connectives which do not fit to one of the syntactic classes distinguished by Pasch et al. (2003) and Pasch (2004). These lexemes (mainly prepositions and specific particles) are summed up by the category 'other types' in figure 1. The usage of prepositions is illustrated by the following extract (speaker 20f), where the PP *vor Schreck* in line 91 is to be translated as *because of being afraid*.

(7) 89 *CHI: da kommt auf einmal aus dem Loch ein [/?] ein Uhu heraus .
    there suddenly an eagle owl is coming out of the hole .
 90 *CHI: und guckt ganz böse .
    and is frowning .
 91 *CHI: vor Schreck fällt der kleine Junge auf den Rücken vom [/?] runter vom Baum .
    because of being afraid the young boy falls down on his back off [/?] off the tree .
 92 *CHI: und liegt jetzt auf dem Boden .
    and is now lying on the ground .

In sum, the age-specific differences can be traced back to the syntactic complexity of certain classes of connectives. Coordinating conjunctions are regarded as being syntactically simple, whereas the usage of subordinating conjunctions requires the ability to deal with hypotaxis. Due to their syntactic behaviour and their morphological structure, adverbial connectives are more complex than coordinating conjunctions. When a preposition is used as a connective, one argument of the coherence relation appears in a rather condensed form. Thus, prepositions used as connectives are semantically more complex than for example coordinating conjunctions.

5.3 Distribution of coherence relations

The explicitly marked coherence relations in the data are for the most part content relations. Since, according to Kyratzis and Ervin-Tripp (1999), the source of coherence relations is to a great degree influenced by the non-linguistic context, the observed results are due to the mere fact that it is typical of narratives to include more content relations than speech act and epistemic relations. This assumption is supported by Spooren and Sanders (2008), who investigate the semantic connections between text segments in picture descriptions made by children aged between six and twelve years. The authors note a proportion of 92.6 % (op.cit.: 2014) for content relations.

The distribution of all explicitly marked coherence relations found in the data is shown in figure 2.

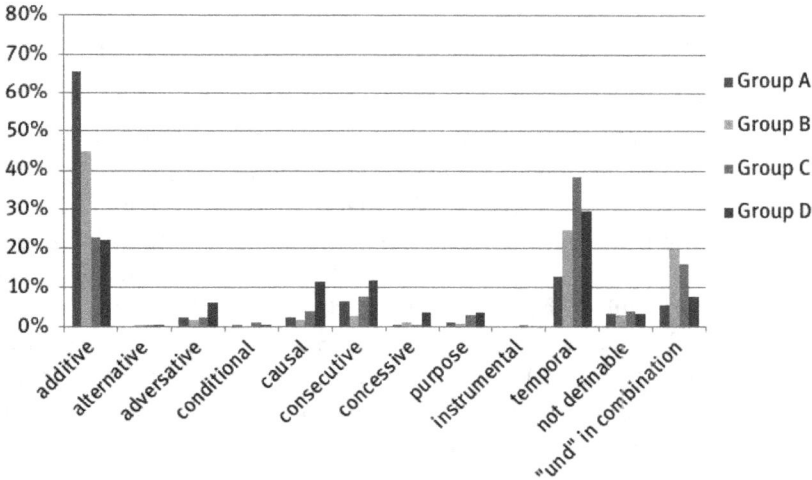

Fig. 2: Specific coherence relations out of all explicit relations

The results indicate that even the youngest children have already acquired coherence relations which are of a relatively high degree of cognitive complexity, e.g. adversative relations as well as some types of causal relations in the broader sense. These results comply with those presented by Bloom et al. (1980), Eisenberg (1980) and Braunwald (1985). Nevertheless, there definitely are some age-specific differences. Especially in the narratives of the three-year old children, the proportion of additive relations is noticeably high (65.7 % for group A as compared to 44.7 % for the five-year-old children and about 22 % for group C and the adults). This can be explained by the low cognitive complexity of this type of relation. Furthermore, the three-year-old children do not always stick to the chronology of events in the picture story. Instead, their narratives resemble a more or less unorganised description of pictures, which increases the number of purely additive relations. For example, in the following extract (speaker 03b), the temporal order of sleeping (line 16) and awakening (line 13) is inverted.

(8) 13 *CHI: da wachen die wieder auf.
   there they are waking up again.
   14 *CHI: da ist der Frosch weg.
   there the frog is gone.
   15 @G: 02a
   16 *CHI: und da schläft der.
   and there he is sleeping.

When children get older, events are presented not just additively but in chronological order so that more temporal relations are marked by connectives (12.9 % for group A, 24.7 % for group B). For the most part, these relations belong to the subtype of immediate temporal sequence (cf. Klein and Stutterheim 1987 for referential movement in narratives). Besides, explicit relations of temporal similarity are found, particularly in the narratives of the older participants. What is also interesting is that the adults use less explicitly marked temporal relations than the nine-year-old children do (29.5 % as compared to 38.5 %). In narratives, events are usually presented in chronological order, and temporal relations are obligatorily marked only if they do not correspond to this pattern (cf. Klein and Stutterheim 1987: 177, Klein 1994: 45). Therefore, the adults do generally consider the chronological order of events and master the 'principle of natural or chronological order' (cf. Clark 1970, 1971) well, but the relations marked by connectives are not always primarily temporal. Instead, more specific relations which logically imply additive and temporal relations between the related segments are made explicit.

This explains why the proportions of causal and consecutive relations in the adults' narratives (causal: 11.6 %, consecutive 11.9 %) are higher than those in the stories told by the children (noteworthy proportions of consecutive relations: 6.5 % for group A, 7.7 % for group C). Since causal and consecutive relations are semantically identical, they can only be distinguished by identifying the internal argument of the connective used to mark the relation. Although, according to the CCR, other relations, namely those having the features 'causal' and 'positive', are not considerably more complex than causal and consecutive relations, they hardly ever occur in the narratives at all, be it explicitly or implicitly. This could be due to the fact that the pictures of the story simply do not suggest such relations between the illustrated events. In general, proportions of causal relations in the broader sense are relatively low in the narratives of group A (10.4 %) and group B (6.1 %), whereas they increase as the speakers get older (group C: 16.2 %, group D: 30.9 %). The most complex relation regarded in this study is the concessive relation. Unsurprisingly, concessive connectives are used with a considerable frequency only by group D (3.7 %).

All in all, the analysis reveals age-specific differences concerning the distribution of explicitly marked relations. The decision to mark a specific relation by using a connective depends on the verbal abilities of the speaker.

5.4 Results for the connective 'und'

Having analysed the distribution of explicit coherence relations in the narratives and the distribution of connectives in terms of their syntactic behaviour, I will now have a detailed look at the most polysemous German connective *und*. In the narratives of all groups compared in this study, *und* is by far the most frequent connective. Similar results are reported by Tribushinina, Valcheva and Gagarina (2017). The calculation of the mean proportions of *und* as related to the numbers of all connectives used by each group gives the following results: group A: 0.85, s=0.14; group B: 0.76, s=0.16; group C: 0.66, s=0.12; group D: 0.57, s=0.08. The comparison of mean values reveals a statistically significant difference between group A and group C (t=3.2425, df=18, p=0.0045, α_1=0.013), whereas the results for all other tested comparisons are not that clear (A vs. B: t=1.3035, df=19, p=0.208, α_4=0.05; B vs. C: t=1.5821, df=18, p=0.131, α_3=0.025; C vs. D: t=2.1808, df=16, p=0.0445, α_2=0.017). Nevertheless, it is not unreasonable to assume that the proportion of *und* decreases as the speakers get older.

In view of this fact, one could expect that *und* is incrementally restricted to additive relations. As set out above, this hypothesis is rejected for the English equivalent *and* by Peterson and McCabe (1987). The authors come to the conclusion that the proportions of the various coherence relations marked by *and* do not significantly change as children get older. In order to find out whether these results are replicable for the German connective *und*, the coherence relations marked by this lexeme are given in figure 3.

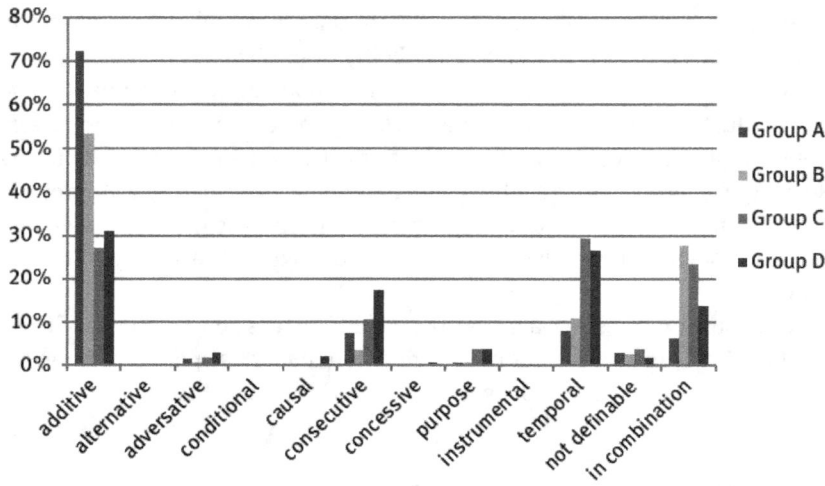

Fig. 3: Specific coherence relations out of all explicit relations marked by *und*

This chart demonstrates the striking semantic diversity of the connective *und*. Besides, there is a remarkable resemblance between these results and the general distribution of coherence relations presented in figure 2: again, the proportion of additive relations decreases with age (group A: 72.4 %, group B: 53.4 %, group C: 27.1 %). At the same time, older children are more likely to connect two events not only by an additive relation but by temporal sequence (29.3 % for group C as compared to 10.9 % for group B). However, there seem to be clear differences between figure 2 and figure 3 concerning the distribution of causal and consecutive relations. This can be traced back to the syntactic behaviour of the coordinating conjunction *und*: When a temporal relation between two events is not additionally marked by other means of cohesion, e.g. by using different tenses in the related clauses, *und* normally introduces the chronologically second event. This explains why as compared to the results in figure 2, the proportions of causal relations decrease, whereas consecutive relations are relatively frequent: the chronologically second event cannot be the cause but only the consequence.

To sum up, because of its polysemy *und* plays an important role for the acquisition of connectives and coherence relations. But as children get older, *und* is neither restricted to additive relations at all. In contrast, the frequency of additive relations even decreases in the analysed data. Furthermore, the findings presented by Peterson and McCabe (1987) do not seem to be applicable to German *und* because the distribution of coherence relations does not remain constant.

5.5 Subsequent analysis of English 'and'

Before going into detail concerning the semantic usage of *and*, I will shortly present some general results. The elementary data for each age group are given in table 3. Besides the relatively high dispersion of MLU values for the two younger groups and the fact that the English narratives are much shorter than the German ones, there are no critical and considerable specifics.

Tab. 3: Elementary data for each English age group (mean values)

Group	Number of words	Number of utterances	MLU	Standard deviation MLU
A_e	123.83	29.2	4.12	1.00
B_e	257.91	43.7	5.87	0.72
C_e	284.58	45.6	6.25	0.38
D_e	518.33	76.9	6.71	0.54

The average number of connectives used per utterance differs strongly between the narratives of the three- and five-year-old participants (group A_e: 0.36, group B_e: 0.98) while connectives are similarly frequent in the narratives of group B_e and group C_e (group C_e: 0.91). These latter frequencies are relatively high as compared to the adult group (0.52), which is partly due to the fact that all children produce remarkably many combinations of two connectives (see below). With regard to different lexemes of connectives, the total number unsurprisingly increases with age (group A_e: 8, group B_e: 9; group C_e: 14; group D_e: 24).

The conjunction *and* is by far the most frequent connective used in the English data (relative frequencies as related to the number of all connectives: group A_e: 0.66, s=0.31; group B_e: 0.62; s=0.17; group C_e: 0.66, s=0.09; group D_e: 0.62, s=0.14). But in contrast to the German data, age does not seem to influence this variable at all (no significant results for comparisons of groups with different mean values: group A_e vs. group B_e: t=0.3455, df=13, p=0.7352; $α_3$=0.05; group A_e vs. group D_e: t=0.4114, df=11, p=0.6887; $α_2$=0.025; group C_e vs. group D_e: t=0.8987, df=18, p=0.3807; $α_1$=0.017). However, it has to be considered that the interviewer of the three-year-old participants O3h to O3l very often intervenes in order to encourage the children to speak. This is illustrated by the following extract (speaker O3k) where the interruptions are marked by "tc":

(9) 12 *CHI: [^ tc: how about there .] he's gone . [+ tc: uhhuh .]
     13 @G: 03b
     14 *CHI: [^ tc: how about that one .] the dog's in (.) the window. [+ tc: ah .]
     15 *CHI: [^ tc: and here] not in the bottle . [+ tc: not in the bottle. ok]

This strategy finds its expression in the fact that these five children use connectives very infrequently – they simply don't get the chance to do so. The exclusion of these narratives leads to an adjusted relative frequency of *and* which is higher than before (0.73); the frequency of connectives used per utterance also increases (0.53).[12]

Now, in order to compare the usage of English *and* to that of German *und*, the distribution of all coherence relations marked by *and* is given in figure 4 below. As already announced for its German counterpart, the results illustrate the striking semantic diversity of the connective *and*. In addition, the overall shape of figure 4 is quite similar to that of figure 3 above: The proportion of additive relations decreases with age (group A_e: 50.0 %, group B_e: 35.0 %, group C_e: 26.6 %, group D_e: 30.8 %), whereby the older participants clearly tend to mark temporal relations (mainly temporal sequence) instead (group A_e: 5.0 %, group B_e: 17.9 %, group C_e: 28.2 %, group D_e: 29.4 %). Nevertheless, the specific proportions of additive relations marked in the narratives of the three- and five-years-olds are much lower than in the German data. The main reason seems to be that these children use *and* in combination with another connective (almost exclusively *and then*) more frequently than their German peers do with the connective *und*. Therefore, these combinations play an important role especially in the early stages of the acquisition of English connectives (group A_e and group B_e). Afterwards this frequency decreases (group A_e: 30.0 %, group B_e: 36.4 %, group C_e: 24.2 %, group D_e: 7.7 %). Furthermore, considerable proportions can also be found for consecutive and purpose relations. As in the German data, older speakers tend to mark more of these cognitively complex relations.

---

12 In my view, the sample wouldn't be representative any more with only seven three-year-old participants. Therefore, I did not exclude them from further analysis.

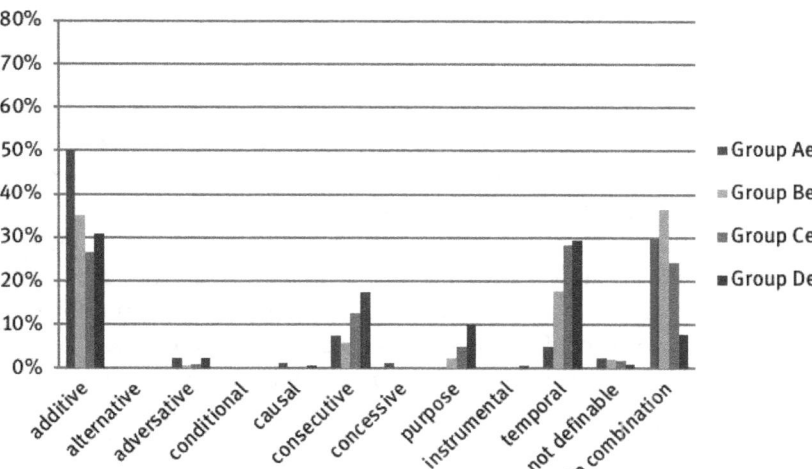

Fig. 4: Specific coherence relations out of all explicit relations marked by *and*

In sum, the usage of *and* in the English frog stories is quite similar to the usage of *und* in the German narratives based on this picture story. Neither is *and* restricted to additive relations as children learn more specific connectives nor do the proportions of different relations marked by *and* remain constant. Therefore, this study also illustrates that the results reported by Peterson and McCabe (1987) cannot be generalized unreservedly over all instances of the connective *and* in narratives. As far as the comparison of German *und* and English *and* within the scope of the present study is concerned, one cannot generally conclude that the underlying mechanisms of acquisition are very different for these two related lexemes. In contrast, taking together all results referred to in the preceding sections, the formal similarity of these coordinating conjunctions apparently finds its analogy in the semantics and pragmatics of these words or – more specifically – in their usage as connectives. However, what could be relevant here is that picture stories like the one used in the CHILDES database narrow down the range of possible relations between text segments while participants can talk about personal experiences more freely in Peterson and McCabe's (1987) study. It has to be examined further in how far the observed usage of the two connectives is dependent on the underlying experimental design, i.e. on different methods of speech elicitation. This would explain the difference between Peterson and McCabe's (1987) results and the facts presented here.

6 Conclusion

The general aim of this study was to trace the usage of German connectives in children's and adults' spoken narratives. This was done by using the so called 'frog stories' provided on the CHILDES database with texts of three-, five- and nine-year-old children and twenty-year-old adults. In order to keep syntactic and semantic acquisition factors apart, two aspects of relational coherence were analysed independently: a) the distribution of connectives in terms of their syntactic classes, and b) the distribution of coherence relations marked by these connectives. As presumed before, age-specific differences were observed indicating that children's usage of connectives is not only influenced by the syntactic behaviour of certain lexemes but also by the cognitive complexity of the coherence relations marked by the connectives. In addition, the German connective *und* was looked at in more detail. The findings show that the relative frequency of this lexeme as compared to other connectives decreases as children get older. But with increasing age of the speakers, *und* is neither restricted to additive relations nor does the distribution of coherence relations expressed by *und* remain constant. Rather, there is a close resemblance between the distributions of coherence relations observed for this connective on the one hand and for all connectives on the other hand. Thus, it was shown that the findings concerning English *and* presented by Peterson and McCabe (1987) cannot be replicated for the German equivalent. However, a subsequent analysis of English frog stories with participants of the same age groups as in the German study reveals striking similarities between the acquisition of these two related lexemes. Since Peterson and McCabe's (1987) data were based on free narratives of personal experiences, it seems reasonable to assume that the choice of elicitation methods influences the usage of *und* or *and*, respectively, in children's narratives.

All in all, this study can function as the basis for further investigation of *und*. Because of the potential differences between English and German it should be tested, for example, whether *und* is used similarly in other contexts. In addition, I suggest to do some research on the role of combinations of different connectives in the early stages of acquisition. With regard to coherence relations in general, it would be interesting to examine in how far their exact distribution is influenced by different text types.

References

Bamberg, M. 1985. Form and function in the construction of narratives: Developmental perspectives. Unpublished doctoral dissertation. University of California, Berkeley.

Becker, A., Cristante, V. & Musan, R. (this volume). The comprehension of coherence relations in expository texts at the age of 10 and 12. In Gagarina, N. & Musan, R. (eds.): Referential and relational discourse coherence in adults and children. Berlin/New York: de Gruyter.

Berman, R. A. & Slobin, D. I. 1994. Relating events in narrative: A crosslinguistic developmental study. Hillsdale, New Jersey etc.: Lawrence Erlbaum Associates.

Bloom, L., Lahey, M., Hood, L., Lifter, K. & Fiess, K. 1980. Complex sentences: Acquisition of syntactic connectives and the meaning relations they encode. *Journal of Child Language* 7, 235–261.

Blühdorn, H. 2008. Subordination and coordination in syntax, semantics and discourse. Evidence from the study of connectives. In Fabricius-Hansen, C. & Ramm, W. (eds.): 'Subordination' versus 'coordination' in sentence and text. A cross-linguistic perspective. Philadelphia/Amsterdam: John Benjamins, 59–85. (Studies in Language Companion Series 98).

Braunwald, S. R. 1985. The development of connectives. *Journal of Pragmatics* 9, 513–525.

Breindl, E. & Waßner, U.H. 2006. Syndese vs. Asyndese. Konnektoren und andere Wegweiser für die Interpretation semantischer Relationen in Texten. Ir Blühdorn, H., Breindl, E. & Waßner, U. H. (eds.): Text – Verstehen. Grammatik und darüber hinaus. Berlin/New York: de Gruyter, 46–70.

CHILDES (Child Language Data Exchange System): http://childes.psy.cmu.edu/browser/index.php?url=Frogs/German-Bamberg/. Accessed 16 February 2014.

Clark, E. 1970. How young children describe events in time. In: Flores d'Arcais, G. B. & Levelt, W. J. M. (eds.): Advances in Psycholinguistics. Amsterdam: North Holland Publishing, 275-293.

Clark, E. 1971. On the acquisition of *before* and *after*. Journal of Verbal Learning and Verbal Behavior 10, 266–275.

Diessel, H. 2004. The acquisition of complex sentences. Cambridge: Cambridge University Press.

Eid, M., Gollwitzer, M. & Schmitt, M. 2013. Statistik und Forschungsmethoden. Lehrbuch. Weinheim, Basel: Beltz Verlag.

Eisenberg, A. R. 1980. A syntactic, semantic, and pragmatic analysis of conjunction. *Papers and reports on child language development* 19, 70–78.

Evers-Vermeul, J. (this volume): Short sentences easy to read? Effects of connectives and layout on text comprehension by beginning readers. In Gagarina, N. & Musan, R. (eds.): Referential and relational discourse coherence in adults and children. Berlin/New York: de Gruyter.

Evers-Vermeul, J. & Sanders, T. J. M. 2009. The emergence of Dutch connectives; how cumulative cognitive complexity explains the order of acquisition. *Journal of Child Language* 36, 829–854.

Fabricius-Hansen, C. 2011. Was wird verknüpft, mit welchen Mitteln – und wozu? Zur Mehrdimensionalität der Satzverknüpfung. http://folk.uio.no/cfhansen/cfh-Satzverkn11.pdf. Accessed 16 February 2014.

French, L.A. & Brown, A.L. 1976. Comprehension of *before* and *after* in logical and arbitrary sequences. *Journal of Child Language* 4, 247–256.

Hartung-Schaidhammer, N. 2012. *Und*-Koordination in der frühen Kindersprache. Eine korpusbasierte Untersuchung. Dissertation, Universität Tübingen. https://bibliographie.uni-tuebingen.de/xmlui/bitstream/handle/10900/46995/pdf/Hartung_Und_Koordination_Kindersprache.pdf?sequence=1&isAllowed=y, Accessed 24 August 2016.

Klein, W. 1994. Time in Language. London/New York: Routledge.

Klein, W. & Stutterheim, C. von. 1987. Quaestio und referentielle Bewegung in Erzählungen. *Linguistische Berichte* 109, 163–183.

Kyratzis, A. & Ervin-Tripp, S. 1999. The development of discourse markers in peer interaction. *Journal of Pragmatics* 31, 1321–1338.

MacWhinney, B. 2000. The CHILDES Project: Tools for analyzing talk. Third Edition. Mahwah, NJ: Lawrence Erlbaum Associates.

MacWhinney, B. 2013. Tools for Analyzing Talk – Electronic Edition. Part 1: The CHAT Transcription Format. Carnegie Mellon University. http://childes.psy.cmu.edu/manuals/CHAT.pdf. Accessed 16 February 2014.

MacWhinney, B. 2014. Tools for Analyzing Talk – Electronic Edition. Part 2: The CLAN Programs. Carnegie Mellon University. http://childes.psy.cmu.edu/manuals/CLAN.pdf. Accessed 16 February 2014.

Mann, W. C. & Thompson, S. A. 1988. Rhetorical structure theory. Toward a functional theory of text organization. *Text* 8, 243–281.

Marchman, V. 1989. Episodic structure and the linguistic encoding of events in narrative: A study of language acquisition and performance. Unpublished doctoral dissertation. University of California, Berkeley.

Mayer, M. 1969. Frog, where are you? New York: Dial Books for Young Readers.

Miller, M. 1976. Zur Logik der frühkindlichen Sprachentwicklung: Empirische Untersuchungen und Theoriediskussionen. Konzepte der Humanwissenschaften. Stuttgart: Klett.

Pafel, J. 2011. Einführung in die Syntax: Grundlagen – Strukturen – Theorien. Stuttgart, Weimar: Metzler.

Pasch, R. 2004. Das „Handbuch der deutschen Konnektoren". In Blühdorn, H., Breindl, E. & Waßner, U. H. (eds.): Brücken schlagen. Grundlagen der Konnektorensemantik. Berlin, New York: de Gruyter. 11–44. (Linguistik – Impulse & Tendenzen 5)

Pasch, R., Brauße, U., Breindl, E. & Waßner, U. H. 2003. Handbuch der deutschen Konnektoren. Linguistische Grundlagen der Beschreibung und syntaktische Merkmale der deutschen Satzverknüpfer (Konjunktionen, Satzadverbien und Partikeln). Berlin/New York: de Gruyter. (Schriften des Instituts für Deutsche Sprache 9)

Peterson, C. & McCabe, A. 1987. The connective 'and': do older children use it less as they learn other connectives? *Journal of Child Language* 14, 375–381.

Renner, T. 1988. Development of temporality in children's narratives. Unpublished doctoral dissertation. University of California, Berkeley.

Roch, C. 2018. Kontextabhängigkeit konditionaler Interpretationen von Präpositionalphrasen. Dissertation, Ruhr-Universität Bochum. https://d-nb.info/116750514X/34, Accessed 20 January 2019.

Rothweiler, Monika. 1993. Der Erwerb von Nebensätzen im Deutschen. Eine Pilotstudie. Tübingen: Niemeyer. (Linguistische Arbeiten 302)

Sanders, T. J. M. & Spooren, W. P. M. 2009. The cognition of discourse coherence. In Renkema, J. (ed.): Discourse, of Course. An overview of research in discourse studies. Amsterdam/Philadelphia: John Benjamins, 197–212.

Sanders, T. J. M., Spooren, W. P. M. & Noordman, L. G. M. 1992. Toward a taxonomy of coherence relations. *Discourse Processes* 15, 1–35.

Spooren, W. P. M. & Sanders, T. J. M. 2008. The acquisition order of coherence relations: On cognitive complexity in discourse. *Journal of Pragmatics* 40, 2003–2026.

Sweetser, E. 1990. From etymology to pragmatics. Metaphorical and cultural aspects of semantic structure. Cambridge: Cambridge University Press.

Tribushinina, E., Valcheva, E. & Gagarina, N. 2017. Acquisition of additive connectives by Russian-German bilinguals: A usage-based approach. In Evers-Vermeul, J. & Tribushinina, E. (eds.): Usage-Based Approaches to Language Acquisition and Language Teaching. Boston/Berlin: de Gruyter, 207–232.

Part 2: **Referential coherence**

Natalia Gagarina, Julia Lomako, Elizabeth Stadtmiller and Katrin Lindner

Text organization in typically developing bilinguals and bilinguals at risk of DLD: what is different and how language independent is it?

Abstract: This study investigates narrative text organization, i.e. well-formedness and coherence of macrostructure in Russian-German sequential bilingual children. Specifically, it compares macrostructure in Russian and German of two groups of children and examines correlations between macrostructure and language proficiency. A total of 74 oral narrative texts in German and Russian were elicited via telling and retelling from 23 children. These children were selected from a larger sample of preschool bilinguals and were divided into two groups: 16 typically developing (TD) children and seven children identified as at risk of a developmental language disorder (DLD) based on their combined language proficiency score in both languages. Both groups were matched by age and nonverbal IQ. Macrostructure of narratives was defined by a multi-dimensional model of text organization and operationalized in terms of the presence of components of story structure and story complexity, as well as the use of forms referring to internal states. In addition, microstructure (i.e. types and tokens) was compared across the TD- and DLD-children and correlated with the composite score of language proficiency. Significant differences between the two groups were found in the organization of narrative texts as well as types and tokens, confirming

---

Note: This work was supported by the DFG Grant „Verbal and Non-Verbal Indicators for Identifying Specific Language Impairment in Successive Bilingual Preschoolers". Grant Numbers: DFG Az. LI 410/5-1 & Az. GA 1424/3-1. The work of Natalia Gagarina was also in part supported by the German Federal Ministry of Education and Research (3MBF) Grant No. 01UG1411.

Natalia Gagarina, Leibniz-Centre for General Linguistics (ZAS), Schützenstraße 18, 10117 Berlin, email: gagarina@leibniz-zas.de
Julia Lomako, email: lomako@web.de
Elizabeth Stadtmiller and Katrin Lindner, Ludwig Maximilian University of Munich, Department I, Deutsche Philologie, Schellingstraße 9, 80799 Munich,
email: edstadtmiller@gmail.com, Katrin.Lindner@germanistik.uni-muenchen.de

https://doi.org/10.1515/9781501510151-005

previous findings on bilingual DLD. No correlation between story complexity and the composite score of language proficiency was found, suggesting its language-independent nature. The study discusses the notion of narrative coherence in terms of macrostructure and its components and proposes a set of assessment tasks for the identification of bilinguals at risk of DLD.

1 Introduction

Texts, i.e., meaningful, contentful sequences of utterances or sentences, accompany our everyday activities. Production und comprehension of texts, provided they are well-formed and comprehensible, enables successful communication, starting at kindergarten age and continuing throughout the lifetime towards old-age (Bliss et al. 1998; Barton 2007; Janks 2010). The organization of texts has a long history of investigation, which started from the seminal study by Berman and Slobin (1994) on the elicited Frog Stories (Mayer 1969, *Frog, where are you?*), in which they applied Stein and Glenn's (1979) *story grammar* to trace the developmental trajectory of the macrostructural organization of oral narratives. While monolingual (narrative) text organization has been investigated representatively as far as age, languages and populations are concerned (Berman and Slobin 1994; Hickmann 2004; Peterson and McCabe 1993), bilingual narrative texts have been examined far less extensively. This is surprising because skills organizing texts are especially interesting in bilinguals, who might know how to organize a text on a macrostructural level, while they might be at a disadvantage with regards to their lexical or grammatical knowledge. The episodic organization of a text at the level of macrostructure, i.e. the event structure and the components of story grammar, is considered to be more language (proficiency)-independent. Microstructure, on the other hand, is expressed by language-specific elements used for the construction of coherent discourse, such as noun and verb phrases, prepositions and connectives (cf. Iluz-Cohen and Walters 2012; Pearson 2002).

Narrative texts as a data source can provide information on both the general cognitive abilities of a story-teller having to deal with the episodic structure, and his/her language-specific skills. They tap into various levels of language and cognition and can be used for the investigation of typically developing children and children with developmental language disorder (DLD). Since the macrostructural level is concerned with a higher-order organization of a text, the question arises of how language independent it is.

In our study, both issues have been investigated: we used oral narrative texts in order to examine the differences between Russian-German bilingual children with either TD or at risk of DLD. Such a comparison has not been carried out before. The two groups of children were selected out of a bigger cohort of bilinguals on the basis of their language proficiency score, which was obtained from a number of tests performed in both of the children's languages. We also discuss the issue of language (in)dependence of text organization. For the evaluation of the text organization we used a multi-dimensional model which taps into story structure, story complexity and internal states (see subsection The Study below). For the evaluation of language proficiency, we used tests measuring both lexical and grammatical knowledge (see the next section for more details).

2 Typical language development and children at risk of DLD

In Berlin, all preschool children undergo obligatory preschool screening around age five, which includes the examination of, for example, motor skills, cognitive abilities, and language skills (*Einschulungsuntersuchung*, Bettge and Oberwöhrmann 2017). On the basis of the linguistic screening, which lasts approximately 15 minutes and involves several tasks, the children are classified into those with no language problems and those with a "combined indicator of language deficits". In 2017, language deficits were found in 8.7% of monolingual German-speaking children and in a much higher proportion of bilingual children speaking Turkish (57.5%), Arabic (68.8%) and Eastern European languages (47.2%); 60.3% of children from low socio-economic status families (i. e. *untere Statusgruppe*) – both monolinguals and bilinguals – showed deficits as well (Bettge and Oberwöhrmann 2017: 106). Parallel to this situation, the medical report of the insurance[1] company *Barmer GEK* states that one in three preschool-aged children is diagnosed with DLD, which should amount to 1.1 million children with DLD in Germany. However, this number does not adequately reflect the real number of bilingual children with DLD – the estimated rate being 5% to 7% for both the US (Tomblin et al. 1997) and Germany. This overestimation of the number of bilingual children with DLD leads to the "medicalization of the social problems of our society" (Fegeler 2004: 22, our translation). One of the reasons for this situation is that the diagnosis of DLD in bilinguals is often difficult and confusing (Genesee, Paradis and Crago 2004; Paradis 2010): the language skills of

---

1 https://presse.barmergek.de/barmer/web/Portale/Presseportal/Subportal/Infothek/Studien-und-Reports/Arztreport/Arztreport-2012/Content-Arztreport-2012.html

sequential bilinguals are generally under-investigated (Marchman, Fernald and Hurtado 2010), and bilingual norms are often unavailable. Recently, however, tools have been developed to test language proficiency in bilinguals and to disentangle bilingual TD and DLD (see Armon-Lotem, Meir and de Jong 2015). Furthermore, tests have been designed targeting the home language in bilingual children (Gagarina, Klassert and Topaj 2010 for home language Russian). One of these tools, Language Impairment Testing in Multilingual Settings - Multilingual Assessment Instrument for Narratives (LITMUS-MAIN, henceforth MAIN, Gagarina et al. 2012, 2015), was used in this study to elicit the telling and retelling of narratives in a large group of preschool bilinguals. Furthermore, LITMUS-battery was developed in the COST Action IS0804 "Language Impairment in a Multilingual Society: Linguistic Patterns and the Road to Assessment" (www.bi-sli.org, Armon-Lotem, de Jong and Meir 2015). Thus, the first rationale for the present study lies in the necessity to differentiate bilingual children with TD from those with DLD and to explore the potential of narratives to differentiate these groups. It was shown that narratives by children with DLD display specific features (Altman, Armon-Lotem, Fichman and Walters 2016; Boerma, Leseman, Timmermeister et al. 2016; Tsimpli, Peristeri and Andreou 2016). These features will be discussed in the next section. Second, there have been discussions recently on the distinction between TD bilingual children and those with DLD with respect to the adaptation of monolingual norms to bilingualism for standardized tests targeting production and perception of lexicon and grammar (see Thordadottir 2015 for an overview and for cutoff criteria for bilinguals, cf. Bedore and Peña 2008). For bilingual children with DLD and L2 German, a study by Hamann et al. (2017) specified the criterion of 1.25 standard deviations below the norm in two language areas (Leonard 1998; Tomblin et al. 1997). They report that, as far as lexical knowledge is concerned, the perceptive, but not the productive vocabulary should be examined. Additionally, they adhere to the cutoffs for bilingual children with DLD at a score below -1.5 SD in two areas in the dominant language and below -2.25 SD in the weaker language (for balanced bilinguals, below -1.75 SD in both languages). In the present study, we further elaborate on the criteria for potential DLD by testing sequential Russian-German bilinguals in their two languages and by applying a test with (preliminary) bilingual norms in the Russian home language. Finally, we examine narrative text organization (on both levels: macro- and microstructure) and the language-(in)dependence of macrostructure. While macrostructure, i.e. event structure and story grammar, reflects the general episodic organization of a text, it is considered to be more language (proficiency)-independent. Microstructure on the other hand, describes the language specific elements that contribute to the production of a cohesive text.

Thus, microstructure is said to be more dependent on language knowledge (cf. Iluz-Cohen and Walters 2012; Pearson 2002).

In the following section, first, we will present relevant research on narratives in bilinguals; then, we will describe the study and the method we used and, finally, we will discuss the results.

3 Narrative's macro- and microstructure in bilingual children: comparing TD- with DLD-children

The results of studies on bilingual children's narratives reveal, on the one hand, some similar patterns as far as the macro- and microstructure in TD children and those with DLD is concerned and, on the other hand, they show dissimilarities. Iluz-Cohen and Walters (2012) examined 17 sequential bilinguals with a mean age of approximately six years: eight children with TD and nine with DLD. The latter group was recruited from special 'language preschools', in which the children had been identified by certified clinicians as having DLD. The narratives were elicited in Hebrew and English utilizing *The Jungle Book* and *Goldilocks and the Three Bears* (books and languages were counterbalanced) and were analyzed using thirty-two measures, which were combined into four sections: narrative (macro)structure, lexis, and morphosyntax (both components of microstructure) and bilingualism. The narrative macrostructure was analyzed based on Stein and Glenn's (1979) story grammar. Here, no differences in the macrostructure score between the groups with TD and with DLD were found. It replicated Pearson's (2002) results on monolingual and bilingual children with TD and with DLD of the same age. However, significant differences were found by Iluz-Cohen and Walters as far as the microstructue, i.e. language performance, was concerned. The authors concluded that while the less language-dependent narrative skills, i.e. the skills necessary for building macrostructure, did not differentiate children with TD from those with DLD, the production of the various elements of microstructural level was significantly lower in preschool bilinguals with DLD and, thus, could be used as a diagnostic cue.

In a longitudinal study Squires et al. (2014) elicited the narratives of 166 Spanish-English bilinguals enrolled in kindergarten and first grade. The children heard a model story, based on pictorial stimuli (e.g. *The Frog Story* by Mayer 1969) and were then asked to retell it. All children were then tested with a battery of standardized tests. Out of this large cohort, 21 bilinguals were identified as having DLD. The narratives of these TD and DLD children were compared with respect to the results on the test measuring macro- and microstructure. The two groups differed significantly as far as macrostructure (i.e. the story grammar score) and microstructure (i.e. the scores for mental and linguistic verbs, adverbs, elaborated noun phrases, and coordinating and subordinating conjunctions) are concerned. It should be noted that this result does not fully corroborate the findings reported in Iluz-Cohen and Walters (2012).

Two recent studies on bilingual children's narratives – by Tsimpli et al. (2016) and Boerma et al. (2016) – used the MAIN methodology (see section Study below) to explore the differences between bilinguals with TD and with DLD, using L2 Greek and Dutch respectively. Monolinguals with TD and with DLD were also part of their studies, but are not considered here. Tsimpli et al. (2016) compared narrated and retold picture-based stories by 15 bilinguals with DLD with those by 15 age-matched TD bilinguals (mean age 9;1) in L2 Greek. Their results revealed significant differences between the two groups of bilinguals in internal state terms (IST), but not in story structure (SS). Although ISTs in the MAIN methodology are analyzed as macrostructural constituents, they are more dependent on language knowledge, specifically (knowledge of) the lexicon, than on story grammar. Boerma et al. (2016) studied the production and comprehension of macrostructure in 33 bilinguals with DLD (mean age 8;7) and 33 bilinguals with TD (mean age 7;1). They found that the children with DLD performed significantly lower than the TD group on all narrative measures both in comprehension and production, with especially few ISTs in the DLD group. Boerma et al. concluded that given such strong differences in all narrative measures, "using narratives to assess children's language abilities can support the identification of DLD in both a monolingual and a bilingual context." (Boerma et al. 2016: 1). In our study, we also used MAIN in order to examine the difference in narratives by Russian-German sequential bilinguals with either TD or at risk of DLD. The two groups of children were selected out of a bigger cohort of bilinguals on the basis of their language proficiency score, which was the result of a number of tests performed in both of the children's languages. The study contributes to the debate on the association between components of macrostructure on the one hand, and language proficiency as measured here by lexicon and grammar tests, on the other (see the next section for more details). Thus, it discusses the issue of language (in)dependence of macrostructure with respect to text organization. For the evaluation of text organization we used a multi-dimensional model which taps into story structure, story complexity and internal states.

4 The Study

The present study had two goals. First, we compared the macro- and microstructure of narratives by bilingual children with TD and bilingual children identified as at risk of DLD, who were matched for age, IQ, and socio-economic status (SES). These children were part of a larger study of Russian-German sequential preschool bilinguals who were tested in both of their languages with a battery of standardized tests (for the identification of children at risk of DLD: see Method). The narrative skills across these two groups were compared separately, first for German and then for Russian. The analyses of the narrative skills were operationalized as a set of scores for the macrostructure constituents: the story structure (SS: quantitative measure), story complexity (SC: qualitative measure) and internal state terms (ISTs). These three components of macrostructure were correlated separately with the overall language score of language proficiency, which was computed on the basis of all language tests, including lexical comprehension, lexical production and grammatical comprehension. The second goal targeted the interconnections between narrative skills and language proficiency. This taps into the theoretical discussion on the language-independence of macrostructure and its particular components. In previous research it has been argued that macrostructure is less language-specific and less dependent on language skills, and is grounded in more general cognitive processes (Trabasso and Nickels 1992). Trabasso and Nickels (1992) used a causal network discourse analysis for the evaluation of macrostructure in narratives by children aged three to five, children aged nine, and by adults. The emphasis was on the expression of the planning of an action by a protagonist.

The present study argues that macrostructure can be analyzed on different structural levels and that different macrostructural constituents, such as the number of SS elements and ISTs, might be more dependent on language skills than elements of SC, which are responsible for the composition of the core narrative skills and for the well-formedness and coherence of macrostructure. In particular, by examining these three components of macrostructure separately in the two languages, we suggest that these constituents depend on language skills to varying degrees, with 1) ISTs being most language-dependent, 2) SC, which taps into the general organization or well-formedness of an episode, being least language-dependent, and 3) SS, as a qualitative measure of narrative skills, in between. In fact, as long as a child knows how to tell a story, i.e. how to compose a full and complex episode, s/he can do so with varying language resources.

These suggestions are grounded in the findings of Pearson (2002), Simon-Cereijido and Gutiérrez-Clellen (2009), and Iluz-Cohen and Walters (2011), who showed strong associations of SS across languages and weak or no correlations of lexical and morpho-syntactic abilities between the two languages of bilingual children. Likewise, Gagarina et al. (2015) found similarities in the SS of bilingual children's narratives for 14 language pairs, even when parents reported that their children's language skills were unbalanced. This cross-linguistic similarity has been explained by the independence of narrative skills from specific language abilities.

Thus, our research questions are: (1) What is the difference in narrative production (telling and retelling) in German and Russian across bilinguals with either TD or at risk of DLD? (2) Are there any correlations within one language between different components of macrostructure, as measured by SS, SC and IST structure and language proficiency and, if so, to what extent are these components of macrostructure (in)dependent of language proficiency?

5 Method

Participants

Out of a larger sample of 70 bilingual Russian-German children aged 4;6-4;11, we selected 23 successive bilinguals with an age of onset (AoO) in German older than 24 months (after Ruberg 2013) and matched for age, IQ and age of exposure. The children were recruited from various preschools in Berlin as well as in and around Munich. Prior to testing, parents signed written consent forms agreeing that their child would participate in the study. In addition, parents filled out a questionnaire providing information about the child's development, the quality and quantity of language input, and the parents' level of education (on the basis of this questionnaire, one child with a reported hearing impairment and seven trilingual children were excluded from testing). Approximately 80% of the mothers had completed the German or Russian equivalent of A-Levels; 45% also held a university degree.

All children had at least one parent who was a native speaker of Russian (in families where only one parent was Russian-speaking, it was always the mother) and thus had acquired Russian since birth. The children were tested on nonverbal IQ with Leiter-3 and showed within-norm development, with no one scoring below 85 (Roid, Miller, Pomplun and Koch 2013). All children performed language proficiency tasks in Russian and German. For German, we used the lexical production and comprehension tasks from the Diagnostic of Specific Language Impairment (PDSS-Patholinguistische Diagnostik bei Sprachentwicklungsstörungen,

Kauschke and Siegmüller 2010), normed and standardized for monolingual children, and the grammar comprehension task Test for Receptive Grammar - TROG-D (Test zur Überprüfung des Grammatikverständnisses, Fox 2011). For Russian, the Russian Language Proficiency Test for Multilingual Children was used (Gagarina et al. 2010). In both languages, similar domains, namely lexical production, and lexical and grammatical comprehension, were assessed. On the basis of these tests, the combined language proficiency score was calculated for each language. For this purpose, the raw scores for each subtest were transformed into z-scores and a mean score was calculated for each child and for each language. The children who scored below average in both languages were placed into a potential language impaired group.[2] In total, seven children were identified as 'at-risk of DLD' and 16 as being TD. No effects between the groups were found for age, age of exposure, or nonverbal IQ. A Welch two-sample t-test to compare these two groups showed that, although the at-risk group scored lower than the TD group in both languages, significant differences were found for language proficiency in German only, $t(16.48) = 4.47$, $p < .001$.

Not all of the 23 sequential bilinguals completed narratives in both languages. For German, the narratives of 15 children with TD and five at-risk children were available. For Russian, we analyzed narratives from 13 children of the TD group and from four children of the at-risk group (see Table 1). Fourteen children completed narratives in both languages, 12 of whom were from the TD group and two from the at-risk group.

Tab. 1: Chronological age, age of onset, language proficiency and IQ of the children who produced narratives in German and in Russian in the TD and at-risk groups of bilingual children (Mean and SD)

German-Russian Bilinguals	TD Mean (SD)	At risk Mean (SD)
German Narratives n = 40 (20 telling and 20 retelling)	n = 15 children	n = 5 children
Age in months	57.4 (2.23)	57.0 (2.30)
Age of Onset in months	33.6 (7.27)	38.6 (7.79)
Language proficiency German (z-score)	0.39 (0.67)	-0.57 (0.28)
Nonverbal IQ	102 (7.18)	101 (4.81)

---

[2] The parents of the children who were identified as potentially having DLD were informed in writing, and it was suggested to them that they contact the relevant child-care centers.

German-Russian Bilinguals	TD Mean (SD)	At risk Mean (SD)
Russian Narratives n = 34 (17 telling and 17 retelling)	n = 13 children	n = 4 children
Age in months	57.5 (2.37)	57.0 (0.81)
Language proficiency Russian as the z-score	0.04 (0.77)	-0.48 (0.42)
IQ	102 (7.13)	98 (4.11)
Age in months	57.5 (2.37)	57.0 (0.81)

Materials and Procedure

The narratives were elicited via MAIN (Gagarina et al. 2012, 2015). The no joint attention procedure of elicitation was carried out as follows: after the warming-up part of the session, the child was shown a set of three envelopes, each containing the same story, either the Cat Story or the Dog Story. The child was asked to pick an envelope, open it, unfold the picture story, and look at all the pictures. After the child had looked at the pictures the experimenter asked, "Are you ready? Now I'm going to tell you the story and then you will tell me the story". After the story was told, the child was asked to retell the same story (the "retelling" condition). When the child had finished the story, the experimenter asked ten comprehension questions and then moved on to the second part of the assessment. The child was asked to pick another envelope from a different set of envelopes. This time all the envelopes contained a picture story of either *Baby Goats* or *Baby Birds*. Again, the child was asked to open the envelope and look at the pictures. The task was to tell the story to the experimenter without having heard the story beforehand and to answer ten comprehension questions (the "telling" condition). Children were tested individually in a quiet room in their kindergarten or home. Testing for German and Russian was conducted on different dates with a minimum interval of two days. German narratives were tested by a native speaker of German, and Russian narratives by a native speaker of Russian. The four stories were counterbalanced by language: each child should perform retelling and telling in each language.

Analysis and Scoring

The children's stories were recorded and transcribed by trained native speakers according to the CHAT format (MacWhinney 2000). Another trained assistant then transcribed one fourth of the recordings and any discrepancies were discussed in order to reach a consensus (which, after the discussions, reached over 90%). The analyses of the macrostructure components SS, SC, and IST were performed in each language according to the MAIN guidelines. For SS we counted the occurrences of setting information (time and place), number of Goals (G), Attempts (A), Outcomes (O) and ISTs as initiating events and reactions. The maximum score for SS was 17 points: two points for Setting, three points each for Goals, Attempts, and Outcomes and six points for ISTs. The scoring of SC was based on Westby (2005). The children were given zero points if G, A, and O were absent, one point for the combination of A and O, two points for the combination of GA or GO and three points for the production of a GAO sequence. Based on these scores, a weighted score was calculated. The IST score indicates the amount of words that denote different internal states, such as: *see, feel, hungry, asleep, sad, want, say, ask*. This score is the percentage of IST tokens in a given story (number of IST tokens / total tokens). As far as microstructure is concerned, we calculated the length of the story, measured in types and tokens without mazes in each language per child.

6 Results

First, we compared the narratives in German across the TD and at-risk groups and performed correlations between narrative skills – operationalized as a macrostructure score – and the combined language proficiency score.

German

To compare the macrostructural story organization of the TD and at-risk children for telling and retelling, a Welch Two-Sample t-test was used. For both retelling and telling, we found significant effects for the two core components of the macrostructure: SS and SC, with at risk children scoring lower than TD children (see Table 2). In addition, the number of types and tokens – i.e. the narrative microstructure – was significantly lower in the at-risk group compared to the TD children.

Tab. 2: Means and results of the group comparisons for German Retelling and Telling macro- and microstructure of the TD and at-risk groups of bilingual children (n.s. = not significant; SS – story structure; SC – story complexity)

German Narratives	TD n = 15 Mean (SD)	At risk n = 5 Mean (SD)	T-Test
Retelling Macrostructure			
SS	4.87 (1.68)	1.60 (2.07)	t(5.87) = 3.19, p < .05*
SC	12.73 (11.68)	2.40 (3.04)	t(17.71) = 3.12, p < .01**
IST	3.65 (2.81)	1.77 (3.14)	n.s.
Retelling Microstructure: Types and Tokens			
Tokens	78.47 (27.70)	42.80 (22.86)	t(8.31) = 2.85, p < .05*
Types	38.00 (9.62)	15.67 (10.26)	t(3.15) = 3.35, p < .05*
Telling Macrostructure			
SS	4.00 (2.47)	1.20 (1.30)	t(13.74) = 3.23, p < .01**
SC	9.13 (7.35)	2.40 (3.05)	t(16.66) = 2.88, p < .05*
IST	2.96 (1.58)	1.28 (1.93)	n.s.
Telling Microstructure: Types and Tokens			
Tokens	79.67 (30.61)	31.40 (28.18)	t(7.44) = 3.24, p < .05*
Types	44.50 (18.50)	10.66 (11.59)	t(5.51) = 3.81, p < .05*

To investigate the relationship between macrostructure and language performance, we calculated separate correlations between the combined score of the German language proficiency and each of the three constituents of macrostructure, as well as the types and tokens. Significant positive correlations with language proficiency were found for SS in both the retelling and telling modes (see Table 3). For IST, a strong significant correlation was found in telling, but not in retelling.

Tab. 3: Correlation coefficients and p-values of German language proficiency scores and macro- and microstructure scores in German narratives (SS – story structure, SC – story complexity)

German Narratives n = 40	Language Proficiency German	
	Retelling (n = 20).	Telling (n = 20)
	Macrostructure	
SS	r(18) = .63, p < .01**	r(18) = .57, p < .01**
SC	n.s.	n.s.
IST	n.s.	r(18) = .78, p < .001***
	Microstructure	
Tokens	r(15) = .63, p < .01**	n.s.
Types	r(15) = .67, p < .01**	n.s.

Russian

Parallel analyses were carried out for the Russian narratives. Although the at-risk children scored lower than the TD children for all analyzed features, this difference was significant for the components of neither macrostructure nor microstructure. Therefore, we combined the data into one group and performed the analyses for thirty-four narratives elicited via telling or retelling. In the retelling mode, language proficiency in Russian correlated significantly with the number of types and tokens measuring the narrative microstructure. No constituent of macrostructure showed any significant correlation with the proficiency score in retelling or telling (Table 4).

Tab. 4: Correlation coefficients and p-values of Russian language proficiency scores and macro- and microstructure scores in Russian narratives

Russian Narratives n = 34	Language Proficiency Russian	
	Retelling (n = 17).	Telling (n = 17)
	Macrostructure	
SS	n.s.	n.s.
SC	n.s.	n.s.
IST	n.s.	n.s.
	Microstructure	
Tokens	r(15) = .63, p < .01**	
Types	r(15) = .67, p < .01**	n.s.

7 Discussion and conclusion

Our study aimed to answer the question of the difference in narrative production (telling and retelling) in German and Russian across age- and SES matched bilinguals with either TD or at risk of DLD. The at-risk group was identified in this study on the basis of the combined language proficiency score in each of the languages of a bilingual child, when both of these scores were lower than 1.75 SD. On a theoretical level, we examined the question of the (in)dependence of narrative text organization, measured on the base of the multidimensional model, on language proficiency.

In order to answer the first question, we elicited and analyzed the macrostructure of narrative texts by the TD and at-risk groups of sequential Russian-German bilingual children in both Russian and German. The evaluation of macrostructure was operationalized as a set of scores for the macrostructural components SS (quantitative measure; a maximal score of 17 can be reached), SC (qualitative measure; the more 'complex' the combination of the components of an episode is, the higher the score is – a maximal score of three can be reached for the GAO combination, which is maximal complexity) and, finally, the number of IST tokens. The IST score (with no possible maximum) sums the tokens of such words as *see, feel, hungry, asleep, sad, want, say, ask*. Each of these three constituents, SS, SC and IST was separately correlated with the overall proficiency score measuring language skills. This score was computed on the basis of a number of tasks tapping into both lexical production and comprehension, as well as comprehension of grammar.

In our findings on German narratives, at-risk children scored significantly lower than TD children for SS and SC (macrostructure) in both retelling and telling. This corroborates Boerma et al.'s (2016) and Squires et al.'s (2014) results. However, Iluz-Cohen and Walters (2012) and Tsimpli et al. (2016) found no significant differences in the SS across both TD- and DLD children.[3] Given these contradictory results, it is still not clear in what way bilingual children with TD and children (at risk of) DLD behave differently while organizing oral texts at the macrostructural level. For all three components of macrostructure, TD children performed better in the retelling modus versus the telling modus, while at-risk children achieved the same results for SC but performed worse for SS. This is probably due to the fact that retelling is more demanding than pure telling as it

---

3 Note that Squires et al. (2014) and Iluz-Cohen and Walters (2012) used procedures different from MAIN.

requires the child to concentrate not only on listening, but also on the reproduction of a given oral text. Furthermore, in our study six children were not diagnosed with DLD, but were identified as *at risk* of DLD. This might have had an impact on the results of the comparison of TD with DLD-children and also on the comparison with the previous studies on children *diagnosed* with DLD.

A more coherent picture can be drawn from previous studies on the use of ISTs, as both Tsimpli et al. (2016) and Boerma et al. (2016) claim that the production of ISTs can be a clear marker of DLD in bilinguals (see Boerma et al. 2016 for further evidence). In their study and in a study by Bamberg and Damrad-Frye (1991) on monolingual DLD, "the children consistently lagged behind in the use of elements related to internal states, i.e., those story elements that are not directly evident from the picture sequence and that represent the narrator's perspective on the events, such as frames of mind" (Boerma et al. 2016: 3). In our study, the at-risk group also scored lower on IST tokens. However, this result was not significant. This might be due to the small sample size of the at-risk group and/or due to the fact that both groups of sequential bilinguals had reduced language exposure and low lexical proficiency in German. This lexical insufficiency in sequential TD bilinguals might explain why they did not produce a number of ISTs high enough to differentiate them from the children in the at-risk group.

As far as microstructure is concerned, our findings support the results of all studies referred to above, which provide a similar picture showing a significantly lower amount of different microstructural components, such as types and tokens, produced by children with DLD (Boerma et al. 2016; Iluz-Cohen and Walters 2012; Squires et al. 2014; Tsimpli et al. 2016).

The next step was to examine the (in)dependence of narrative macrostructure from language proficiency. Analyses of the correlations between each macrostructural component, SS, SC and ISTs, and the combined language proficiency score were performed. We predicted that SS - the quantitative element of macrostructure (the number of episodic elements) – would be more dependent on language abilities, and that SC - the qualitative component of macrostructure (the combination of episodic elements) – would be less dependent on language knowledge. The qualitative component of macrostructure assesses the very core of narration. A quantitative estimate or quantitative score is based on how much the child substantially says about the story organization, whereas a qualitative estimate considers the co-occurrence of the episodic components, Gs, As and Os, thus measuring the skill to combine single events into a whole with causal relationships. Technically, one can produce a high number of SS elements, but no maximally complex and complete episodes including all three GAO components (McCabe and Peterson 1984; cf. Trabasso and Nickels 1992). No significant correlations in either language were found between language performance and SC, the core component of macrostructure. This confirms our prediction that the skill of verbalizing a universal organization of the episodic structure is independent of language proficiency.

For SS in the retelling and telling modus, moderate positive correlations were found. This can be explained by the quantitative nature of the SS scoring system, i.e. MAIN evaluates the total number of elements produced and includes ISTs as initiating events and reactions. The observation that SS shows more language dependence seems to be due to the fact that one needs lexical knowledge to produce the relevant items. ISTs correlations were found only for telling. This outcome might show that retelling does not reflect (only) the skill of using ISTs, but instead involves the participation of working memory and is associated with children's ability to listen attentively, memorize and repeat the texts.

For narrative text organization to claim that it is language independent, it seems not to be enough to merely count the components of language proficiency. Texts should be comprehensive and coherent as far as well-formedness of episodes is concerned. A full complex episode consists of a co-occurrence of elements, describing the causal flow of what is happening: description of an event or a problem, actions of the protagonist and a kind of result/outcome.

Finally, the two microstructural features - types and tokens - positively correlated with language performance in both languages in retelling only. This result is rather surprising, given that the length of stories was expected to be associated with language knowledge and children's overall language performance. This result can be attributed to the small sample size and to the considerable learner-specific differences, i.e. a large individual variation in the production of types and tokens.

In conclusion, this study provides evidence that macrostructure scores in bilingual children's narratives might be used as an identification cue for bilinguals at risk of DLD, as these scores were significantly lower in the at-risk group as compared to the TD children. This result confirms Tsimpli et al.'s (2016) and Boerma et al.'s (2016) findings, which underline the value of macrostructure analyses, especially for bilingual DLD children. All in all, this study contributes to the growing body of evidence that sequential bilinguals at risk of DLD might be identified by a set of assessment 'instruments', e.g. by language proficiency tests in both of the children's languages, and by the examination of the macro- and microstructure in elicited narratives.

Finally, by applying the theoretical model of story organization for macrostructure analyses, the study shows evidence for a 'non-monolithic' nature of story grammar, evaluated from a quantitative perspective, i.e. SS, and qualitative perspective, i.e. SC, whereas the core component of macrostructure, SC, is independent of language proficiency.

References

Altman, C., Armon-Lotem, S., Fichman, S. and Walters, J. 2016. Macrostructure, microstructure, and mental state terms in the narratives of English-Hebrew bilingual preschool children with and without specific language impairment. *Applied Psycholinguistics* 37 (1), 165–193.

Armon-Lotem, S., Meir, N. and De Jong, J. (eds.). 2015. *Assessing multilingual children: Disentangling bilingualism from language impairment*. Bristol, UK: Multilingual Matters.

Bamberg, M. and Damrad-Frye, R. 1991. On the ability to provide evaluative comments: Further exploration of children's narrative competencies. *Journal of Child Language* 18, 689–710.

Barton, D. 2007. *Literacy: An Introduction to the Ecology of Written Language*. Oxford: Willey-Blackwell Publishing.

Bedore, L. M. and Peña, E. D. 2008. Assessment of Bilingual Children for Identification of Language Impairment: Current Findings and Implications for Practice. *International Journal of Bilingual Education and Bilingualism* 11 (1), 1–29.

Berman, R.A., & Slobin, D.I. 1994. *Relating events in narrative: A crosslinguistic developmental study*. Hillsdale, NJ: Erlbaum.

Bettge, S. and Oberwöhrmann, S. 2015. Grundauswertung der Einschulungsdaten in Berlin 2014. *Gesundheitsberichterstattung Berlin*.

Bliss, L., McCabe, A. and Miranda, E. 1998. Narrative assessment profile: Discourse analysis for school-age children. *Journal of Communication Disorders* 31, 347–363.

Boerma, T.D., Leseman, P.P.M., Timmermeister, M., Wijnen, F.N.K. and Blom, W.B.T. 2016. Narrative abilities of monolingual and bilingual children with and without language impairment: implications for clinical practice. *International Journal of Language and Communication Disorders* 51 (6), 626–638.

Chilla, S. and Şan, N. H. (subm.) Möglichkeiten und Grenzen der Diagnostik erstsprachlicher Fähigkeiten: Türkisch-deutsche und türkisch-französische Kinder im Vergleich?

Cleave, P. L., Girolametto, L. E., Chen, X. and Johnson, C. J. 2010. Narrative abilities in monolingual and dual language learning children with specific language impairment. *Journal of Communication Disorders* 43 (6), 511–522. http://doi.org/10.1016/j.jcomdis.2010.05.005.

Duinmeijer, I., De Jong, J. and Scheper, A. 2012. Narrative abilities, memory and attention in children with a specific language impairment. *International Journal of Language & Communication Disorders* 47 (5), 542–555.

Fox, A. 2011. *Test zur Überprüfung des Grammatikverständnisses (TROG-D)*. 5. Auflage. Idstein: Schulz-Kirchner Verlag.

Fegeler, U. 2004. Alarmierender Anstieg von Entwicklungsstörungen bei Kindern. Übereinstimmendes Bild in verschiedenen Bundesländern. *Berliner Ärzte* 41 (9), 22–24.

Gagarina, N. 2013. First language diagnostics in multilingual children (using the example of Russian). *Sprache. Stimme. Gehör* 37, 196–200.

Gagarina, N. 2016. Narratives of Russian-German preschool and primary school bilinguals: Rasskaz and Erzählung. *Applied Psycholinguistics* 37 (1), 91–122.

Gagarina, N., Klassert, A. and Topaj, N. 2010. Sprachstandstest Russisch für mehrsprachige Kinder/ Russian language proficiency test for multilingual children. *ZAS Papers in Linguistics* 54.

Gagarina, N., Klop, D., Kunnari, S., Tantele, K., Välimaa, T., Balčiūnienė, I., Bohnacker U. and Walters, J. 2012. MAIN – Multilingual Assessment Instrument for Narratives. *ZAS Papers in Linguistics* 56.

Gagarina, N., Klop, D., Kunnari, S., Tantele, K., Välimaa, T., Balčiūnienė, I., Bohnacker, U. and Walters, J. 2015. Assessment of Narrative Abilities in Bilingual Children. In S. Armon-Lotem, J. de Jong and N. Meir (eds.), *Assessing multilingual children: Disentangling bilingualism from language impairment* 259–275. Bristol, UK: Multilingual Matters.

Genesee, F., Paradis, J. and Crago, M. 2004. *Dual Language Development and Disorders: A Handbook on Bilingualism and Second Language Learning.* Baltimore: Brookes Publishing.

Hamann, C., Solveig C., Gagarina, N. and Ibrahim, L. A. 2017. Syntactic Complexity and Bilingualism: How (a)typical bilinguals deal with complex structures. In E. Di Domenico (ed.), *Complexity in acquisition* 142–177. Newcastle upon Tyne: Cambridge Scholars Publishing.

Hickmann, M. 2004. *Children's Discourse: Person, Space and Time across Languages.* Cambridge Studies in Linguistics.

Iluz-Cohen, P. and Walters, J. 2012. Telling stories in two languages: Narratives of bilingual preschool children with typical and impaired language. *Bilingualism: Language and Cognition* 15 (Special Issue 01), 58–74.

Kauschke, C. and Siegmüller, J. 2010. *Patholinguistische Diagnostik bei Sprachentwicklungsstörungen (PDSS)* (Vol. 4). Elsevier, Urban & Fischer Verlag.

Leonard, L.B. 1998. Children with specific language impairment. Cambridge, MA: MIT Press.

MacWhinney, B. 2000. *The CHILDES Project: Tools for analyzing talk* (3rd ed.). Mahwah, NJ: Lawrence Erlbaum Associates.

Mayer, M. 1969. *Frog, where are you?* New York: Dial Press.

Marchman, V. A., Fernald, A. and Hurtado, N. 2010. How vocabulary size in two languages relates to efficiency in spoken word recognition by young Spanish–English bilinguals. *Journal of Child Language* 37 (4), 817–840.

Miranda, A. E., McCabe, A. and Bliss, L. S. 1998. Jumping around and leaving things out: A profile of the narrative abilities of children with specific language impairment. *Applied Psycholinguistics* 19, 647–667.

Pankratz, M. E., Plante, E., Vance, R. and Insalaco, D. M. 2007. The diagnostic and predictive validity of the Renfrew Bus Story. *Language, Speech, and Hearing Services in Schools* 38 (4), 390–399.

Paradis, J. 2010. The interface between bilingual development and specific language Impairment. *Applied Psycholinguistics* 31, 227–252.

Pearson, B. Z. 2002. Narrative competence among monolingual and bilingual school children in Miami. In D. K. Oller and R. E. Eilers (eds.), *Language and literacy in bilingual children,* 135–174. Clevedon, UK: Multilingual Matters.

Peterson, C. and McCabe, A. 1983. *Developmental psycholinguistics: Three ways of looking at a child's narrative.* New York, NY: Plenum Press.

Plante, E. and Vance, R. 1994. Selection of Preschool Language Tests. A Data-Based Approach. *Language, Speech, and Hearing Services in Schools* 25 (1), 15–24.

Roid, G.H., Miller L., Pomplun M. and Koch C. 2013. *Leiter International Performance Scale* (3rd ed.). Wood Dale, IL: Stoelting.

Rothweiler, M. 2013. Specific Language Impairment in multilingual children. *Sprache. Stimme. Gehör* 37, 186–190.
Ruberg, T. 2013. Problembereiche im kindlichen Zweitspracherwerb. *Sprache. Stimme. Gehör* 37, 181–185.
Schneider, P., Hayward, D. and Dube, R. V. 2006. Storytelling from pictures using the Edmonton Narrative Norms Instrument. *Journal of Speech Pathology and Audiology* 30 (4), 224-238.
Schröder, A. 2010. *Vergleichende Analyse interaktiver Erzählfähigkeiten bei sechsjährigen Kindern mit einer sogenannten spezifischen Sprachentwicklungsstörung und Kindern mit unauffälligem Spracherwerb.* Unpublished Doctoral dissertation. Technische Universität Dortmund.
Simon-Cereijido, G. and Gutiérrez-Clellen, V. 2009. A cross-linguistic and bilingual evaluation of the interdependence between lexical and grammatical domains. *Applied Psycholinguistics* 30 (2), 315–337.
Squires, K. E., Lugo-Neris, M. J., Peña, E. D., Bedore, L. M., Bohman, T. M. and Gillam, R. B. 2014. Story retelling by bilingual children with language impairments and typically developing controls. *International Journal of Language & Communication Disorders* 49 (1), 60-74.
Stein, N. L. and Glenn, C. G. 1979. An analysis of story comprehension in elementary school children. In R. Freedle (ed.), *Discourse processing: Multidisciplinary perspectives*, 53–120. Norwood, NJ: Ablex.
Stein, N. L. and Trabasso, T. 1982. Children's understanding of stories: A basis for moral judgement and dilemma resolution. In C. J. Brainerd and M. Pressley (eds.), *Verbal processes in children: Progress in cognitive development research*. New York: Springer-Verlag.
Tomblin, C., Records, L., Buckwalter, P., Zhang, X., Smith, E. and O'Brien, M. 1997. Prevalence of specific language impairment in kindergarten children. *Journal of Speech Language and Hearing Research* 40 (6), 1245–1260.
Tracy, R. and Schulz, P. 2010. *LiSe-DaZ. Linguistische Sprachstandserhebung – Deutsch als Zweitsprache.* Hogrefe.
Trabasso, T. and Nickels, M. 1992. The development of goal plans of action in the narration of picture stories. *Discourse Processes* 15, 249–275.
Tsimpli, I. M., Peristeri, E. and Andreou, M. 2016. Narrative production in monolingual and bilingual children with specific language impairment. *Applied Psycholinguistics* 37 (1), 195-216.
Westby, C. E. 2005. Assessing and facilitating text comprehension problems. In H. Catts and A. Kamhi (eds.), *Language and reading disabilities*, 157–232. Boston MA: Allyn & Bacon.

Hana Klages and Johannes Gerwien
Referential coherence: Children's understanding of pronoun anaphora. Insights from mono- and bilingual language acquisition

Abstract: In this study we investigated how monolingual and bilingual learners of German between five and ten years of age resolve anaphoric pronouns. We employed a visual world design to measure what parts of a visual stimulus participants attend to while presented with short spoken texts, in which a sentence beginning with an anaphoric pronoun follows a sentence which includes two referents. In order to shed light on pre- and post-pronominal processing we manipulated (1.) 'gender' and (2.) syntactic function/position in the preceding sentence of the referents (in the following the latter will be referred to as, 'antecedent type'). Results suggest that the reliable cue 'gender' is acquired earlier than the probabilistic cue 'antecedent type', which is in line with previous findings in the field. However, our findings show that in monolingual and bilingual children the reliability of the gender cue steadily increases even up to age 9. With respect to 'antecedent type', as a probabilistic cue in German anaphoric pronoun resolution, our results suggest differences between acquisition types. Monolinguals use this cue during pre-pronominal processing at an early age, and only at later ages during post-pronominal processing, together with the gender cue. Bilinguals, on the other hand, do not use the cue at an early age, and when they do at age seven, they use it during post-pronominal processing. Only the oldest bilingual participants use 'antecedent type' information for pre-pronominal processing. Taken together, our study shows that all factors manipulated in our experiment (age, acquisition type, cue type) have to be considered when explaining how anaphoric pronoun resolution is acquired by language learners.

Hana Klages and Johannes Gerwien, Department for German as Foreign Language Philology, University of Heidelberg, Plöck 35, 69117 Heidelberg, email: klages@idf.uni-heidelberg.de, gerwien@idf.uni-heidelberg.de

https://doi.org/10.1515/9781501510151-006

1 Introduction

An important part of discourse comprehension is establishing referential coherence. There are numerous possibilities in which a speaker can refer to an entity previously mentioned in discourse again, e.g., by using nouns, descriptions, or expressions with attenuated meanings, such as pronouns. In this article, we will focus on the latter.

Previous research has shown that the resolution of anaphoric pronouns in discourse relies on several factors. Some relate to information encoded in the pronoun itself, i.e., grammatical information of the pronoun (gender, number, case[1]), or its form (e.g., personal pronoun, demonstrative pronoun). Others relate to formal-syntactic features of the context, e.g., the syntactic functions of potential antecedents or their position in the previous sentence. Furthermore, global coherence (global topic), as well as the local relations between successive utterances in the discourse play an important role. In addition, the process is driven by inferences related to probability or plausibility considerations that are mediated by the semantic environment of the pronoun (verb semantics), by world knowledge, or by knowledge about the current situation (e.g., Colonna et al. 2014; Järvikivi et al. 2013; Colonna et al. 2012; Ellert 2010; Koornneef and Sanders 2013; Bouma and Hopp 2007; Arnold et al. 2000; Ariel 2013; Arnold 2013; McKoon and Ratcliff 1992; Tyler 1983; Terhorst 1995). Competent language users consider all of these factors in a highly automatized fashion. But is this also the case in children acquiring a language? In the current study, we ask: How do mono- and bilingual children integrate different types of information when they face the task of anaphoric pronoun resolution? How does this competence develop between the age of 5 and 10?

Previous research has demonstrated that some of the cues mentioned above may be characterized in terms of their reliability, and we will discuss this in more detail in section 2. In general, we follow Tanenhaus and Trueswell's (1995) assumption about the role of cue reliability in anaphoric pronoun resolution, which states that more reliable cues are weighted higher compared to less reliable cues. For cases in which more than one cue is available (e.g., gender and syntactic role of the antecedent), the authors assume a processing mechanism which will calculate the probability of each cue in order to identify the referent intended by the speaker: the more reliable a cue, the higher the probability that anaphoric pronoun resolution will rely on that cue. Furthermore, following Hopp (2013) we wish to make a distinction between 'internally' and 'externally' reliable cues. A cue is

---

1 Note that we will not deal with number and case in the present study.

considered as 'internally reliable' when it is reliable within the individual language system of a recipient. A cue is considered as 'externally reliable' when it is reliable in the language system as a whole (e.g., because of its *grammaticalization*). In contrast to external cue reliability, internal cue reliability is influenced – among other things – by the exposure to the input, as well as the current state of the internal language system. Thus, the internal cue reliability is not in a stable state but may undergo changes over time, i.e., during language acquisition.

In the current study, we focus on two types of information relevant to anaphoric pronoun resolution in German: a) gender information of the pronoun and of the antecedent, and b) 'antecedent type', i.e., the syntactic role of the antecedent (subject vs. object), or its position in the preceding sentence (preverbal/first mentioned vs. postverbal/last mentioned), respectively. Note that both information types can be considered as cues of different quality. In German, gender information is highly reliable because all nouns are specified with respect to this category in the mental lexicon. Gender information surfaces in many ways, e.g., articles and adjectives. Most importantly for our purposes, gender is encoded in the third person singular form of the pronoun. 'Antecedent type', on the other hand, is less reliable (see below), and can be categorized as a probabilistic cue. Both cues differ with respect to when they can be processed during the pronoun resolution process: while processing 'antecedent type' can be initiated *before* the pronoun is perceived, gender information can only trigger processes *after* the pronoun has been perceived. Following Arnold (2013: 63), we will refer to these processes as 'pre-pronominal' and 'post-pronominal'.

Manipulating the cues gender and 'antecedent type' should allow to investigate: (1.) whether children between 5 and 10 years of age and of two different acquisition types (monolingual vs. bilingual) process multiple cues relevant to anaphoric pronoun resolution in the same manner; (2.) whether both cues show different effects on the time course of the resolution process depending on age and acquisition type; (3.) whether reliable cues are acquired and used earlier than probabilistic cues.

We measured children's eye movements in a 'visual world' design to answer these questions. This method enables us to shed light on natural (implicit) processing mechanisms, since it does not rely on any explicit task, which could potentially direct attention to what is being investigated. Furthermore, this method has been shown to be informative about the different phases of the on-line anaphoric pronoun resolution processes (cf. Arnold 2013).

This article is structured as follows: in section 2 we will discuss general processes involved in anaphoric pronoun resolution, as well as the specific role of gender and referent type information. Here we will also show what can be expected for mono- and bilingual children of different ages on the grounds of previous research. In section 3 we will report an experiment in which we manipulated the factors age, acquisition type, and 'antecedent type'. In section 4 we will discuss our results. Our conclusions will be presented in section 5.

2 Background

Processes in anaphoric pronoun resolution

Anaphoric pronouns in texts are resolved on the basis of two types of processes. Both types can be distinguished with respect to *when* they are initiated relative to the onset of the pronoun. On the one hand, there are processes that focus solely on information extracted from the current state of the discourse, and this information is processed *before* the pronoun is perceived. We refer to these processes as 'pre-pronominal'. Among the most important factors at play during pre-pronominal processing are features of referents in the current discourse, e.g., syntactic function (Järvikivi et al. 2005; Frederiksen 1981) and order of mention (Gernsbacher 1988; Arnold et al. 2007). In general, these features are regarded as cues about the probability with which a referent will be referred to again in the following discourse, e.g., with a pronoun. Thus, the probabilities result from predictions made by the recipient about the upcoming discourse; they form the basis on which pronouns encountered later during the comprehension process are resolved. Processes which are initiated based on such probabilities have also been called 'forward-looking processes': they aim at parts of the discourse which are yet to come (Grosz et al. 1995; Gordon et al. 1993).

On the other hand, anaphoric pronoun resolution is affected by processes that are initiated only *after* a pronoun has been processed. We will refer to those processes as 'post-pronominal'. Among the factors that play a role during post-pronominal processing is the information carried by the pronominal form itself, e.g., gender and number, but also information which can be derived from the fact that a pronoun is an expression with attenuated meaning that refers to highly salient referents in preceding discourse (cf., Ariel 1988; Givón 1983; Gundel et al. 1993). Note that in German, a referent which is the subject of a sentence, or which is mentioned first, has been reported to be perceived as more salient compared to other referents (Ahrenholz 2007; Ellert 2010; Musan 2010). Processes that are initiated based on the pronoun itself have also been called 'backward-looking processes' (Grosz et al. 1995; Gordon et al. 1993).

The role of 'antecedent type'

A number of theoretical accounts make predictions about what the influence of 'antecedent type' in anaphoric pronoun resolution may be. The 'Expectancy Hypothesis' (Arnold et al. 2007) proposes that the position of the antecedent in the preceding sentence, or its syntactic role, respectively, is the basis for forward-directed assumptions about the referent(s) mentioned in the next sentence. Other approaches, like 'Givenness Theory' (Gundel et al. 1993) or 'Accessibility Theory' (Ariel 1988, 2001), highlight the importance of 'antecedent type' for what has been called 'backward looking'. Based on information encoded in an anaphoric pronoun, a recipient identifies the antecedent within the discourse representation in a backward fashion. Proponents of the 'Expectancy Hypothesis' (Arnold et al. 2007) assume that the position of a referential expression (which in some languages correlates with a specific syntactic function) affects the degree of its 'expectancy', i.e., the probability of the referent of the expression to be referred to again in the following discourse. First-mentioned expressions generally have a higher degree of expectancy. 'Accessibility Theory' and 'Givenness Theory' highlight the interrelation between a referential expression and the degree of its accessibility, or givenness, respectively, i.e., the saliency in the discourse representation of the recipient. Referential expressions like personal pronouns are regarded as markers that encode a specific degree of saliency: the more reduced a referential expression is – for example, with respect to its lexical content or its phonological size – the higher the degree of saliency of the corresponding referent in the discourse model. Thus, one may conclude that 'antecedent type' does not only play a role for pre-pronominal processing, in that predictions about which referent is most likely to be mentioned next are derived from information extracted from the current sentence/discourse, but that it also plays a role during post-pronominal processing, in that it is the referential expression, e.g., an anaphoric pronoun and its associated features, which triggers the backward search for an antecedent with matching saliency values.

'Antecedent type' is as a probabilistic cue, i.e., a cue that does not represent absolute certainty. Even though, in (some languages) subjects or first-mentioned referents are referred to more often in the succeeding discourse than other referents, one can only assume a default setting, but not a rule. Some studies have shown that whether the sentence subject is referred to or not in the following sentence may depend on the modality (written/oral) or on semantic environment of the anaphoric pronoun (Ahrenholz 2007; Pyykkönen et al. 2010).

The probabilistic nature of 'antecedent type' as a cue in anaphoric pronoun resolution is linked by some authors to the observation of its late acquisition and use by language learners. Arnold et al. (2007), for example, observed the use of this cue in monolingual English children at the age of 5. However, counter evidence was also obtained. Song and Fisher (2006, 2007) showed that monolingual English children between 2 to 3 years of age preferably identify syntactic subjects/first-mentioned referents as the antecedent of a pronoun. Results obtained by Järvikivi et al. (2013) showed the same preference for 4 year-olds in L1 German.

The role of gender

Gender agreement between an anaphoric pronoun and an antecedent noun phrase is obligatory in languages which provide this grammatical category. Violations of this rule generally result in ungrammaticality[2]. Thus, grammatical gender is a highly (externally) reliable cue in establishing coreference between an anaphoric pronoun and an antecedent.

The question about what role the gender cue plays in establishing coreference has already been discussed in the early 1980s; however, results and assumptions differ somewhat. Some authors assumed that anaphoric pronoun resolution is accomplished fast and more or less automatic on the basis of the gender cue, (if it is available in a given language and a given context). Other factors, like the 'antecedent type', were thought to play a minor role only (e.g., Crawley et al. 1990; Ehrlich 1980; see also Shillcock 1982; Arnold et al. 2000). Tanenhaus and Trueswell (1995), for example, suggested that, if different cues are available, those that are reliable are weighted higher in the process of anaphoric pronoun resolution. Thus, gender as a reliable cue should play a prominent role in anaphoric pronoun resolution in German.

Arnold et al. (2000, 2005, 2007) did obtain evidence for a very early influence of gender information in anaphoric pronoun resolution by employing an eye tracking procedure. The effect was observed in children as well as in adults. The authors showed that children at age 4 resolve the anaphoric pronoun based on semantic gender (sexus) and that only at age 5, children consider order of mention as a cue in anaphoric pronoun resolution. The authors interpreted their findings with

---

2 There are cases in which an anaphoric pronoun is gender-incongruent with its antecedent, namely when a speaker refers to an aformentioned referent on the basis of its natural gender instead of its grammatical gender: „Das Mädchen ging in den Wald. Sie fand dort einen großen Pilz". In the last sentence the girl (das Mädchen, neutral gender) is referred to with the anaphoric pronoun sie (feminine gender).

respect to the reliability of the two different cues: cues that are more reliable are acquired before probabilistic cues.

To the best of our knowledge, so far there have been no studies that directly investigated how gender information is used in the context of anaphoric pronoun resolution in bilingual participants. Still, to some extent we can draw on findings in bilingual gender processing in other contexts. These findings may illustrate what can be expected when bilinguals process gender information encoded in pronouns under the task of establishing coreference with an antecedent. In a production study, Irmen and Knoll (1999) found that adult learners of German whose L1 does not encode grammatical gender (Finnish) have considerable problems with assigning gender in their L2. Their performance was highly influenced by their L2 competence. But also learners with an L1 that does encode grammatical gender only profit from their experience (in the context of word recognition), if they exhibit a high competence in their L2 (Hopp 2013). In another word recognition study, Weber and Paris (2004) showed that even very advanced learners are hardly able to block gender information stemming from their L1. Guillelmon & Grosjean (2001) found effects of the onset of language acquisition (OLA) in gender processing. In an auditory naming study it was shown that native and early L2 speakers of French (L1 English) were sensitive to the manipulation of the factor gender in the experiment, whereas late L2 speakers did not show an effect. Thus, OLA seems to play an important role in gender processing in adults. Furthermore, children who learn a second language were found to have difficulties in acquiring the gender system in their L2 (for results in L2-German Kaltenbacher & Klages 2012).

Taken together, gender is an internally reliable cue for native speakers of a gender-language like German. Despite some exceptions, matching the gender information encoded in the pronoun and in the corresponding referent is always necessary when a pronoun establishes coreference with an antecedent. Thus, following Arnold et al. (2000, 2005, 2007) and Tanenhaus and Trueswell (1995), the gender cue should be acquired earlier than other cues and recipients should rely on it more, or at least to the same extent compared to other cues, because it is reliable. On the other hand, previous research has shown that grammatical gender is difficult to acquire for L2 learners. Even advanced learners do not seem to process gender information like native speakers. In this sense, gender is a highly externally reliable cue, but the internal reliability can be assumed to be different for native and L2 learners. With respect to when in the time course of anaphoric pronoun resolution the gender cue is processed, we can conclude that it only plays a role in post-pronominal processing, because it is the anaphoric pronoun and its gender features which trigger the backward search for a matching antecedent.

In the present study, we are interested in how native language learners and early learners of German as a second language use both gender and 'antecedent type' in anaphoric pronoun resolution. More specifically, we ask in how far the differing degrees of external cue reliability attributed to both cues play a role in children of different ages and of different acquisition types. Moreover, we focus on the time course of cue processing (pre- and post-pronominal processing), and ask when the two cues are used by our participants, and whether differences can be observed depending on age and/or acquisition type.

3 Present Study

Participants

The data in this study stem from 117 monolingual German and successive bilingual Russian-German children. At the time of data collection, all children regularly attended an educational institution, either a day nursery or a school. There were six participant groups based on age (5, 7 and 9 year olds) and learning type (German as L1 and German as L2). The majority of the bilingual children was born in Germany[3] and had received regular German input between the ages of one and three. All bilinguals spoke Russian at home, and most of them had regular contact with Russian outside of the family context (clubs, Russian school). All children had normal or corrected to normal sight and hearing. None of the children had any language learning deficiencies. Table 1 gives an overview of the number of children and their sex in each subject group. The data were collected separately for each child either at the Eye-Tracking laboratory at Heidelberg University or in the educational institution the children attended. The children received a compensation of 10 € for their time/participation.

Tab. 1: Overview of the participants

	L1-German	L2-German
Gr. 1	N= 19, 10 male, 9 female; age range: 5;00-6;06, mean: 5;05	N= 19, 10 male, 9 female; age range: 4;10-6;07, mean: 6;00

---

[3] Eight children from age group 3 and one child from the age groups 1 and 2 respectively were born in Russia.

	L1-German	L2-German
Gr. 2	N=23, 8 male, 15 female; age range: 6;10-8;09, mean: 7.01	N=20, 8 male, 12 female; age range: 7;00-8;09, mean: 8;08
Gr. 3	N=18, 9 male, 9 female; age range: 8;11-10;00, mean: 9;03	N=18, 6 male, 12 female; age range: 8;11-10;10, mean: 9;04

Experimental design and materials used

The method used for this experiment is the 'visual world' paradigm (Cooper 1974; Tanenhaus et al. 1995; Tanenhaus and Trueswell 1995). The material used in the experiment consists of 30 stimuli with one acoustic (texts and questions about the texts) and one visual component (pictures).

Acoustic Materials

There were 20 test and 10 filler items in this experiment. Each item was composed of three main clauses, which together formed a short text: An introduction sentence, an antecedent sentence and the test sentence. The introduction sentence was used to set the general frame. It was composed of a definite NP + a verbal phrase (*The friends were playing in the sandbox*) or of an unsubstantial *es* in the role of subject + a verbal phrase that included the verb to be (*It was night*). The antecedent sentence was composed of two definite NPs and an action verb with a middle or high level of transitivity[4]. The NPs served as potential antecedents for the anaphoric personal pronouns in the test sentence and in the critical trials, each NP was specified for a different gender (feminine or masculine). The test sentence was composed of an anaphoric personal pronoun and a verb phrase. For each text four versions were created by manipulating the order of the two NPs in the antecedent sentence (keeping the canonical SVO word order) and by manipulating the gender of the anaphoric pronoun in the test sentence (feminine/masculine). The introduction sentence was the same for each version. All texts were presented in past tense.

---

[4] The degree of semantic transitivity was determined using a rating technique with 15 adult German mother tongue speakers. This rating technique was taken from Kako (2006) and adapted for use with German speakers.

Example

Introduction sentence (same for all four versions):
Die Freunde haben im Sandkasten gespielt.
'The friends have in+the sand box played'

Antecedent sentence (same for feminine subject and masculine object)
Die Fee hat den König im Sand eingebuddelt.
DET (f, sg, Nom) fairy has DET (m., sg, ACC) king in+the sand burried

Antecedent sentence (same for feminine object and masculine subject)
Der König hat **die** Fee im Sand eingebuddelt.
DET (m, sg, Nom) king has DET (f., sg, ACC) fairy in+the sand burried

Test sentence (same for feminine subject and feminine object)
Sie war zum ersten Mal in diesem Sandkasten.
PRONOUN (f., sg., Nom) was for the first time in this sand box

Test sentence (same for masculine subject and masculine object)
Er war zum ersten Mal in diesem Sandkasten.
PRONOUN (m., sg., Nom) was for the first time in this sand box

This text material (20 texts x 4 versions) was distributed over four experimental lists in order to counterbalance the text versions and to make sure that each participant encounters only one version of each text, but at the same time is exposed to all conditions. There were always 5 tokens of each version in each list.

Filler items showed an identical structure. Ten animal names from all three gender classes were used with the corresponding pronouns. Note that in the filler items the pronoun was always ambiguous because the two NPs in the antecedent sentence were specified for the same gender. This was done to ensure that the participants would not develop a strategy by which they would exclusively rely on the gender cue but use all cues available to them. The same filler items were used for all four experimental lists.

The order of test and filler items was pseudo-randomized in each list. All lists were created so that there were never more than two succeeding trials that contained the same gender or the same 'antecedent type'. Also, there was never more than one filler in between critical trials.

In addition to the critical and filler items we recorded 10 questions (2 filler items and 8 test items) which asked the subjects about specifics mentioned in the texts[5]. These questions had the goal of making sure the children were listening carefully. Furthermore, the number of correct answers determined whether the data were later included in the analysis, or not. If a subject answered more than four questions incorrectly, he/she was excluded from the analysis. Subjects responded by saying the answer aloud. All texts and questions were recorded by a male German native speaker thereby controlling for normal speed, intonation, and emphasis.

Visual Materials

Visual stimuli consisted of colored pictures on white background depicting the two characters mentioned in the texts. They were positioned equally far away to the left and the right from the center of the screen. In order to avoid 'strategic viewing' we created two versions for each text. The 'parallel version' showed the picture corresponding to the sentence's subject on the left hand side and the picture corresponding to the sentence's object on the right hand side of the screen. The 'non-parallel versions' showed the pictures the other way around. For one half of all trials we used the parallel version and for the other half we used the non-parallel version (c.f. Dussias et al. 2013). Parallel and non-parallel versions were randomized in each experimental list.

---

[5] Since asking questions about the figures draws attention to the potential antecentends and thus could indirectly influence the anaphoric resolution process, we abstained from any questions about the figures (cf. Constens 2004, Dussias et al. 2013 on how explicit questions can make the participants aware of the object of investigation).

Fig. 1: Structure of the antecedent components of the stimuli

Structure of trials

Each stimulus consisted of a total of 5 components: (1.) a fixation cross; (2.) the antecedent component (AC), in which the introduction and the antecedent sentence was played and the visual stimulus was shown; (3.) a second fixation cross; (4.) the test component (TC), in which the test sentence was played and the same visual stimulus as in the AC was shown again; (5.) the end component, in which the subjects heard a comprehension question (in ten out of thirty trials) or the experimenter just proceeded to the next trial by pressing a button. If a component contained visual and audio material, both began simultaneously. Figure 2 shows the structure of a trial, as well as the length of each component.

Apparatus

Eye movements were recorded with a remote *Eye Follower* eye tracker (LC Technologies, Inc.). The gaze point sampling rate was 120 Hz, with a 0.45 degree gazepoint tracking accuracy. Stimuli were displayed on a 20" TFT monitor.

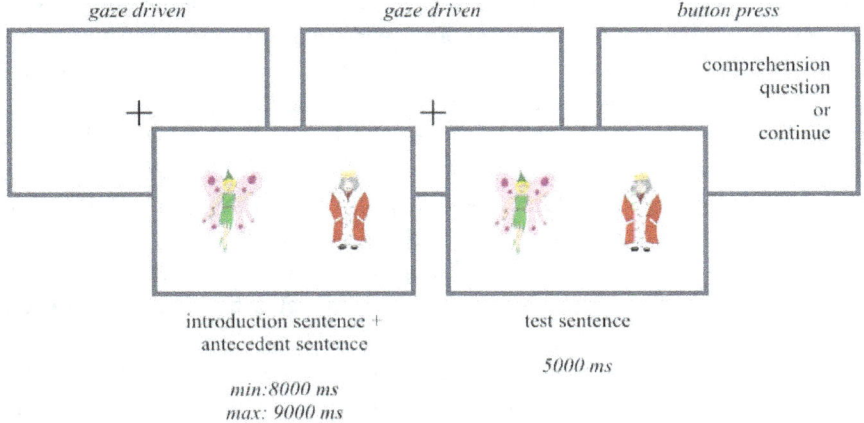

Fig. 2: Structure of one trial

Procedure

Participants were seated approximately 65 cm from the screen. They were instructed to listen to short stories while viewing pictures presented on the computer screen and to answer questions if they encountered one.

Data treatment and analysis

We analyzed target fixation proportions transformed into elogits over time as suggested by Barr (2008), focusing on effects of age, language, condition, and possible interactions between these variables[6]. Time was regarded as a continuous variable. We used the statistic software R, version 2.15.2 and the lme4 package, version 0.999999-2. After choosing a particular analysis window (see below), we asked if our variables (1.) yield differences in the overall target fixation proportions within the entire analysis window; (2.) yield differences with respect to the rate with which target fixation proportions increase over time (slope); (3.) yield differences with respect to what may be called anticipatory target fixations.

---

[6] Elogits were calculated as follows: elogt = log (target fixation + 0.5 / total of fixations -target fixations +0.5)

Before carrying out any analysis we cleaned our data by removing all fixations initiated before 200 ms after the onset of the auditory stimulus. This was done to ensure that all fixations entering the analyses were due to the presentation of the critical stimuli (auditory/visual) and were not artifacts related to our experimental design. In addition, fixations lasting shorter than 100 ms were excluded from further analyses. The output of the eye tracking system was transformed into a table that specified a binary value (yes/no) for every 50 ms, indicating whether a fixation was registered in the target Area of Interest (AoI), or not. Data were aggregated by subjects[7]. Since all items were counterbalanced across conditions we will not describe results from the by-items aggregation here (cf. Raaijmakers et al 1999).

We chose 375 ms after stimulus onset as the left boundary of the time window to be analyzed. There are several reasons for doing so. First, it is known that programming and launching a fixation takes about 200 ms. Since the phonological length of the pronouns used in the current study was between 150 and 200 ms, we expected any fixations driven by full processing of the pronoun only to occur between 350 and 400 ms. Furthermore, choosing 375 ms after pronoun onset as the left boundary of the analysis window does not mean that our analyses ignore possible fixations carried out earlier, though, we argue, that those fixations reflect rather anticipatory effects, since they must have been planned and launched before full processing of the pronoun had finished. The right boundary of the analysis window was set to 1000 ms after pronoun onset. We chose this specific interval because we were mainly interested in the initial phase of post-pronominal processing. Furthermore, a first exploration of the pre-processed data suggested a breakpoint at 1000ms after stimulus onset, that is, the steady increase of the mean elogits, as observed up to this point, stagnated.

To test the impact of the experimental factors, we set up a number of linear mixed effects models. There were two types of models: The first tested for possible effects concerning the proportions of target looks within the entire analysis window, as reflected in the values of the elogits[8]. This type ignored time as a variable. The second type of models always included an interaction term for time and the predictor under focus. This way it was possible to estimate (1.) by what value the elogits would increase for every value the time variable increases by one (slope), and (2.) the means of the elogit values at bin 0 (375 ms after pronoun

---

[7] If the variable "condition" was included as a factor we aggregated over items from the same conditions.
[8] Note that the value of the elogit depends on the sum of fixations carried out at the same time (within the same 50 ms-time bin) after pronoun onset across items.

onset), i.e., the left boundary of the analysis window. We argue that target fixation proportions indicate how much attention participants allocate towards the target under different experimental conditions while identifying the visual target as the antecedent, and that the slopes indicate how fast participants arrive at the target under the different experimental conditions. Furthermore, we interpret the elogits at the baseline (bin 0) as to reflect the proportion of target looks launched before full processing of the pronoun is finished, i.e., anticipatory target looks. All models included a random intercept for participants (with a random slope for time in the time-sensitive analyses). The models testing for effects of 'antecedent type' additionally included a term specifying that this manipulation was within-subject. Finally, weights[9] were also included in all models, because the variance of the elogit depends on the mean (Barr 2008).

Results

For better readability, we will here only describe the effects of our predictor variables in words. All formulas and model outputs can be found in the Appendix. If differences are mentioned, they are statistically significant. We interpreted t-values of at least 2 or -2 as statistically significant. Since main effects are not as relevant in the present study as the interactions between our predictor variables, we will not report them here. The interested reader is referred to the Appendix.

Let us first turn to the two-way interactions of the factors 'age' and 'language'[10]. It will be clear how 'antecedent type' contributes to our findings below, where we will partly report the three-way interaction of all experimental factors. Our model detected that bilinguals within the group of children at age 5 showed significantly fewer target looks than the monolinguals at the same ages, whereas no differences were detected within the other groups. With respect to differences in slope, we found that target fixation proportions increased more slowly in bilinguals at age 9 than in monolinguals at age 9. No differences were detected in the other groups. More anticipatory looks were found within the group of children at age 5, where monolinguals showed more target fixations at the left boundary of the analysis window. There were no differences within the other age groups (see figure 3).

---

9 Weights= (1/target fix + 0.5) + (1/total - target fix + 0.5)
10 All results can be found in the Appendix

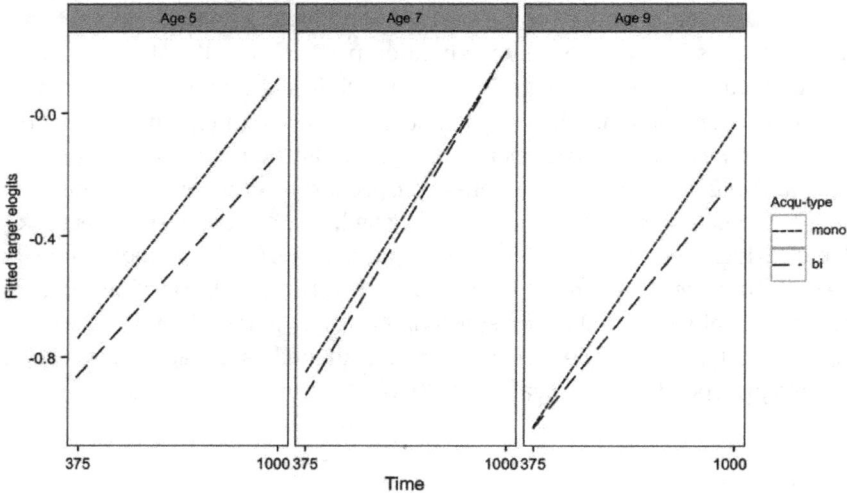

Fig. 3: Age over Acquisition type

To complete the picture, let us look at the age groups within the monolingual and bilingual participant groups separately. With respect to overall target fixation proportions, in the group of monolinguals, children at age 5 and 7 exhibited more target looks than children at age 9, whereas there was no difference between the former. In the group of bilinguals, children at age 7 showed higher target fixation proportions than children at age 5 and 9. No differences between the latter two were detected. With respect to slope effects, in the monolingual group there were no differences between children at age 5 and 9 and between children at age 7 and 9, but 7 year old children showed a faster increase in target fixation proportions than 5 year old children. In the bilingual group, this is different. Here, we found that target fixation proportions increase faster in children at age 7 compared to children age 5 and age 9 (no difference between age 5 and 9). Concerning our third dependent variable we found that in the group of monolinguals children at age 9 showed fewer anticipatory target looks than children at age 5 and 7. There was no difference between children at age 5 and 7. In the group of bilinguals, we found marginally significantly fewer anticipatory target looks in children age 9 compared to children age 5. The other comparisons did not yield significant or near-significant results.

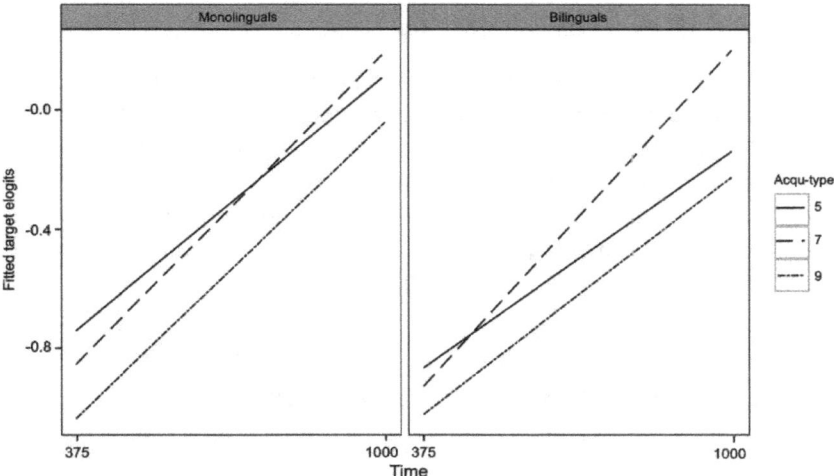

Fig. 4: Acquisition type over age

'Antecedent type' – Children Age 5

In monolinguals, we found lower overall target fixation proportions in the subject condition than in the object condition. In bilinguals there were no differences between conditions. With respect to slope, no differences between conditions were found in the group of monolinguals, nor in the group of bilinguals. In the object condition, we found more anticipatory target looks than in the subject condition for monolinguals, there was no difference between conditions in bilinguals.

'Antecedent type' – Children age 7

In children at age 7 we detected only two significant differences. There were higher fixation proportions in the object condition than in the subject condition for bilinguals. There was a steeper slope in the object condition than in the subject condition in bilinguals.

'Antecedent type' Children age 9

In monolinguals, we found higher target fixation proportions in the object condition than in the subject condition, no difference between conditions were found in bilinguals. A steeper slope was found in the object condition relative to the subject condition in monolinguals, and the same pattern was obtained in bilinguals. We found no differences between conditions with respect to anticipatory target looks in monolinguals. In bilinguals, there was a higher rate of anticipatory target looks in subject condition relative to the object condition.

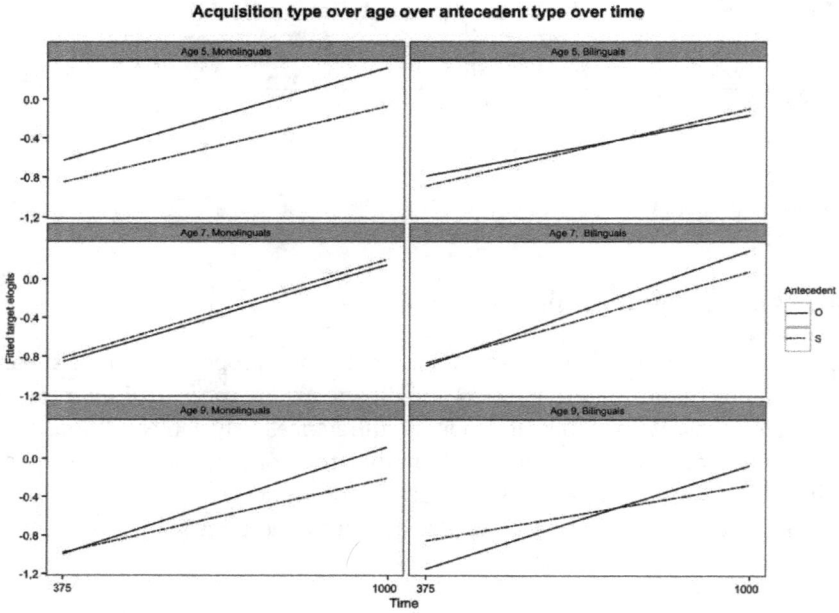

Fig. 5: Language over age over condition

Discussion

The present study focused on how children of different ages and different acquisition types accomplish pronoun resolution in real time. In particular, it was investigated how two different cues – gender and 'antecedent type' – are being used during the task. Both cues differ with respect to cue reliability and the point in time when their processing may be initiated. We will discuss the findings for mono- and bilinguals in turn.

Monolinguals

Our findings suggest that monolingual children in all age groups effectively use the gender cue within the first second after pronoun onset. This is evidenced by the fact that all children allocated more attention to the referent which is gender-congruent with the pronoun (target) compared to the referent which is not (competitor). Note that matching the gender encoded in the pronoun with the gender of the antecedent is the only way to successfully establish coreference with the antecedent in our task.

Surprisingly, we found differences with respect to total target fixation proportions between the age groups. Monolingual children at age 9 exhibited fewer target fixations compared to monolinguals at age 5 and 7. We interpret this in the following way: The decrease in target fixation proportions in older children could reflect a higher level of automatized gender cue processing; fewer cognitive resources are needed which results in a lower level of attention allocation to the target referent in the same time window compared to children of the other age groups. Children at age 9 generally resolve the pronoun faster as the younger children, which directly affects the total time spent gazing at the target referent within the first second after pronoun onset.

With respect to findings from the slope analyses, which we generally interpret to be informative about how quick children in the different age groups arrive at the gender-congruent referent (and thus establish coreference), we found that here it is the group of children age 5 which stands out the most: while children at age 7 and at age 9 do not show significant differences concerning this measure, children at age 5 exhibited a shallower slope compared to both other groups.

The way the slope is calculated, of course, allows several reasons for why this finding was obtained, but still, we argue that the fact that target fixation proportions increase more homogenously along the time course across items and participants in older children suggests that accessing the gender cue to resolve the anaphoric pronoun proceeds faster in children at age 7 and 9. Theoretically there are three reasons for why this could be the case: a) The gender cue is the most internally reliable cue compared to all other cues available at age 7 and age 9; this could be due to a longer exposure to the input; b) interference from other previously acquired cues is reduced; c) the gender cue is reinforced by processing other cues ('antecedent type').

In order to decide which of those explanations is most plausible we will now discuss our findings with respect to the 'antecedent type' manipulation. Note that the 'antecedent type' manipulation also allows us to shed light on the above mentioned distinction between pre- and post-pronominal resolution processes. In contrast to the gender cue, the position of the referent in the preceding sentence or its syntactic function, respectively, allows the children to make predictions about how the discourse will proceed even before the anaphoric pronoun is processed (pre-pronominal processing). At the same time the position of the referent also contributes to post-pronominal processing, in the sense that all cues associated with the referent's position may work "hand in hand" with the gender cue, or interfere with it. We argue that pre-pronominal processing is directly reflected in the proportions of anticipatory looks, but partly also in the slope[11].

In monolingual children at age 7 we did not find differences with respect to the 'antecedent type' manipulation, neither in the analysis of overall fixation proportions, nor in the analysis of anticipatory looks, nor in the analysis of the slope. We will get back to this after we have discussed the findings from the other two age groups where we did detect differences between the two 'antecedent type' conditions: in both groups we found higher target fixation proportions in the object condition compared to the subject condition. There are at least three possible interpretations for this finding: a) the object antecedent attracts more attention after the anaphoric pronoun has been processed ('post-pronominal' processing), because object reference is what the children perceive as an exception to the default case (since the probability of subject reference in everyday speech is higher). This way object referents can be considered to be more salient than subject referents at the current stage of language acquisition, because reference to objects appears to be "new" or relevant to learning information structuring rules. This could imply that already at age 5 children have acquired knowledge about or experience with what the default is in discourse structuring in German[12] (subjects tend to be preferred antecedents of anaphoric pronouns) and that they now devote themselves to acquiring exceptions. A similar, but slightly different explanation could be that, b) because children at their current state of language acquisition have found

---

11 It cannot completely be ruled out that the slope differences we found in the different age groups is not only an indicator for how fast language processing takes place in the groups we investigated but that it also reflects physiological abilities at a given age. Under this view the slopes we calculated would rather, or additionally, represent the general ability to move the eyes towards a specific object. However, previous studies have shown that already at age 5 children only move their eyes marginally slower than adults (Snedeker and Trueswell 2004).
12 Cf. Song and Fisher (2007) for evidence for the subject preference in early language acquisition in English.

evidence in the input that also objects can be referred to in the next sentence, they direct more attention towards object referents than towards subject referents, even before the anaphoric pronoun is encountered. They look at the object referent and wait if it will be referred to in the succeeding sentence; thus, higher fixation proportions on objects would be a result of this higher awareness in pre-pronominal processing. Once the children found their predictions to be correct (the object is the target in the object condition) their level of attention remains high. Another alternative explanation could be that c) the higher degree of attention allocation may reflect that objects are in the focus of attention because they were encountered last (recency strategy).

Even though all three explanations might hold to some extent for children at age 5, we favor interpretation b). This is based on our finding that we did detect significantly more anticipatory looks in the object condition compared to the subject condition, i.e., children in this age group direct more attention to object referents before the anaphoric pronoun is fully processed. A difference in anticipatory looks should not be obtained if 'antecedent type' as a cue would only play a role in 'post-pronominal' processing. At the same time we cannot completely rule out interpretation c), since syntactic objects were always last mentioned in our study. Note, however, that following a 'recency strategy' would not necessarily lead to the anticipatory effect we found. If we assume that applying a 'recency strategy' has an effect on 'post-pronominal' processing, then the elevated total target fixation proportions found in the object condition should not be interpreted as a result of applying 'antecedent type' as a cue (extracted from the anaphoric pronoun); it should rather be regarded as the result of a local strategy.

In children at age 9 we did not find a difference with respect to the proportion of anticipatory target looks in the two 'antecedent type' conditions, which rules out interpretation b). The higher overall target fixations and the steeper slope found in the object condition suggest that children at age 9 not only attend more to objects, but also arrive faster at the target, if this is an object antecedent. Taken together, we favor explanation a) for this group of children. Object reference is more salient at this age because children acquire exceptions to the default (subjects are preferred antecedents).

The interpretation that 'antecedent type' in general plays a role for pre-pronominal processing in children at age 5 and that the same type of information plays a role for post-pronominal processing in children at age 9 is also supported by the fact that, irrespective of condition, children at age 9 showed fewest anticipatory looks. In this age group, children seem to be able to apply all cues available to them in a more flexible fashion. They adjust better to task requirements, in that they "understand" that pre-pronominal processing lets them perform less well in our task.

Let us now return to children at age 7. Even though we did not find a difference between the two 'antecedent types' – neither in the measures associated with pre-nor post-pronominal processing –, we also did not detect significantly lower overall anticipatory target fixations compared to children at age 5: similar to children at age 5, children at age 7 still seem to generate probabilities about which referent will be mentioned next before full processing of the pronoun is finished. The absence of the condition effect, thus, can only be explained by an increase in anticipatory subject target looks and – at the same time – a decrease in anticipatory object target looks. This implies that the higher degree of attention during pre-pronominal processing on object referents observed in children at age 5 is abandoned in favor for elevated attention allocation towards subject referents. Thus, children age 7 seem to give up their interest in the non-default cases during pre-pronominal processing.

With respect to overall target fixation proportions we did not detect a difference between children at age 5 and at age 7. In both age groups the same amount of cognitive resources is spent during the resolution process. But similar to the absence of the 'antecedent type' effect in anticipatory target fixations, we also did not obtain any difference between subject and object targets with respect to overall target fixations. Again, this can only be interpreted as an increase in (post-pronominal) attention allocation on subject referents and – at the same time – a decrease in (post-pronominal) attention allocation on object referents (compared to the 5 year-olds). We interpret this as to reflect the beginning of establishing 'antecedent type' as a relevant cue for 'post-pronominal' processing while at the same time the gender cue becomes more internally reliable. Gender and referent-type are both used as sources of information extracted from the pronoun. The absence of the 'antecedent type' effect could indicate that gender is the primary cue 7 year-olds use, while 'antecedent type', though, also clearly used, serves as a secondary cue at this age.

Comparing children at age 5 and children at age 7, the steeper slope in the older children could also be interpreted as an indicator for the increasing importance of 'antecedent type' as a cue relevant to 'post-pronominal' processing: after, or while, processing gender information encoded in the pronoun, the referent-type cue supports the accessibility of the antecedent. Gender information and 'antecedent type' together, lead to an earlier identification of the (correct) referent. Note, however, that though the identification of the antecedent proceeds faster (compared to 5 year-olds), children at age 7 still allocate more attention towards the target, if compared to children at age 9. This could be interpreted as to reflect that the coordination of the two cues puts high processing demands on children at age 7. These findings may be interpreted as to reflect that age 7 marks a stage in language acquisition at which using 'antecedent-type' as a discourse cue in post-pronominal processing begins.

Taken together, our findings suggest that children do get better with respect to gender cue processing between the age of 5 and 9. Though, in children at age 5 and 7 approximately the same amount of cognitive resources is needed to establish coreference between the antecedent and the pronoun, the distribution of available resources is different. While children at age 5 spend most resources available on processing gender information, children at age 7 use their resources on processing gender *and* 'antecedent type' information. We interpret this shift as to reflect an increase in the internal gender cue reliability from age 5 to age 7: More reliable cues are processed faster. Children at age 7 need fewer resources to process gender and this way more capacities are available for processing 'antecedent type' information ('post-pronominal'). At age 9 cognitive resources needed for anaphoric pronoun resolution are lowest, even though we found clear signs for processing gender information and 'antecedent type' information. We argue that this indicates that processing the gender cue has become an automatized process at age 9.

From the findings obtained in our experiment we can conclude that acquiring knowledge or processing routines about how to make use of the gender cue in anaphoric pronoun resolution develops at least up to 9 years of age. Our conclusions are not in line with Arnold et al. (2007). On the basis of their eye tracking study the authors concluded that processing gender during anaphoric pronoun resolution in English monolingual children at age 5 overlaps with the performance of monolingual adults. This result was interpreted as to show that the acquisition of and the ability to apply the gender cue is completed by children at age 5. Of course, the performance of children at age 5 may very well be similar to the performance of adults. In fact, from results obtained in our experiment we cannot conclude the contrary, because we did not test an adult control group. Still, since we did detect differences in the performance between all age groups investigated we reject the aforementioned conclusion from the Arnold et al. (2007) study. The different conclusions, however, could of course also be related to the languages investigated. One cannot rule out that the acquisition of the gender cue proceeds faster in English, which could correlate with the fact that the gender system is rather opaque in German, whereas gender marking in English is more transparent, because it is restricted to natural gender. Furthermore, the statistical approach chosen for data analysis was different in our study compared to the one applied in Arnold et al. (2007).

With regard to processing 'antecedent type' information we found the following pattern: monolingual children begin using this cue for pre-pronominal processing at age 5 (probably even before). At this age children attend to non-default cases (in German). At age 7 acquisition of 'antecedent type' as a discourse cue seems to come to an end: in pre-pronominal processing no preference for either subject or object referents were detected. At age 9 children even seem to be able to inhibit the use of that cue during pre-pronominal processing, because this is beneficent for task requirements in our experiment.

Considering 'antecedent type' as a relevant cue in post-pronominal processing begins at the age of 7, i.e., that age at which acquiring this cue as a feature of the discourse (pre-pronominal processing) is ceasing. Thus, the acquisition of 'antecedent type' as a cue in anaphoric pronoun resolution progresses at least up to age 9 and the way in which this acquisition proceeds may be characterized as follows: at age 7 children generally consider 'antecedent type' as a basic feature of the anaphoric pronoun. They attend increasingly to default cases (higher degree of attention to subject referents in comparison to the youngest participants). At age 9, processing the cue ('post-pronominal') becomes somewhat more automatized and meanwhile non-default cases are in the focus of attention. If we assume that attending to non-default cases marks the last sequence of acquiring a phenomenon by a language learner, children at age 9 in our study are going towards the end of acquiring the relevance of 'antecedent type' during 'post-pronominal' processing. Considering 'antecedent type' for 'post-pronominal' processing generally seems to support the identification of the antecedent based on the gender cue in two distinct ways: the accessibility of the antecedent becomes higher and fewer cognitive resources are required.

To summarize, in monolingual children between age 5 and 9, anaphoric pronoun resolution is accomplished on the basis of the externally most reliable cue, which is gender. With increasing age (from age 7 years on), the externally less reliable cue 'antecedent type' supports 'post-pronominal' processing. During pre-pronominal processing, the cue shows an effect in the early stages of language acquisition; in our study, it was evident in children at age 5.

Bilinguals

Results obtained in the bilingual group suggest that children resolve the anaphoric pronoun within the first second after pronoun onset, as can be inferred from our finding that participants allocated significantly more attention to the gender-congruent compared to the gender-incongruent referent. Contrary to our findings in the monolingual group, in bilinguals, we found a U-shape with respect to total target fixation proportions: children at age 7 showed the highest degree of attention allocation towards the target, whereas both, children at age 5 and children at age 9 allocated significantly less attention to the target within the first second after pronoun onset. We will interpret this pattern by discussing the increase between children at age 5 and 7 and the decrease between children at age 7 and 9 in turn. It will become clear that the low overall target fixation proportions in 5 year-olds and 9 year-olds have different reasons.

We propose that the gender cue becomes more internally reliable between age 5 and 7 in bilinguals. Based on our results, we assume that compared to children at age 5 more children at age 7 look at the target referent in the first second after pronoun onset because gender information extracted from the pronoun is being matched with the gender information extracted from the corresponding antecedent. This in turn suggests that the 5 year-olds generally have a low competence in processing gender information in their L2, a finding which relates to previous research (Kaltenbacher & Klages 2012). Thus, the gender cue is internally less reliable. This could be related to the fact that the 5 year-olds had less contact with their L2 compared to the 7 year-olds. Furthermore, the higher degree of the gender cue reliability in children at age 7 may additionally allow processing 'antecedent type' (post-pronominal). Processing an externally reliable cue and at the same time processing a probabilistic cue should require more cognitive resources than processing one cue (which is of only low internal reliability) only. This is what we observed comparing bilingual children at age 5 and 7.

Now, how can the decrease in overall target fixation proportions between age 7 and 9 be explained? There are two possibilities: First, bilinguals at age 9 have a low competence with respect to gender, just as bilinguals at age 5. An influence of their L1 could be responsible for that. As all children in our study reported to have L1 contact on a daily basis, gender processing in their L2 could suffer from interference from their L1. Second, one could apply the same logic as for the monolingual children at age 9: the decrease in overall target fixation proportions could reflect an increase in automatized gender cue processing. Because there was no indication in the participant data that bilingual children at age 9 differed with respect to the intensity of contact to their L1 compared to children at age 7 and thus there are no grounds to assume that interference from their L1 is greater, we favor our second interpretation.

In terms of the slope analysis, we obtained the same pattern of results as for the total target fixation proportions (U-shape). We argue that in bilingual children at age 7, the gender cue is most accessible which is supported by the strongest increase in target fixation proportions over time within the entire bilingual group.

Again, this could be related to the supportive effect of 'antecedent type' during post-pronominal processing.

With respect to the 'antecedent type' manipulation we did not obtain any effect in bilingual children at age 5, for neither of the dependent variables we analyzed. Thus, there is no evidence that the youngest bilinguals in our study use the cue associated with the position/syntactic function of the referent in the preceding sentence, neither during pre-pronominal, nor during post-pronominal processing. In bilingual children at age 7, on the other hand, we do find effects with respect to the 'antecedent type' manipulation: attention allocation to object referents was higher relative to subject referents. In addition, the proportion of looks to targets increased faster in the object condition compared to the subject condition (steeper slope). Object referents seem to be more salient than subject referents, which we interpret to reflect that bilinguals at age 7 have begun to use the 'antecedent type' cue as encoded in the content of the anaphoric pronoun (rather reduced form compared to full NPs) to establish coreference. This implies that children in that age group have begun to acquire knowledge about other cues than the gender cue. However, note that we did not obtain effects indicating differences during pre-pronominal processing between conditions. Information about the position or the syntactic function of the referent in the preceding sentence, thus, only plays a role in post-pronominal processing.

The finding that object referents are more salient but that this only affects 'post-pronominal' processing could be due to an increasing awareness of the default rules for text structuring in German. Object reference violates the default in the L2 and leads to faster and higher attention allocation. If this was the case, the behavior observed in seven-year old bilinguals may be attributed to the same reasons as in the five-year old monolinguals (see above). However, for the bilinguals there is one further alternative interpretation for their preference to attend to objects, which essentially may be related to an interference effect from their L1: Russian is regarded a weak pro-drop language. Here the zero-anaphor competes with the anaphoric pronoun in the context of subject coreference (Gagarina 2007). The personal pronoun, thus, is not the only anaphor with which speakers of Russian refer to the subject in the preceding sentence. The lack of an exclusive relation between a pronoun and the subject referent in Russian could be a factor which explains why object reference attracts more attention in the children's L2. Furthermore, personal pronouns are regarded as most neutral with respect to indicating continuity of reference (Gagarina 2007).

In bilingual children at age 9 we did not find evidence for a different degree of overall attention allocation towards the target depending on 'antecedent type' within the time window analyzed. What we did find was that the 'antecedent type' manipulation led to differences with respect to anticipatory target fixation proportions. This group of participants was the only group in our study which showed significantly higher anticipatory target fixation proportions in the subject condition compared to the object condition. This finding suggests that at age 9, our bilingual participants *begin* to use 'antecedent type' information during pre-pronominal processing: they devote themselves to the default-case in German (subjects/ first-mentioned referents tend to be next-mentioned) to generate predictions about the succeeding discourse.

Taken together, we conclude that bilingual children at age 5 predominantly use the gender cue to establish coreference between the pronoun and the antecedent, even though their competence in gender processing is relatively low. At age 7, the reliability of the gender cue increases and at the same time the 'antecedent type' cue begins to gain importance, but only for post-pronominal processing. At this stage of language acquisition, children attend to non-default cases. At age 9, anaphoric pronoun resolution proceeds to be accomplished on the basis of the gender cue *and* 'antecedent type' information (in a more and more automatized fashion). At this age, so we interpret our findings, learners begin to consider 'antecedent type' as a feature of the discourse, which is used during pre-pronominal processing.

To summarize, in bilingual children between the age of 5 and 9, anaphoric pronoun resolution is accomplished on the basis of the externally reliable cue (gender). Its internal reliability increases with increasing age. Also with increasing age, less reliable cues ('antecedent type') support the resolution process during 'post-pronominal' processing. It seems that in bilingual language learners the acquisition of externally reliable cues precedes the acquisition of probabilistic cues, at least with respect to 'post-pronominal' processing. The use of less reliable cues gains importance only at later stages in bilingual language acquisition, i.e., bilinguals are first devoted to the acquisition of cues they can use in 'post-pronominal' processing, and only if this stage is completed they begin to acquire cues relevant to pre-pronominal processing.

Comparison between mono- and bilinguals

A comparison of the two acquisition types shows that monolingual and bilingual children are most similar at age 7. In this age group, children spend approximately the same amount of cognitive resources on identifying the target. One difference, though, is that bilingual children were more sensitive to the 'antecedent type' manipulation during 'post-pronominal' processing. With respect to pre-pronominal processing, we did not detect differences between the two acquisition types at this age. Youngest and oldest children in the two acquisition types showed differences that are more pronounced. In children at age 5, we found differences with regard to pre- and post-pronominal processing. Monolinguals clearly made predictions about the referent to be mentioned next before full processing of the pronoun was finished, whereas bilinguals did not use such a strategy. Also later in the time course, monolinguals at age 5 direct more attention to object antecedent than subject antecedents; again an effect which we did not observe in bilingual children in this age group. At age 9 we found a similar, but reversed pattern: while in monolinguals, 9-year old children are the only ones for which *no* clear signs of pre-pronominal processing of 'antecedent type' as a discourse cue was found, 9 year-old children are the only ones in the bilingual group for which we did detect signs of pre-pronominal processing.

To summarize, monolingual language learners between the age of 5 and 9 exhibit signs for both pre- and post-pronominal cue processing. What considering the 'antecedent type' cue at different stages in the time course of anaphoric pronoun resolution at different ages revealed, can be interpreted to correlate with what is acquisition-relevant at a given stage in language learning. Bilingual language learners, on the other hand, show a different pattern: they do not use the externally less reliable 'antecedent type' cue during pre-pronominal processing at early ages, that is, before the internal reliability of the gender cue has reached a certain level. In how far both acquisition types differ with respect to how well they are able to coordinate both cues during post-pronominal processing cannot be derived from our findings. It remains to be said that the focus placed on one specific type of antecedent (subject/object) differs depending on acquisition type. Based on our findings, we conclude that monolinguals make a start using 'antecedent type' as a cue by using it during pre-pronominal processing first, whereas bilinguals approach the acquisition of this cue via post-pronominal processing. Lastly, in both acquisition types the internal reliability of both cues increases with increasing age, albeit, the performance of bilinguals stays below the performance of the monolinguals.

Conclusion

Our three most important findings are the following: (1.) With respect to our experimental manipulation of the factor 'age' we showed that both, the acquisition of gender, as well as the acquisition of 'antecedent type' as cues in anaphoric pronoun resolution is not completed at least up to the age of 9. We obtained different results under the same task in all age groups. In monolingual children, the gender cue reliability increases at least up to approximately age 7; after the cue has been established as reliable, its use becomes more and more automatized. 'Antecedent type' is used in pre-pronominal processing by youngest, but in post-pronominal processing by older monolingual children. (2.) With respect to the manipulation of 'acquisition type', we conclude that bilingual children (L1 Russian, L2 German) perform less well and that their way of acquiring cues relevant to anaphoric pronoun resolution differs compared to monolinguals. However, based on the results presented in this article, we could not ultimately decide what factors are responsible for the difference between L1 and L2 children. (3.) With respect to the question in what order, or when in language acquisition reliable and probabilistic cues are acquired, we were able to show that indeed externally reliable cues are acquired first by bilinguals. For monolinguals we cannot make a clear statement in this regard, since already the youngest participants in our study used both cues. However, we discussed evidence that 5 years of age might be exactly that point in monolingual language acquisition when learners begin to consider probabilistic cues. In bilinguals, the acquisition of different cues relevant to anaphoric pronoun resolution clearly lags behind that of monolinguals, most probably due to difficulties in processing gender information irrespective of task. (4.) In research on anaphoric pronoun resolution it is worth to distinguish between pre- and post-pronominal processing. Our analyses revealed that a specific cue, in our case 'antecedent type, may be used differently by children of different ages. The analysis of what we have called anticipatory looks showed that monolingual children at age 5, as well as bilingual children at age 9 use the 'antecedent type' cue for pre-pronominal processing, whereas children in other age groups used the same cue for post-pronominal processing. Thus, considering the differentiation between pre- and post-pronominal processing makes it possible to track shifts of cue usage under different conditions.

References

Ahrenholz, B. 2007. Verweise mit Demonstrativa im gesprochenen Deutsch. Grammatik, Zweitspracherwerb und Deutsch als Fremdsprache. Berlin, Boston: de Gruyter.
Ariel, M. 1988. Referring and accessibility. In *Journal of Linguistics* 24 (1), 67–87.
Ariel, M. 2001. Accessibility theory: An overview. In: Sanders, T. J. M., Schilperoord, J., Spooren, W. (eds): Text representation: Linguistic and psycholinguistic aspects. Amsterdam: John Benjamins, 29–87.
Ariel, M. 2013. Centering, accessibilty and the next mention. In *Theoretical Linguistics* 39 (1–2), 39–58.
Arnold, J. 2013. What should a theory of pronoun interpretation look like? Commentary on Kehler and Rohde (2013): A probabilistic reconciliation of coherence-driven and centering-driven theories of pronoun interpretation. In *Theoretical Linguistics* 39 (1–2), 59–73.

Arnold, J. E., Brown-Schmidt, S., Trueswell, J. C., Fagnano, M. 2005. Children's use of gender and order-of-mention during pronoun comprehension. In Trueswell, J. C., Tanenhaus, M. K. (eds.): Approaches to studying world-situated language use: Bridging the language-as-product and language-as-action traditions. Cambridge, London: *The MIT Press*, 261–281.

Arnold, J. E. 2013. What should a theory of pronoun interpretation look like? Commentary on Kehler and Rohde (2013): A probabilistic reconciliation of coherence-driven and centering-driven theories of pronoun interpretation. In *Theoretical Linguistics* 39 (1–2), 59–73.

Arnold, J. E., Brown-Schmidt, S., Trueswell, J. 2007. Children's use of gender and order-of-mention during pronoun comprehension. In *Language and Cognitive Processes* 22 (4), 527-565.

Arnold, J. E., Eisenband, J. G., Brown-Schmidt, S., Trueswell, J. C. 2000. The rapid use of gender information: Evidence of the time course of pronoun resolution from eyetracking. In *Cognition* 76 (1), B13–B26.

Barr, D. J. 2008. Analyzing 'visual world' eyetracking data using multilevel logistic regression. In: *Journal of Memory and Language* 59 (4), 457–474.

Bouma, G., Hopp, H. 2007. Coreference preferences for personal pronoun in German. In Bittner, D., Gagarina, N. (eds): Intersentential Pronominal Reference in Child and Adult Language. ZASPiL 48. Berlin: Zentrum für allgemeine Sprachwissenschaft, Typologie und Universalienforschung, 53–74.

Colonna, S., Schimke, S., Hemforth, B. 2012. Information structure effects on anaphora resolution in German and French: A cross-linguistic study of pronoun resolution. In *Linguistics* 50 (5), 991–1013.

Colonna, S., Schimke, S., Hemforth, B. 2014. Information structure and pronoun resolution in German and French: Evidence from the visual-world paradigm. In Hemforth, B., Mertins, B., Fabricius-Hansen, C. (eds.): Psycholinguistic approaches to meaning and understanding across languages, 175–195.

Consten, M. 2004. Anaphorisch oder deiktisch? Zu einem integrativen Modell domänengebundener Referenz. Tübingen: Niemeyer.

Cooper, R. M. 1974. The control of eye fixation by the meaning of spoken language. A new methodology for the real-time investigation of speech perception, memory and language processing. In *Cognitive psychology* 6, 84–107.

Crawley, R. A., Stevenson, R. J., Kleinman, D. 1990. The use of heuristic strategies in the interpretation of pronouns. In *Journal of Psycholinguistic Research* 19 (4), 245–264.

Dussias, P. E., Valdés Kroff, J. R., Guzzardo Tamargo, R. E., Gerfen, C. 2013. When gender and looking go hand in hand. Grammatical Gender Processing in L2 Spanish. In *Studies in Second Language Acquisition* 35 (2), 353–387.

Ehrlich, K. 1980. Comprehension of pronouns. In *Quarterly Journal of Experimental Psychology*, 32 (2), 247–255.

Ellert, M. 2010. Ambiguous Pronoun Resolution in L1 and L2 German and Dutch. In *MPI Series in Psycholinguistics* 58. Wageningen: Ponsen and Looijen.

Ellert, M., Roberts, L., Järvikivi, J. 2011. Verarbeitung und Disambiguierung pronominaler Referenz in der Fremdsprache Deutsch: Eine psycholinguistische Studie. In Krafft, A. and Spiegel, C. (eds.): Sprachliche Förderung und Weiterbildung-Transdisziplinär. Frankfurt am Main: Peter Lang, 51–68.

Frederiksen, J. R. 1981. Understanding anaphora: Rules used by readers in assigning pronominal referents. In *Discourse processes* 4, 323–347.

Gagarina, N. 2007. The hare hugs the rabbit. He is white...Who is white? Pronominal anaphora in Russian. In *ZAS Papers in Linguistics* 48, 133–149.
Gernsbacher, M. A., Hargreaves, D. J. 1988. Accessing sentence participants: The advantage of first mention. In *Journal of Memory and Language* 27 (6), 699–717.
Givón, T. 1983. Topic continuity in discourse: An introduction. In Givón, T. (ed.): Topic continuity in discourse: A quantitative cross-language stud., Amsterdam: John Benjamins Publishing, 1–42.
Gordon, P. C., Grosz, B. J., Gilliom, L. A. 1993. Pronouns, names, and the centering of attention in discourse Cognitive Science 17, 311–347.
Grosz, B., Joshi, A.K., Weinstein, S. 1995. Centering: A framework for modeling the local coherence of discourse. In *Computational Linguistics* 21 (2), 203–225.
Guillelmon, D., Grosjean, F. 2001. The gender marking effect in spoken word recognition: the case of bilinguals. In *Memory and Cognition* 29 (3), 503–511.
Gundel, J., Hedberg, N., Zacharski, R. 1993. Cognitive status and the form of referring expressions in discourse. *Language* 69 (2), 274–307.
Hopp, H. 2013. Mehrsprachig sehen – Was die Augen uns über bilinguale Sprecher verraten. Vortrag am 12.12.2013, „Mehrsprachigkeit". FiSS Herbstschule Mannheim.
Irmen, L., Knoll, J. 1999. On the use of the grammatical gender of anaphoric pronouns in German. A comparison between Finns and Germans. In *Sprache & Kognition* 18 (3-4), 123–135.
Järvikivi, J., Pyykkönen-Klauck, P., Schimke, S., Colonna, S., Hemforth, B. 2013. Information structure cues for 4-year-olds and adults: tracking eye movements to visually presented anaphoric referents. In *Language, Cognition and Neuroscience* 29 (7), 877–892.
Järvikivi, J., van Gompel, R.P., Hyönä, J., Bertram, R. 2005. Ambiguous pronoun resolution: Contrasting the first-mention and subject preference accounts. *Psychological Science* 16 (4), 260–264.
Kako, E. 2006. Thematic role properties of subjects and objects. In *Cognition* 101 (1), 1–42.
Kaltenbacher, E., Klages, H. 2012. Sprachprofil und Sprachförderung bei Vorschulkindern mit Migrationshintergrund. In Ahrenholz, B. (ed.): Kinder mit Migrationshintergrund. Spracherwerb und Fördermöglichkeiten. 3. Aufl. Freiburg: Fillibach, 80–97.
Koornneef, A.W., Sanders, T.J.M. 2013. Establishing coherence relations in discourse: the influence of implicit causality and connectives on pronoun resolution. In *Language and Cognitive processes* 28 (8), 1169–1206.
Musan, R. 2010. Informationsstruktur. Heidelberg: Winter.
Pyykkönen, P., Matthews, D., Järvikivi, J. 2010. Three-year-olds are sensitive to semantic prominence during online language comprehension: A visual world study of pronoun resolution. In *Language and Cognitive Processes* 25 (1), 115–129.
Raaijmakers, J. G., Schrijnemakers, J. M., Gremmen, F. 1999. How to Deal with "The Language-as-Fixed-Effect Fallacy": Common Misconceptions and Alternative Solutions. In *Journal of Memory and Language* 41 (3), 416–426.
Shillock, R. 1982. The on-line resolution of pronominal anaphora. In *Language and Speech* 25 (4), 385–401.
Snedeker, J., Trueswell, J. C. 2004. The developing constraints on parsing decisions: The role of lexical-biases and referential scenes in child and adult sentence processing. In *Cognitive Psychology* 49 (3), 238–299.
Song, H., Fisher, C. 2006. Who's "she"? Discourse structure influences preschooler's pronoun interpretation. In *Journal of Memory and language* 52 (1), 29–57.

Song, H., Fisher, C. 2007. Discourse prominence effects on 2.5-year-old childerens's interpretation of pronoun. In *Lingua* 117 (11), 1959–1987.

Tanenhaus, M. K., Spivey-Knowlton, M. J., Eberhardt, K. M., Sedivy, J. C. 1995. Integration of visual and linguistic information in spoken language comprehension. In *Science* 268 (5217), 1632–1634.

Tanenhaus, M. K., Trueswell, J.C. 1995. Sentence Comprehension. In Miller, J. L., Eimas, P. D. (eds): Speech, language, and communication. Handbook of perception and cognition 11, San Diego, CA, US: *Academic Press*, 217–262.

Tanenhaus, M.K., Trueswell, J.C. 2005. Eye-movement as a tool for bridging the language-as-product and language-as-action traditions. In Trueswell, J.C., Tanenhaus, M.K. (eds): Approaches to studying world-situated-language-use. Bridging the language-as-action and language-as-product traditions. Massachusetts: *MIT Press*, 3–38.

Terhorst, E. 1995. Textverstehen bei Kindern: Zur Entwicklung von Kohärenz und Referenz. Opladen: Westdeutscher Verlag.

Tyler, L. 1983. The development of discourse mapping processes: the on-line interpretation of anaphoric expressions. In *Cognition* 13 (3), 309–341.

Weber, A., Paris, G. 2004. The origin of the linguistic gender effect in spoken-word recognition: Evidence from non-native listening. In Forbus, K., Gentner, D., Tegier, T. (eds.): Proceedings of the 26th Annual Meeting of the Cognitive Science Society. Mahwah, NJ: Erlbaum.

Appendix

```
## Main effect 'Language'
##### reference-level: German
Formula: (elogit ~ Language + (1|vp)
                 Estimate  Std. Error  t value
(Intercept)     -0.34674    0.02021   -17.153
LanguageR       -0.09775    0.02899    -3.372

## Main effect 'Age'
##### reference-level: Age 5
Formula: (elogit ~ Age + (1|vp)
            Estimate  Std. Error  t value
(Intercept) -0.38565   0.02521    -15.3
Age7         0.08386   0.03461     2.423
Age9        -0.12896   0.03623    -3.559

## Main effect 'reference type'
##### reference-level: object
Formula: elogit ~ condition + (1 + condition | vp)
             Estimate  Std. Error  t value
(Intercept) -0.33649   0.02147    -15.67
conditionS  -0.08939   0.02354    -3.797

## Interaction 'Language', 'Age'
### within age 5
Formula: elogit ~ Language + (1 | vp)
             Estimate  Std. Error  t value
(Intercept) -0.26691   0.02881   -10.307
LanguageR   -0.17697   0.04079    -4.338

Formula: elogit ~ t1 * Language + (1 + t1 | vp)
              Estimate  Std. Error  t value
(Intercept)  -0.74384    0.03936   -18.898
t1            1.43603    0.09188    15.63
LanguageR    -0.11863    0.05574    -2.128
t1:LanguageR -0.22433    0.13012    -1.724

### within monolinguals
##### reference-level: age 5, German
Formula: elogit ~ Age + (1 | vp)
            Estimate  Std. Error  t value
```

```
##### reference-level: German
Formula: (elogit ~ t1*Language + (1+t1|vp)
              Estimate  Std. Error  t value
(Intercept)  -0.86946   0.02978   -29.193
t1            1.62127   0.05256    30.844
LanguageR    -0.06547   0.04272    -1.532
t1:LanguageR -0.13174   0.07545    -1.746

##### reference-levels: Age 5
Formula: (elogit ~ t1*Age + (1+t1|vp)
            Estimate  Std. Error  t value
(Intercept) -0.80381   0.03729   -21.554
t1           1.32543   0.06532    20.291
Age7        -0.0806    0.05123    -1.573
Age9        -0.22201   0.05367    -4.137
t1:Age7      0.48816   0.08978     5.437
t1:Age9      0.17239   0.09416     1.831

##### reference-level: object
Formula: elogit ~ t1 * condition + (1 + t1 | vp)
               Estimate  Std. Error  t value
(Intercept)   -0.872308  0.033513  -26.029
t1             1.637984  0.068892   23.776
conditionS     0.003838  0.031104    0.123
t1:conditionS -0.278668  0.086655   -3.216

### within age 7
Formula: elogit ~ language + (1 | vp)
             Estimate  Std. Error  t value
(Intercept) -0.29128    0.03065   -9.442
LanguageR   -0.02097    0.04523   -0.464

Formula: elogit ~ t1 * Language + (1 + t1 | vp)
              Estimate  Std. Error  t value
(Intercept)  -0.84882    0.04599   -18.458
t1            1.74669    0.08099    21.801
LanguageR    -0.07553    0.06745    -1.12
t1:LanguageR  0.14375    0.11722     1.209
```

```
##### reference-levels: Age 7
Formula: (elogit ~ Age + (1|vp)
              Estimat Std. Errot  t value
(Intercept)  -0.302    0.02371   -12.727
Age5         -0.084    0.03461    -2.423
Age9         -0.213    0.03521    -6.044

### within age 9
Formula: elogit ~ language + (1 | vp)
             Estimate  Std. Error  t value
(Intercept) -0.472    0.04646   -10.164
LanguageR   -0.095    0.06579    -1.446

Formula: elogit ~ t1 * Language + (1 + t1 | vp)
              Estimate  Std. Error  t value
(Intercept)  -1.033    0.07241   -14.26
t1            1.6657   0.10665    15.618
LanguageR    -0.003    0.102613   -0.026
t1:LanguageR -0.304    0.155325   -2.007

##### reference-level: age 7, German
Formula:  elogit ~ Age + (1 | vp)
              Estimate  Std. Errot value
```

```
##### reference-levels: Age 7
Formula: (elogit ~ tl*Age + (1+tl|vp)
              Estimate Std. Error  t value
(Intercept)  -0.88442   0.03512  -25.18
t1            1.81359   0.0616    29.443
Age5          0.0606    0.05123    1.573
Age9         -0.14141   0.05218   -2.71
t1:Age5      -0.48816   0.08978   -5.437
t1:Age9      -0.31577   0.09161   -3.447
```

Formula: elogit ~ tl*Age + (1+t1 | vp)
         Estimate Std. Errot value

Sarah Schimke, Saveria Colonna and Maya Hickmann†
Reference in French and German: A developmental perspective

Abstract: The present study investigates how French and German adults and 7- and 10-year-old children introduce and maintain reference to entities in short stretches of connected discourse. Data consisted of retellings of video clips in which a protagonist was promoted from a "new" to two degrees of "given" statuses. In the adult data, retellings were denser and forms were leaner in French than in German. Results for children showed common tendencies within age groups and across languages, in particular an overuse of definite forms for referent introduction and the use of less reduced forms for reference maintenance than in the adults. There were also differences between age groups across languages; in particular, adult-like clause structures were used earlier in French than in German children. Overall, our results show that an adult-like discourse organization is not fully acquired even by age ten. Moreover, they provide further evidence that similar developments in discourse construction across languages interact with language-specific grammatical properties in the acquisition of adult-like means of reference (similar to Hickmann, 2003; von Stutterheim, Halm and Carroll 2011).

1 Introduction

Introducing discourse participants and maintaining reference to them is one of the main tasks that speakers have to accomplish when producing a coherent discourse. In order to do so, speakers have to mark the information status of a referent, that is, whether and to which degree this referent is "new" or "given" in the discourse. Cross-linguistically, this marking can be achieved by local means, for example by morphological markings of the noun phrase referring to the referent, and global means, in particular, the position of the referring noun phrase in the clause. Although both types of markings interact with language-specific grammatical constraints and serve different functions in each language in addition to

---

Sarah Schimke, TU Dortmund University, Emil-Figge-Straße 50, 44221 Dortmund, email: sarah.schimke@tu-dortmund.de
Saveria Colonna, Université de Vincennes - Paris 8, 2 rue de la Liberté, 93526 Saint-Denis
Maya Hickmann, Université de Vincennes - Paris 8, 2 rue de la Liberté, 93526 Saint-Denis

https://doi.org/10.1515/9781501510151-007

marking the discourse status of information, there are cross-linguistically valid tendencies in the way they are realized. In typical cases, new referents are introduced in postverbal position, and referred to with full indefinite noun phrases, whereas given referents are introduced before the verb and referred to with definite noun phrases (see between others Chafe 1976; Clark and Haviland 1977; Givón 1983; Lambrecht 1994). Full definite noun phrases are typically used when reference needs to be disambiguated between several discourse participants that have a similar degree of salience, whereas leaner forms, such as pronouns, can be chosen when one participant is clearly the most salient participant and therefore the most likely referent to be denoted at that point in the discourse (Ariel 1990; Gundel, Hedberg and Zacharski 1993). This can be the case for instance because it has been repeatedly referred to in previous utterances, or because it has occupied a particularly important role in previous utterances. To sum up, cross-linguistically common forms and positions for different types of referents are presented in Table 1, along with (made-up) English examples.

Tab. 1: Common markings for different types of referents across languages

Context	Form	Postverbal position	Preverbal position
Introduction	Indefinite N	There is *a boy* and a little dog	
Maintenance, two salient protagonists	Definite N		*The boy* plays with the dog
Maintenance, one salient protagonist	Lean form		Then *he* goes home

A large number of studies in language acquisition has investigated whether children can use markings of information status appropriately. These studies have come to conflicting conclusions. While some conclude that children use correct forms from their very first utterances on (e.g. De Cat 2011), others claim that the acquisition of means of reference continues up to adolescence (Hickmann 2003; von Stutterheim et al. in 2011).

Part of these conflicting findings can be explained by differences in research methodologies and objective (as shown in detail by Hickmann 2003). For example, past research did not always take the nature and extent of mutual knowledge into account, which has been shown to have a strong impact on children's uses of referring expressions (Kail and Hickmann 1992; Hickmann, Kail and Roland 1995).

In addition, researchers who claim early competence frequently look at spontaneous productions in situations that are not sufficiently controlled to allow for unambiguous interpretations. Moreover, they frequently do not make fine-grained distinctions between properties other than morphological forms (positions and roles in the clause) and multiple functions of the same forms (e.g. indefinite nouns serve intralinguistic referent introductions, but also non-specific reference and deictic labeling, see Karmiloff-Smith 1979). Typically, evidence for early competence is provided by studies that look at local markings in isolated utterances and decide whether these markings are a **possible way** of encoding the information status of the referent in that language (e.g. De Cat 2011).

In contrast, studies that point to differences between children and adults do not focus on whether children use a **possible** way of encoding reference, but rather on whether they are able to encode reference in the way that is **preferred** by adult speakers of their language. They also extend the investigation to connected stretches of discourse in order to find out whether children can combine markings when organizing utterances in long stretches of discourse in the same (language-specific) way as adults, (Berman and Slobin 1994; Hickmann 2003; von Stutterheim et al. 2011). These studies have shown that differences between adults and children persist even in school-aged children. These differences are not yet fully understood, however. This is in part due to the fact, which will be illustrated below, that the acquisition of means of reference interacts with the acquisition of language-specific grammatical means. To determine what is typical for children's discourse in general, independently of a specific language, it is thus necessary to conduct carefully controlled cross-linguistic studies in which the same set of data can be compared across languages and age groups. Only few such studies are available to date, however (see in particular Berman and Slobin 1994; Hickmann 2003).

The current study aims at contributing to this line of research, by comparing preferred ways of introducing and maintaining reference to entities in a new database, which provides small stretches of connected discourse produced by children of 7 and 10 years as well as by adult speakers of French and German. In the following background section, properties of French and German that are relevant for the expression of reference will be summarized, and a brief overview will be given on the existing evidence of how 7-10 year old French and German children acquire the use of means of reference. Subsequently, the methodology and results of the current study will be presented and discussed. It will be shown that children have not fully acquired adult-like means of reference by age 10. This is true in both target-languages, but in line with previous studies (Hickmann 2003), we find that deviations from the adult pattern are stronger and longer-lasting in German, where the V2-constraint makes it particularly hard for children to achieve an adult-like discourse organization.

2 Background

2.1 Referential means in French and German

The cross-linguistically common tendencies summarized in Table 1 can be observed in French and German as well. French and German differ, however, in how often speakers deviate from these basic tendencies, due to language-specific grammatical properties.

With respect to global markings, the basic word order in French is SVO, but there are frequent deviations from this in written and even more in oral French. First, word order differs when objects are pronominalized, in which case they must be placed before the verb. Second, word order variations also occur due to specific syntactic constructions that are related to information structure and frequent in particular in spoken French. Specifically, full noun phrases referring to topical elements are dislocated in oral French (Lambrecht 1994; De Cat 2007). Moreover, there is a large range of presentational constructions that allows for new or focused elements to appear in postverbal position. Due to these properties, it has been claimed that oral French is a discourse configurational language (Kiss 1995), with a particularly transparent mapping between discourse statuses of entities and morphosyntactic referential means (Lambrecht 1994; Hickmann 2003; De Cat 2007).

In German, word order is more flexible. Most sentence constituents can occupy several different positions in a sentence. The position of the finite verb is fixed, however, and depends on the syntactic status of the clause. In main clauses, the finite verb has to appear in second position, which is referred to as the "V2-constraint". This leads to subject-verb inversion as soon as a non-subject constituent occupies the first position, and grants a special information-structural status to the one constituent that is placed in initial position in any given sentence. Studies have shown that overall, there are different conflicting tendencies as to how this position is filled. In particular, it may be filled with topical, but also with focal elements (see e.g. Bohnacker and Rosén 2008; Fandrych 2003). In simple narratives as the ones studied below, however, a clear tendency has been established to fill the sentence-initial position with topical elements, in particular, expressions referring either to the main protagonist of a narration or expressions referring to the (topic) time (Caroll and von Stutterheim 2002; von Stutterheim and Carroll

2005). Crucially, when a sentence contains both an adverbial denoting a topical time and an expression denoting a topical protagonist, the V2-constraint causes a conflict, because only one of them can appear in initial position, while the other has to appear in postverbal position. While in spoken narrations, adults have been shown to more often select the topical referent than the adverbial for the initial position (von Stutterheim and Carroll 2005), the reverse order is possible as well, leading to referential expressions appearing immediately post-verbal, in the so-called Wackernagel position. Overall, the V2-constraint thus leads to a less transparent mapping between pre- vs. postverbal position of a referring expression and the discourse status of the referent in German compared to French main clauses. In subordinate clauses, the finite verb appears clause-finally in German, so that all other expressions appear preverbally, leading likewise to a less transparent mapping of the position of a referent and its information status.

As for local markings, both languages mark definiteness on full noun phrases by means of articles. Both languages have a range of different lean forms. In oral French, the most frequently used lean forms are weak (clitic) personal pronouns. Zero pronouns are rare, but can occur under certain syntactic conditions. There is also a series of strong pronouns that can be stressed as well as a series of demonstrative pronouns. Frequently used lean forms in German consist of two series of personal pronouns, the so-called *er*-series, usually considered the 'standard' personal pronouns in German, and a series of so-called *der*-pronouns which are sometimes claimed to behave more like demonstrative pronouns (which also exist as a separate *dieser*-series) (see Ahrenholz 2007). Oral German is a topic-drop language in which clause-initial topical elements can be omitted when they can be recovered from the discourse or situational context (Fries 1988). Zero subject anaphora are thus overall more frequent in (oral) German than in French. Note that in both languages, zero anaphora are possible in clause-initial position only.

In the following, we will summarize the available evidence on how children between 7 and 10 years of age deal with these different linguistic systems in comparison to adult native speakers.

2.2 Previous findings on reference in French and German 7-10 year olds

As mentioned in the introduction, differences between children and adults are found in particular in studies that look at preferred ways of using local and global markings of referent status in discourse.

The results of these studies show on the one hand a strong overuse of definite forms for referent introductions in both languages, in particular for children aged 7 (or younger) (Kern 1997; Lambert and Lenart 2004, for French; Bamberg 1987, for German, Hickmann, Hendriks, Roland and Liang 1996; Hickmann 2003, for both French and German). For reference maintenance, many authors observe a (less pronounced) underuse of lean forms in 7-10 year old children as compared to adults, and, in particular, a near-absence of zero anaphora (Kern 1997; Lambert and Lenart 2004 for French; Hickmann and Hendriks 1999; Hickmann 2003 for both French and German). Bamberg (1988) reports that while children from 9 to 11 years of age underuse lean forms, children under age 9 tend to overuse lean forms in his data, but this might be due to the presence of mutual knowledge between the child and the experimenter in his study. As for differences between the acquisition of French and German, only Hickmann and colleagues (Hickmann et al. 1996; Hickmann and Hendriks 1999; Hickmann 2003) make direct comparisons between these two languages. They note that the overuse of definite forms for referent introduction is equally pronounced in both languages, but that the underuse of lean forms for reference maintenance is more pronounced in German than in French children. This might be related to another difference between the two languages, namely the use of the position of the referring expression in the clause. While in French, children and adults are consistent in using mostly a postverbal position for referent introduction, and mostly a preverbal position for maintenance of reference, German children very frequently use the postverbal position both for reference maintenance and introduction. Hickmann (2003) suggests that the use of this position might attract the use of full as opposed to lean form even for maintained referents. This idea is taken up and further developed in a study by von Stutterheim et al. (2011). According to these authors, adult speakers of German center narrative retellings around the main protagonist, who typically appears in sentence-initial position and is frequently denoted by means of a zero anaphor, while temporal adverbials appear after the verb. Children, on the other hand, structure their discourse according to a strictly temporal principle, linking each clause to the next by the adverbial "and then" or other temporal adverbials. As temporal adverbials thus receive a particularly important role, they are placed before the verb, leaving the postverbal position for protagonists. To sum up, children acquiring both languages have been reported to sometimes deviate from the cross-linguistically common markings of information status summarized in Table 1. French and German children differ in that deviations appear to be stronger in German children, in particular for maintained reference, where they tend to overuse the postverbal position and full as compared to lean forms. Direct comparison between French and German children with the same set of data have been made only by Hickmann and colleagues (Hickmann et al. 1996; Hickmann and Hendriks 1999; Hickmann 2003), however. The stimuli used in any given study can have a strong impact on the results, as subtle differences in to-be-retold stories can elicit very different types of retellings (e.g. means of reference might be used quite differently according to for example the length of a story, the number of characters, and so on, see Hickmann 2003, for a detailed discussion of such effects). In the current study, we thus want to test in a new dataset, in which the number and type of discourse contexts were carefully controlled, whether differences between French and German children can be replicated and if so, further explore them. In particular, we will investigate whether and to which degree French and German children deviate from the cross-linguistically common mappings between information status and morphosyntactic means. We will compare the two language groups to each other and to a control group of adults of each language. Chi-square or Fisher's exact tests will be used to test whether differences with respect to the control group are reliable within each language. In the result section, we will comment on these differences, but also provide a more qualitatively oriented description of the main data patterns within each age group and language.

3 Methods

3.1 Elicitation materials

Data consisted of retellings of video clips. Retellings of eight different clips were analyzed. The clips all had a very similar structure: they all displayed a puppet theater in which two animal figures performed a series of actions, subdivided in three different scenes. The video clips were designed such that one animal (hereafter the *main* protagonist) appeared first on stage and was the agent of all actions, while the other animal (hereafter the *secondary* protagonist) appeared second and did not take an agentive role in any of the subsequent actions. In our analysis, we will focus on how participants refer to the main protagonist throughout the three scenes.

In the first scene, the main protagonist appears on the screen and greets the (imaginary) audience. This scene thus provides a context for the introduction of a new referent. The main protagonist is then followed by the secondary protagonist, which appears on the screen without any particular action. Subsequently, in the second scene, a transitive action such as hitting or kissing happens in which the main protagonist is the agent and the secondary protagonist the patient. This provides a context in which reference to the main protagonist needs to be maintained from the first to the second scene. Depending on how participants decide to retell the story, this can constitute a case of reintroduction (when speakers choose to mention explicitly the appearance of the secondary protagonist between these two scenes) or of maintained reference (when speakers choose not to mention the appearance of the secondary protagonist). In the third scene, the main protagonist leaves the stage and comes back holding an object with which it performs an intransitive action, such as drinking out of a cup. The secondary protagonist remains on the screen but does not perform any action. This again provides a context for maintained reference to the main protagonist, which in this scene should be facilitated by the fact that this referent had taken on an agentive role in the previously performed transitive action. As an illustration, the two retellings below in French and German illustrate the changing means of reference to this protagonist throughout the three scenes. In this and all subsequent examples, the scene number is provided between square brackets, the crucial references to the main protagonist are printed in bold. English word-by-word translations are provided with all examples[1].

(1) [1] donc bien alors on a vu   **un ours** saluait le public.
so well then we have seen   **a bear** *greeted the audience*
Puis est entré un loup ou un renard.
then has entered a wolf or a fox
[2] Le **l'ours**   lui donne trois tapes dans le dos
the **the bear**   *it gives three hits in the back*
[3] puis ø revient   avec un tambourin
then ø comes back   *with a tambourine*
et puis s'en suit une danse puis le rideau se ferme.
and then follows a dance then the curtain closes

(2) [1] **Ein Bär** kommt auf die Bühne,   verbeugt sich dreimal,
a bear *enters*   *the stage*   *bows*   *three times*
Puis est entré un loup ou un renard.
then has entered a wolf or a fox
[2] äm **der Bär** haut...kratzt den Fuchs dreimal am Rü...

---

[1] In the English word-by-word translations, care was taken to make the position and form of the analyzed referring expressions (printed in bold) transparent. For the remaining sentence parts, we aimed at rough translation equivalents of all lexical items, sometimes omitting the translation of discourse particles or grammatical elements to make the translations more readable.

auf dem Rücken
the bear *hits   scratches the fox   three times*
on the back

[3] äm **der Bär** verschwindet dann
the bear *disappears   then*
und kommt wieder mit einem Schellenkranz auf die Bühne
and returns   with a   tambourine   onto the stage

Each participant saw and retold two out of the eight clips. The clips were distributed evenly across participants, such that each clip was used a constant number of times within each age group and language. A description of the eight clips is provided in the appendix[2].

3.2 Participants

Participants were 16 French and 12 German adults as well as French and German 7- and 10-year-old children. Information about the age and sex of the children is displayed in Table 2.

Tab. 2: Information about the four child participant groups

Language	Number (male/female)	Mean age (range)
French	16 (7/9)	7;4 (6;8 – 7;10)
French	16 (13/3)	10;5 (9;8 – 11;3)
German	16 (8/8)	7;4 (6;8 – 7;9)
German	16 (8/8)	10;2 (9;10 – 10;7)

3.3 Procedure

We aimed at eliciting retellings in a situation in which there was no mutual knowledge. Participants were thus told that they were going to see a series of

---

[2] Next to the two clips per participant which were used for the current study, each participant saw 14 other experimental clips as well as a number of filler and warm-up clips. None of these clips had exactly the same structure as those analyzed for the current study, and these retellings will not be further analyzed here.

videos that they should retell to somebody who had not seen the videos. The adults were told that they should imagine an interlocutor. For the children, a blind-folded puppet was placed in front of them and they were told to retell the videos to the puppet. Participants watched each video clip until the end and then retold what had happened. Each clip lasted between 22 and 28 seconds.

4 Results

In the following, we will discuss the results for each of the three scenes. For each scene, we will discuss first the adult and then the child data, and pay special attention to deviations from the cross-linguistically expected pattern in each case.

4.1 Scene 1: Referent introduction

For the analysis of the retellings of the first scene, we coded all first mentions of the main protagonist for the form of the referring noun phrase (definite vs. indefinite) and for its position with respect to the finite verb. In this context, the cross-linguistically most common option would be to use an indefinite form, and a post-verbal position. The results are displayed in Table 3, with the expected, cross-linguistically common, options printed in bold.

Tab. 3: Utterance patterns for referent introductions in the first scene (absolute numbers)

Age		French			German		
		Indef	Def	% position	Indef	Def	% position
Ad	Pre V	7	1	26	9	1	39
	Post V	**20**	**0**	**65**	**9**	**0**	**39**
	No Verb	3	0	10	5	0	22
	% form	97	3		96	4	
7 y	Pre V	0	1	3	0	2	6
	Post V	**29**	**1**	**97**	**25**	**5**	**94**
	No Verb	0	0		0	0	
	% form	94	6		78	22	
10 y	Pre V	0	1	4	0	2	6

Age		French			German		
		Indef	Def	% position	Indef	Def	% position
	Post V	27	0	96	28	1	94
	No Verb	2	0		0	0	
	% form	97	3		90	6	

The French child groups did not differ reliably from the adult control group with respect to definite vs. indefinite forms (both $\chi2 < 1$). In German, there was no difference between 10 year olds and adults ($\chi2(1) = .61$, ns), and a marginal difference between 7 year olds and adults ($\chi2(1) = 3.51$, $p = .06$), because 7-year olds used a higher percentage of definite forms. With respect to syntax, children used reliably more postverbal positions than adults in both languages (French adults vs. 7 year olds: $\chi2(1) = 7.31$, $p < .01$; French adults vs. 10 year olds: $\chi2(1) = 6.49$, $p < .05$; German adults vs. 7 year olds: $\chi2(1) = 14.3$, $p < .001$; German adults vs. 10 year olds: $\chi2(1) = 13.8$, $p < .001$).

We start our discussion with a description of the adult behavior. In both languages, new referents are introduced with an indefinite form in almost all cases. There is one exception to this in each language:

(3) [1] **Le lapin** et le renard veulent repeindre leur maison.
    the hare and the fox want to repaint their house
(4) [1] **Der Hase** streichelt den Fuchs ganz lieb   übers Fell
    the hare pets   the fox   very gently on the fur

It has been reported before that introduction of new referents with definite articles is a (marginal) possibility even in adults (Bamberg 1988; De Cat 2011). In the current case, speakers might have chosen this option precisely to create the impression that the protagonists are already known to the listener, thereby giving the listener the feeling of being placed in the middle of the action.

As for syntactic options, the cross-linguistically common use of a postverbal position for new referents is realized more consistently in French than in German adults. Speakers of French make use of the high number of presentational constructions that exist in this language, as in (5) through (7).

(5) [1] C'est l'histoire   d'**un éléphant** et d'un tigre.
        this is the story of **an elephant** and a tiger
(6) [1] On a   une marionette ours.
        we have a marionette   bear

(7) [1] Donc y'a **une vache blanche et noire**, puis une girafe
    so there is **a cow** **white and black** *then a giraffe*

In German, postverbal position is a result of spatio-temporal adverbials appearing in the preverbal position, e.g. (8) and (9):

(8) [1] Als erstes erscheint **ein Bär**, der sich dreimal verbeugt.
    first appears **a bear** *who three times bows*
(9) [1] In dem Video ist **ne Katze** und ne Gans.
    in the video clip is **a cat** *and a goose*

In both languages, there are also some cases in which referents are introduced in verbless utterances, as in (10) and (11).

(10) [1] **Une marionette vache** qui se présente.
     a marionette cow *who appears*
(11) [1] Gut. Zunächst **ein Eselchen**.
     good first **a little donkey**

This pattern is similar to postverbal introductions as referents appear clause-finally here as well. This type of utterances might be analyzed as containing implicit presentational structures. They have previously been described for French (Hickmann 2003; Leclercq 2008), but our data show that verbless introductions exist in German as well. Strikingly, however, all of the French verbless introductions are followed by a subordinate clause, as in (10), whereas this is not the case for any of the German examples.

In about 40 % of the cases in German and about a quarter of the cases in French, speakers prefer to introduce the new referent in preverbal position. Most of these sentences consist of a subject (the new referent) and an intransitive motion verb, such as "appears" or "comes":

(12) [1] **Une vache** apparaît sur la gauche de l'écran.
     a cow *appears on the left of the screen*
(13) [1] **Ein Elefant** erscheint, tanzt oder verbeugt sich zumindest.
     an elephant *appears dances or bows in- any-case*

Finally, there are two remaining cases in German, where there is no particular introduction at all, and the story starts with a description of the transitive action which at the same time introduces the two referents:

(14) [1,2] **Eine Kuh** küsst ein anderes Tier.
     a **cow** *kisses another animal*

To sum up the findings for the adults, new referents are, as expected, regularly introduced with local indefinite markings in both languages. In French, the preferred syntactic structure are presentational constructions, leading to a postverbal position of the new referent. In German, referents are often introduced after the verb, when an adverbial occupies the first position in the clause, but equally frequent appear before an intransitive motion verb, so that position is a less consistent cue in German as compared to French. We now turn to local and global markings provided by the child participants.

As for local markings, children, similarly to the adults, clearly prefer indefinite noun phrases over definite ones in this context. There are exceptions to this pattern, however, in particular in the German 7-year-olds, leading to the marginal difference mentioned above. Contrary to the adults cases (see 1 and 2), these definite introductions can occur in syntactic constructions typically reserved for the introduction of new referents, as in (15) to (17), which were all provided by 7-year-old children.

(15) [1] Ben en fait c'est **le koala.**
     in fact this is **the koala**
(16) [1] Also das war **die Ente.**
     so that was **the goose**
(17) [1] Da kam **der Bär.**
     there came **the bear**

The remaining cases in particular in the 10-year-olds (example 18) are similar to the adult utterances in (3) and (4) in that they take the listener directly into the action:

(18) [1] Also **der Bär** hat sich zuerst verbeugt.
     So **the bear** *has first bowed*

Definite markings are also used in three cases (one in French, two in German), in which no particular referent introduction is produced and children start directly with the transitive action, similar to example (14) from the adult data:

(19) [1,2] **L'ours** frappe le loup pour faire de la musique.
    the bear slaps the wolf to make music
(20) [1,2] **Der Löwe der** geht erst auf den Fisch.
    the lion this-one goes first onto the fish

Overall, these examples confirm the observation that overuse of definite articles can occur up until 10 years of age, although this clearly concerns a small minority of cases in the current dataset.

As for syntax, there is an overwhelming tendency in both 7- and 10-year-old children to present referents in postverbal position, which is significantly different from the adult behavior in both languages. The French 7-year-olds use the past tense presentational construction "il y avait" in almost all cases, whereas the German 7-year-olds use the closest German equivalent to this, a spatial adverbial in preverbal position followed by a past-tense copula verb:

(21) [1] Y avait **un éléphant** et y avait un tigre.
    *there was **an elephant** and there was a tiger*
(22) [1] Da war **nen Esel,** da war nen Affe.
    *there was **a donkey** there was a monkey*

French 10-year-olds use a larger variety of presentational constructions than the 7-year-olds, and do so consistently in the present tense:

(23) [1] Y a **une vache** elle salue les gens et y a un taureau
    *there is **a cow** it greets the people and there is a bull*
    qu'arrive
    who arrives
(24) [1] C'est **une vache** avec une girafe
    *this is **a cow** with a giraffe*
(25) [1] Alors c'est l'histoire d'**un ours** et d'un loup.
    *so this is the story of **a bear** and of a wolf*

German 10-year-olds use the same construction as the German 7-year-olds, again with the exception that some 10-year-olds use it in the present tense:

(26) [1] Äm da sind **eine Gans** und eine Katze.
    there are **a goose** *and a cat*

To sum up, children use indefiniteness for new referents descriptively less consistently than adults, in particular the 7-year-old German children. Moreover, all children have a consistent preference for postverbal referent introductions. For French, children exploit the rich repertoire of presentational constructions. In German, children seem to privilege a spatial reference as the starting point for their story, similarly to what has been described by Stutterheim et al. (2011). Overall, this leads to both French and German children following a pattern that is relatively common in French adults, but less common in the German adults, who, contrary to all other groups, do not privilege the post- over the preverbal position for referent introduction.

4.2 Scene 2: Maintained reference to one of two new protagonists

For the retellings of the second scene, we selected all productions in which the main protagonist had been introduced in the previous description of the first scene, and coded how the next reference to this protagonist was achieved. We coded whether the form used to refer to the protagonist was a full or a lean form (demonstrative, personal, relative or zero pronoun in finite or nonfinite clauses), and whether it appeared pre- or postverbally. The cross-linguistically common pattern in this context are full forms in preverbal position. The data are presented in Table 4.

Tab. 4: Utterance patterns for reference maintenance in the second scene (absolute numbers)

Age		French			German		
		full	lean	% position	full	lean	% position
Ad	Pre V	17	11	100	15	2	81
	Post V	0	0	0	4	0	19
	% form	61	39		90	10	
7 y	Pre V	20	6	100	9	2	61
	Post V	0	0	0	5	2	39
	% form	77	23		78	22	

Age		French full	French lean	% position	German full	German lean	% position
10 y	Pre V	12	12	96	19	2	78
	Post V	1	1	4	5	1	22
	% form	52	48		89	11	

There was no significant difference between the child groups and the adult control group in either of the languages regarding morphology (all χ2 < 2). The discussion will focus on a qualitative description of the data patterns. In the adults, as expected, the most frequent pattern in both languages are preverbal full definite noun phrases. These noun phrases are realized as subjects of transitive verbs along with an object noun phrase referring to the secondary protagonist. The object NP can be pronominalized (29 and 30), given that the secondary protagonist is often mentioned in the preceding clause.

(27) [1] Donc y'a une vache blanche et noire, puis une girafe.
 so there is a cow white and black then a giraffe
 [2] **La vache** fait trois bisous à la girafe.
 the cow gives three kisses to the giraffe
(28) [1] äm da kommt erst nen Löwe und dann nen Delphin oder so.
 there comes first a lion and then a dolphin or so
 [2] Und **der Löwe** zieht dem Delfin dann an der Flosse.
 and **the lion** pulls the dolphin then at the fin
(29) [1] Un panda arrive, salue le public, un pingouin vient le rejoindre.
 a panda arrives greets the audience a penguin comes it join
 [2] **Le panda** lui tape sur la tête.
 the cow gives three kisses to the giraffe
(30) [1] Ja da ist am Anfang äm nen Panda,
 there is first a panda
 und dann kommt nen Pinguin dazu,
 and then comes a penguin
 [2] und **der Panda** haut ihn oder tätschelt ihn.
 and **the panda** hits it or strokes it

A less frequent variation of this pattern occurs in German when speakers choose to link the description of the first and second scene by a temporal adverbial and to place this adverbial before the verb:

(31) [1] Da war eine Kuh und ae dann kam noch   eine Giraffe dazu,
there was a cow and   then came as well   a giraffe
[2] und dann hat **die Kuh** die Giraffe geküsst, auf die Wange.
*and then has **the cow** the giraffe kissed   on the cheek*

Strikingly, deviations from the dominant pattern of full definite reference occur much more frequently in French than in German: while 90 % of the forms are full forms in German, there are only 61 % of full forms in French. A closer look at the data reveals that the use of lean forms in the second scene in French is related to the form that was used in the first scene. Typically, lean forms are used to describe the second scene when for the first scene, the main protagonist has been introduced in postverbal position or in a verbless sentence, and the secondary protagonist has not been introduced. In this configuration, French speakers exploit the fact that the new referents presented clause-finally can easily be followed up by one or even several relative clauses, which are then used to introduce both the secondary protagonist and the transitive action. This pattern is illustrated in (32) and (33).

(32) [1] y'a un oiseau   [2] **qui** frappe un ours avec son bec.
         there is a bird   **who** *hits   a bear   with his beak*
(33) [1] une marionnette vache qui se présente
         a marionette   cow   who appears
     [2] et   **qui**   après   fait un bisou à une marionette girafe.
         *and **who** afterwards gives a kiss to a marionette giraffe*

The frequent use of relative clauses following referent introductions in French has been observed before (Dasinger and Toupin 1994; Hickmann 2003; Kern 1997; Lambert and Lenart 2004; Lambrecht 1994). For the retellings of the current video clips, this provides a condensed way of achieving the introduction of both referents and retelling of the transitive action within one single sentence. At the same time, the syntactic construction reflects the fact that the first referent occupies a more important and active role in the story than the second referent, given that all other information is expressed in constituents that are syntactically dependent of the noun phrase introducing the main referent. Relative pronouns make up 7 out of the 11 uses of lean forms in the French natives in scene 2. By contrast, there is not a single example of this type in German.

The remaining four cases of lean forms in French and two in German correspond to simple personal pronouns as in (34) or (35).

(34) [1] Un canard apparaît. [2] **Il** va donner des coups de bec au chat
a duc appears *it will give hits of beak to the cat*
qui venait de le rejoindre.
who came of him join

(35) [1] euh une marionnette en forme de zèbre sur la gauche,
a marionette in the shape of zebra to the left
qui secoue un peu sa tête.
who shakes a bit its head
Après y'a un singe [2] **Elle** frappe le singe.
qui arrive. *it hits the monkey*
afterwards there is a monkey who arrives

In these cases, contrary to the relative clause cases, there is no systematic connection as to whether the referent has been mentioned before the verb in the first scene or not, and whether the secondary protagonist has been previously mentioned or not.

To sum up, mentions of a referent that has been previously introduced are most often made in preverbal position by adult speakers of both languages. In German, second reference to this referent in the current context almost always is done by a full form. In French, however, there are many lean forms. This difference is mainly due to the fact that speakers of French often choose to present both the secondary referent and the transitive action in a relative clause following a previously clause-finally introduced main referent. Although such a construction would be grammatically possible in German, German speakers never use it in this context. We now turn to the child data for the second scene.

As in the adults, the most frequent morphological forms are full definite noun phrases appearing mostly before the verb in transitive sentences. Examples (36) and (37) illustrate this for 7-year-olds, and (38) and (39) for 10-year-olds.

(36) [1] y avait un éléphant et... et un tigre... et un lion.
there was an elephant and and a tiger and a lion
[2] et puis, après **le... le lion il** avait tapé le l'éléphant.
*and then afterwards **the the lion it** had hit the the elephant*

(37) [1] Da war ne Kuh und ne Giraffe.
there was a cow and a girafe
[2] **Die Kuh** hat die Giraffe drei Mal geküsst.
***the cow** has the giraffe three times kissed*

(38) [1] alors y a y a   un lion qui arrive
        so there is there is a lion   who arrives
        euh après   y a   hm y a   un poisson euh un gros poisson
        afterwards there is   there is a   fish   a big   fish
        qui qui sort.
        who who comes out
    [2] et **le lion il** le,   i va un peu le manger
        *and **the lion it** it it will a bit   it eat*
        donc il essaye de le tirer comme ça.
        so   it tries   to it pull like this
(39) [1] Also da war   ein Esel und ein Affe.
        so there was a donkey and a monkey
    [2] **Der Affe, der**   hat den Esel   erst gestrei..streichelt.
        ***the monkey this-one** has the donkey first stroked*

In French, full NPs are dislocated in nearly all cases (19/20) in the seven year-olds, and very frequently (9/12 cases) in the 10-year-olds, but only in one case among the adults, demonstrating that adults choose a more formal variety of French than the children. In German, there are no dislocations except for three cases of d-dislocations in the 10-year-olds.

Exceptions from the dominant pattern concern use of postverbal instead of preverbal positions. German children use the postverbal position more often than French children, and the German 7-year-olds use it even more often (39 % of the cases) than the 10-year-olds (22 %) and adults (19 %) respectively, even though these differences are not significant as observed in previous studies (Hickmann and Hendriks 1999; Hickmann 2003; von Stutterheim et al. 2011), this is due to the frequent use of preverbal placement of temporal adverbials. This pattern occurs particularly often in the 7-year-olds, who use the formula "und dann" (and then):

(40) [1] Also zuerst war ein Panda und dann is'n Pinguin dahin gekommen
        so first   was a panda and then is a penguin there came
    [2] und dann hat **der Panda** den Pinguin geschlagen
        *and then has **the panda** the penguin hit*

Note that use of the same formula ("et puis" or "et après") is equally wide-spread in the retellings of 7-year-old French children:

(41) [1] Y avait un ours et   puis y avait aussi un loup.
        there was a bear and then there was also a wolf

[2] Et puis **le, le loup** il avait tapé le l'ours.
and then **the the wolf** *it had hit the bear*

Connecting utterances by clause-initial temporal adverbials is thus a frequently used strategy in children from both languages. But only in the German children does this have the consequence of removing the protagonist from the preverbal position, due to the V2-constraint.

As for the use of lean forms, which were found to be underused by children in previous studies, the same tendency can be observed here in the French data, where in particular 7-year-olds use less lean forms than 10-year-olds. In the 10-year-olds, however, they make up almost 50 % of the cases. Strikingly, these children use the same type of form under the same type of conditions as the adults, namely, relative clauses following postverbal or verbless introductions of the main protagonist:

(42) [1] C'est un ours [2] **qui** tape dans le dos d'un renard.
that is a bear **who** *hits in the back of a fox*

If 7-year-old children do use lean forms, the same structure can be found (in four out of the six lean forms):

(43) [1] C'est un ours [2] **qui** griffe un loup.
that is a bear **who** *scratches a wolf*

The remaining lean forms in the French children and all of the German children concern personal pronouns:

(44) [1] Da war ein Löwe und son Fisch oder Delphin.
There was a lion and such a fish or dolphin
[2] Und dann hat **der** dann hat der da dran gezogen.
and then has **this-one** *then has this-one this-at pulled*

In German, children choose the *der*-series instead of the *er*-series of pronouns more commonly found in the adults. Contrary to French 7-year-olds, German 7-year-olds use a comparable number of lean forms when compared to adults and older children.

Summing up, French 7-year-olds differ descriptively from older children in using less lean forms. When they do use lean forms, they often use the relative clause construction found in older children and adults. Except for the use of dislocations, there are no striking differences between 10-year-olds and adults in French. As expected, German children have an overall stronger tendency to place referents after the verb, because they often reserve the preverbal slot for a temporal adverbial. They use lean forms as frequently as the adults, and these lean forms are mostly personal pronouns in all German age groups. The absence of any difference in the number of lean forms between German children and adults might well be due to the low number of lean forms overall even in the adults, to which we will come back below.

4.3 Scene 3: Maintained reference to the subject of a transitive action

For this last scene, we coded all productions in which the transitive action had been previously reported. As reference continues, this should foster the use of lean forms, which should typically appear in preverbal position. Results are reported in Table 5, with again the cross-linguistically common pattern printed in bold.

Tab. 5: Utterance patterns for reference maintenance in the third scene (absolute numbers)

Age		French			German		
		full	lean	% position	full	lean	% position
Ad	Pre V	11	**18**	**100**	4	7	50
	Post V	0	0	0	7	4	50
	% form	35	**65**		50	50	
7 y	Pre V	11	**11**	**92**	0	0	0
	Post V	1	1	8	13	7	100
	% form	50	**50**		65	35	
10 y	Pre V	6	**18**	**100**	1	2	11
	Post V	0	0	0	15	9	89
	% form	25	**75**		59	41	

There were no significant differences between the child groups and the respective adult control group with respect to morphology (all $\chi 2 < 1.1$). With respect to syntax, the French children did not differ from the French adults, but both German child groups used more postverbal placement than the adults (adults vs. 7 year olds: $\chi2(1) = 13.5$, $p < .001$; adults vs. 10 year olds: $\chi2(1) = 13.5$, $p < .001$). Again, we start our discussion with the adult groups.

As expected, preverbal lean forms are the dominant pattern in the adults in French. The use of lean rather than full forms is thereby dependent on which type of form was used in the previous scene. More precisely, in a large number of the cases in which a lean form is used in the third scene, the main protagonist has been referred to with a lean form in the immediately preceding sentence as well (in 9 out of 18 cases), while this is less frequently the case for full forms (3 out of 11 cases). Thus, it seems that a lean form in the second scene fosters the further use of lean forms in the third scene. Typically, such a lean form following a previous lean form is more reduced than the previous one. As a consequence, while lean forms in the second scene where always overt (relative or personal) pronouns, there are 8 cases of zero forms in the French data. This promotion to increasingly lean forms creates very condensed retellings that capture all three scenes in a single sentence, as illustrated in (45) and (46).

(45) [1] Une marionnette vache qui se présente
    a marionette cow   who appears
 [2] et qui   après   fait un bisou à une marionnette euh girafe
    and who afterwards gives a kiss to a marionette   giraffe
 [3] pour après   ø passer le balai.
    to afterwards   ø sweep

(46) [1] y'a un oiseau   [2] qui frappe un ours avec son bec
    there is a bird   who hits a bear with its beak
 [3] et ensuite ø va chercher un sifflet pour siffler.
    and then ø fetches   a whistle to whistle

Zero anaphora, which are usually assumed to be more frequent in German than in French, thus can appear in French as well. They usually appear in coordinated finite clauses, as in (46). The example in (45) is the only example of a zero anaphor appearing in a non-finite clause.

In the German adults, there is more variation both in position and form. Speakers show a strong tendency to always mark the transition from the second to the third scene by a temporal adverbial. They often place this adverbial in postverbal position, reserving the initial position for the main protagonist (47), but in about half of the cases, they make the opposite choice and place the temporal adverbial in preverbal position (48 and 49). Use of the postverbal position for the protagonist is thereby often associated with full forms (48), although personal pronouns are possible as well (49).

(47) [1] Da war ein Esel und ein kleiner Affe,
there was a donkey and a small monkey
[2] und äm am Anfang hat der Esel den Affen immer so weggerammt,
and in the beginning has the donkey the monkey always pushed
[3] äm ø ist dann kurz verschwunden und ist dann wiedergekommen
ø is then briefly disappeared and is then came-back
mit einer Flasche im Maul und hat getrunken.
with a bottle in-the mouth and has drunk

(48) [1] OK. Eine Kuh ist zunächst auf der Bildfläche.
ok a cow is first on the scene
Ein Schweinchen trifft dazu. [2] Die Kuh stupst das Schweinchen an.
a little-pig joins there the cow nudges the little pig
Dies zeigt sich davon unbeeindruckt.
this-one shows of-this not-impressed
[3] Dann geht **die Kuh** nochmal zurück und holt einen Pinsel
then goes the cow once-more back and fetches a paint-brush

(49) [1] In dem Video ist ne Katze und ne Gans.
in the video-clip is a cat and a goose
[2] Und die Gans hackt so'n bisschen nach der Katze mit dem Schnabel.
and the goose picks such a little-bit after the cat with the beak
[3] und dann verschwindet **sie** kurz und holt ne Trillerpfeife
and then disappears it briefly and fetches a whistle
und pfeift dann vermutlich auf der.
and whistles then probably on it

When the temporal adverbial is placed after the verb, speakers often use a zero anaphor, as in (47) (5/7 cases). The fact that this structure, which has been reported to be very frequent in German adults (von Stutterheim et al. 2011; von Stutterheim and Carroll 2005), is not more frequent in the current data might be related to the fact that the discourses produced here are relatively short, and that German speakers do not seem to find a way to refer to the main protagonist with a lean form by scene 2. As a consequence, the protagonist might not yet be well enough established to be denoted with a zero pronoun in the third scene.

Summing up, while there are frequent uses of preverbal lean forms in both languages, this pattern is much more systematic in French than in German. There are more lean forms in French than in German, presumably because speakers of French can build onto the lean forms used in the description of the previous scene, and do not have to solve a conflict between temporal adverbials and protagonist for the preverbal position. If lean forms are used, they are more often zero forms in the description of scene 3 than has been the case in the descriptions of scene 2. We now turn to the discussion of the child data.

French children typically use a preverbal position for referents. In the 10-year-olds, these forms are typically lean. As in the adults, there is a relation with the way the previous scene has been told: in 14 out of the 18 lean forms, the main protagonist had been referred to with a lean form in the previous scene as well, while this is only the case in 3 out of the 6 cases of full forms. Contrary to the adults and in line with previous findings, there are no zero pronouns in the children. All lean forms consist of overt personal pronouns, independent of the type of form used in the previous description:

(50) [1] C'est un éléphant [2] qui tire les moustaches d'un tigre
  that is a elephant *who pulls the mustache of a tiger*
  [3] **I** part et i revient avec un camion.
  it leaves and it comes-back with a truck.

(51) [1] Alors c'est l'histoire d'un ours et d'un loup.
  so this is the story of a bear and a wolf
  [2] Et l'ours euh griffe le loup.
  and the bear scratches the wolf
  [3] et après **i** joue avec un euhm...uhm un tambourin je crois... ?
  *and afterwards **it** plays with a.. a tamburine I think*

The 7-year-olds use descriptively less lean forms than the 10-year-olds or adults. However, when they use lean forms, they do so particularly often after previous uses of lean forms at 7 years as well (6 out of the 11 lean forms follow a previous use of a lean form for the main protagonist, but only 3 out of the 12 full forms). Similarly to the 10-year-olds, all lean forms are personal pronouns.

Full forms are either simple full definite NPs or dislocated definite NPs, which can occur even after the same structure has been used in the previous scene, as in the following example produced by a 7-year-old:

(52) [1] En fait y a une vache, après y a un y a une girafe qui arrive.
  in fact there is a cow then there is there is a giraffe who arrives
  [2] La vache elle fait des bisous à la girafe.
  the cow it gives kisses to the giraffe
  [3] euh, **la vache elle** redescend,
    ***the cow it** goes-down-again*
  elle remonte avec un balais, et puis c´est fini.

it comes-back-up with a broom and then that is finished

Dislocated full NPs occurred occasionally (3/6 cases) in the 10-year-olds and more frequently (10/13 cases) in the 7-year-olds.

In the German children, utterance patterns are radically different. This is due to the fact that in all of the utterances produced by 7-year-olds, and most of the utterances produced by 10-year-olds, children choose to place a temporal adverbial utterance-initially, similarly to what has been described by von Stutterheim et al. (2011). This leads to the significant difference in placement compared to the adult group.

(53) [1] Da war'n Esel und 'nen Affe.
there were a donkey and a monkey.
[2] Der Esel hat den Affen 'nen paar Mal geschubst.
the donkey has the monkey a few times husteled
[3] und dann hat **der Esel** so ne Tröte geholt und dann getrötet.
*and then has **the donkey** such a noisemaker fetched and then madenoise.*

Most of the noun phrases used by the children are full definite noun phrases, presumably fostered by the postverbal position and by the low rate of lean forms in the previous scene. Lean forms occur descriptively more often in the 10-year-olds than in the 7-year-olds, and occur as overt personal pronouns in these cases:

(54) [1] Da is n Hase. [2] Und der kitzelt den Fuchs aus.
there is a hare *And this-one tickles the fox out*
[3] Und dann malt **er** irgendwas.
and then paints it something.

As in the adults, lean forms are more likely when there has been a lean form in the previous scene, but this effect is less strong than in the French children, presumably due to the fact that there is a lower number of lean forms in the second scene overall. Similarly to the French children, German children do not use any zero forms, but use forms either from the *er*-series or the *der*-series. The absence of zero forms is not surprising given the fact that almost all forms appear in postverbal position.

To sum up, lean forms and preverbal positions are much more common in French children than in German children. Within each language, lean forms are descriptively more common in older than in younger children. If children use lean forms, they use overt personal pronouns, whereas adults are more likely to use zero forms.

5 Discussion

The current study has replicated some known differences between French and German, on the one hand, and between children and adults, on the other hand, as well as provided new details about these differences. In the following discussion, we will first compare the patterns found in the two languages, and then turn to a comparison of the different age groups.

5.1 Reference in French vs. German

As has been observed in the previous literature, the mapping between pre- and postverbal positions, on the one hand, and the information status of referents, on the other hand, is more consistent in French than in German. This is due to the fact that French speakers make use of presentational constructions for referent introductions and of preverbal lean forms for reference maintenance. It is thereby precisely the introduction of new referents in clause-final position that makes it possible to subsequently attach a relative clause to this referent, providing a first lean reference (scene 2), which can then be built upon with even leaner forms in the next sentence (scene 3). These observations in our data confirm the claim that (oral) French belongs to the type of languages which have particularly transparent means for the marking of discourse statuses (Hickmann 2003; Kiss 1995; de Cat 2007; Lambrecht 1994).

In German, the mapping between information structure and position is less clear. This is mainly due to the fact that speakers often choose to place adverbials in initial position, leading to many postverbal positions of given referents (V2 constraint). While the problem of reserving the preverbal position for referents is known for child German (Hickmann 2003; von Stutterheim et al. 2011), it is at first sight surprising that even German adults rarely chose a preverbal position, and, probably related to this, that they rarely chose lean forms for given referents. Von Stutterheim et al. (2011) cite previous studies of German adult narrative retellings in which German productions were characterized by a particularly high amount of preverbal positions and zero anaphora encoding the main protagonist. The finding that this pattern is more restricted in the current data replicates observations by Hickmann (2003), however, who observes a particularly low number of preverbal positions and of lean and zero forms in German adults compared to speakers of other languages. It might be that the difference is related to the type of discourse elicited by different stimuli. Von Stutterheim et al. refer to data elicited with the *Quest*-film featuring a single animated main protagonist who encounters many inanimate objects during a much longer story about his quest for water. The Cat and Horse stories used by Hickmann (2003), as well as the stimuli used in the present study, involve shorter stories with more different protagonists. It might be that the "German way" of constructing a coherent discourse around one main protagonist can better be realized in the first type of retelling. This is not to say that Germans cannot describe scenes involving more different protagonists, but they might have a less strong tendency to produce condensed retellings for these types of stimuli. This stands in contrast to the very condensed French retellings.

Summarizing, the present study has confirmed that the cross-linguistically common mappings between the information status of a referent and certain morphosyntactic forms can be observed both in French and in German, but more consistently so in French. In the type of short retellings examined here, the difference between French and German is particularly strong. In our data, oral French reveals itself again as particularly apt to express distinctions situated on the discourse level, in particular by means of presentational constructions, relative clauses and zero anaphora. In German, the expression of discourse distinctions is in the current data often overridden by a grammatical principle, the V2-constraint, according to which the second element in independent or matrix clauses must always be the finite verb. In the present narrative data, since speakers used frequent adverbial expressions to connect clauses (typically *und da* or *und dann* 'and there/then'), subject-verb inversions were obligatory so that more referring expressions occurred in postverbal position, regardless of their discourse status, as compared to French. Our data thus clearly show a different weight of discourse as compared to grammatical or sentence-level principles in the two languages.

In previous studies, it had been observed that on top of general differences between French and German adults, German children deviated particularly strongly from the adult pattern compared to French children. In the following, we will discuss in how far we could replicate this difference, and how it might be explained.

5.2 How 7- and 10-year-old children differ from adults

Our findings replicate the observations that in both target languages, children up to age 10 can overuse definiteness markings for referent introduction, and underuse lean forms for maintained reference in comparison to adults. Even though the morphological differences between age groups do not reach significant in the current relatively small data sets, we think that they are suggestive in that they replicate known patterns. Moreover, we have confirmed the reliability of this pattern in a fuller analysis of more data that included and extended the present ones by analyzing descriptions of a larger number of video clips by the same participants (Schimke, Colonna and Hickmann 2015).

The overuse of definiteness markings does not seem to interact with specific language-specific properties of French or German in the current data. The underuse of lean forms in children, however, occurs to different degrees in different groups and interacts with language-specific grammatical properties in complex ways. We will thus examine this finding in more detail in the following.

In both languages, 7-year-olds show a strong tendency to connect utterances to each other by temporal connectives. This way of structuring the discourse seems to be typical for this age group, independent of the specific language. It has, however, different consequences in the two languages. Whereas in French the temporal adverbial can share the preverbal position with a form referring to the protagonist, in German, the expressing referring to the protagonist has to be placed after the verb when the preverbal slot is occupied by an adverbial. As a consequence, German children use the postverbal position for given referents, deviating from the target pattern, while French 7-year-olds can follow the target pattern with respect to the position of the referring noun phrase. French children do, however, use a full form more frequently than older children and adults. This might be due to the fact that they do not yet master the adult way of condensing the description of several scenes into one syntactic structure by means of subordination. If they avoid this type of structure due to its complexity, this explains why they also do not use the lean forms that are typically used in such structures. To sum up, both groups of 7-year-olds use fewer lean forms, at least in the description of the last scene, than older children and adults. In German this might be due to difficulties with acquiring the preverbal position for reference to protagonists, while in French it might be related to the complexity of the language-specific condensed ways of retelling. Against this background, it is not surprising that deviations from the target-pattern are more persistent in German than in French 10-year-olds. Like the adults, French 10-year-olds use subordinate clauses in scene 2 and might therefore also use lean forms as frequently for both scene 2 and scene 3. Their preference for personal pronouns over zero forms shows, however, that they are still not able to use increasingly reduced forms throughout discourse as adults do. German 10-year-olds show a strong tendency to use temporal adverbials in preverbal position. This pattern seems to be hard to overcome, and prevents them from using zero anaphora although these are extremely widespread in the German input.

This finding suggests that claims as to when children acquire adult-like means of reference cannot be made independently of specific languages, as some languages might make it harder to acquire target-like means than others. In our case, the V2-constraint in German reveals itself again as a strong factor hindering the establishment of target-like means of reference in German children, even at age 10. The transparent mapping of discourse functions and morphosyntax in oral French, however, has been acquired to a large degree by French children of the same age.

References

Ahrenholz, B. 2007. Verweise mit Demonstrativa im gesprochenen Deutsch. Grammatik, Zweitspracherwerb und Deutsch als Fremdsprache. Berlin and New York: de Gruyter.
Ariel, M. 1990. *Accessing Noun-Phrase Antecedents*. London: Routledge.
Bamberg, M.G.W. 1987. The acquisition of narratives: learning to use language. Berlin: Mouton de Gruyter.
Berman, R.A. and Slobin, D.I. (eds.). Different ways of relating events in narrative: a cross-linguistic developmental study. Hillsday, NJ: Lawrence Erlbaum.
Bohnacker, U. and Rosén, C. 2008. The clause-initial position in L2 German declaratives: Transfer of information structure. *Studies in Second Language Acquisition* 30 (4), 511–538.
Carroll, M. and Stutterheim, C. von 2002. Typology and information organisation. perspective taking and language-specific effects in the construction of events. A. Ramat (Ed.), *Typology and Second Language Acquisition* (pp. 365–402). Berlin: de Gruyter.
De Cat, C. 2007. *French Dislocation. Interpretation, Syntax, Acquisition*. Oxford: OUP
De Cat, C. 2011. Information tracking and encoding in early L1: linguistic competence vs. cognitive limitations. *Journal of Child Language* 38 (4), 828–860.
Chafe, W. 1976. Givenness, contrastiveness, definiteness, subjects, topics and point of view. In C.N. Li (ed.), *subject and topic*. New York: Academic Press.
Clark, H.H. and Haviland, S.E. 1977. Comprehension and the given-new contract. In R.O. Freedle (ed.) *Discourse processes: Advances in Research and Theory, Vol. 1: Discourse production and comprehension*. Norwood, NJ: Ablex.
Dasinger, L.K. and Toupin, C. 1994. The development of relative clause function in narrative. In R.A. Berman & D.I. Slobin (Eds), *Relating Events in narrative. A crosslinguistic developmental study*. Hillsdale, New Jersey, Lawrence Erlbaum, 457–515.
Fandrych, C. 2003. Zur Textlinguistik des Vorfelds. In Thurmair, Maria and Willkop, Eva-Maria (Eds.), *Am Anfang war der Text. 10 Jahre Textgrammatik der deutschen Sprache*. München, Iudicium, 173–196.
Frey, W. 2004. *The grammar-pragmatics interface and the German prefield. Sprache und Pragmatik* 52, 1–39.
Fries, N. 1988. Über das Nulltopik im Deutschen. In *Sprache und Pragmatik* 3, 19–49.

Givón, T. 1983. Topic continuity in discourse: a quantitative cross-linguistic study. Amsterdam: John Benjamins.
Gundel, J.K., Hedberg, N. and Zacharski, R. 1993. Cognitive status and the form of referring Expressions in Discourse. *Language* 69, 274–307.
Hickmann, M. 2003. Children's discourse: person, time, and space across languages. Cambridge: Cambridge University Press.
Hickmann, M., Kail, M. and Roland, F. 1995. Cohesive anaphoric relations in French children's narratives as a function of mutual knowledge. *First Language* 15, 277–300.
Hickmann, M., Hendriks, H., Roland, F. and Liang, J. 1996. The marking of new information in children's narratives: A comparison of English, French, German and Mandarin Chinese. *Journal of Child Language* 23, 591–619.
Hickmann, M. and Hendriks, H. 1999. Cohesion and anaphora in children's narratives: a comparison of English, French, German and Chinese. *Journal of child Language* 26, 419–52.
Kail, M. and Hickmann, M. 1992. French children's ability to introduce referents in narratives as a function of mutual knowledge. *First Language* 12, 73–94.
Karmiloff-Smith, A. 1979. A functional approach to child language: a study of determiners and reference. Cambridge: Cambridge University Press.
Kern, S. 1997. Comment les enfants jonglent avec les contraintes communicationnelles, discursives et linguistiques dans la production d'une narration. Presses Universitaires du Septentrion, ANRT, thèse à la carte, Sciences du Langage, Lyon.
Kiss, K. 1995. *Discourse configurational languages*. New York, Oxford: Oxford University Press.
Lambert, M. and Lenart, E. 2004. Incidence des langues sur le développement de la cohésion en L1 et en L2: étude de la gestion du statut des entités dans une tâche de récit. *Langages* 155, 14–32.
Lambrecht, K. 1994. *Information structure and sentence form*. Cambridge: Cambridge University Press.
Leclercq, P. 2008. L'influence de la langue maternelle chez les apprenants adultes quasi-bilingues dans une tache contrainte de verbalisation. *Acquisition et interaction en langue étrangère* 26, 51–69.
Schimke, S., Colonna, S. and Hickmann, M. 2015. The development of discourse cohesion in French and German: General and language-specific determinants. *Child Language Symposium*. University of Warwick, Coventry 20-21 Juli 2015.
Stutterheim, C. von and Carroll, M. 2005. Subjektwahl und Topikkontinuität im Deutschen und Englischen. *Zeitschrift für Literaturwissenschaft und Linguistik* 139, 7–27.
Stutterheim, C. von, Halm, U. and Carroll, M. 2011. Macrostructural principles and the development of narrative competence in L1 German: the role of grammar (8-14-year-olds). In Watorek, M., Benazzo, S. and Hickamnn, M. (Ed.). *Comparative Perspectives to Language Acquisition: Tribute to Clive Perdue*. Multilingual Matters.

Appendix

I Description of experimental videos

1. [1] A cow enters the stage and greets the public, followed by a giraffe.
   [2] The cow kisses the giraffe three times.
   [3] Then the cow disappears from stage, comes back with a broom and starts sweeping the floor.
2. [1] A donkey enters the stage and greets the public, followed by a monkey.
   [2] The donkey hustles the monkey three times.
   [3] Then the donkey disappears from stage, comes back with a bottle of milk and starts drinking from it.
3. [1] A panda enters the stage and greets the public, followed by a penguin.
   [2] The panda slaps the penguin three times.
   [3] Then the panda disappears from stage, comes back with a telephone and starts speaking on it.
4. [1] A duck enters the stage and greets the public, followed by a cat.
   [2] The duck hits the cat in the face with her beak three times.
   [3] Then the duck disappears from stage, comes back with a whistle and starts whistling.
5. [1] An elephant enters the stage and greets the public, followed by a tiger.
   [2] The elephant pulls the moustache of the tiger three times.
   [3] Then the elphant disappears from stage, comes back with a toy car and starts playing with it.
6. [1] A bear enters the stage and greets the public, followed by a wolf.
   [2] The bear hits the wolf on his back three times.
   [3] Then the bear disappears from stage, comes back with a drum and starts drumming.
7. [1] A lion enters the stage and greets the public, followed by a shark.
   [2] The lion pulls the fin of the shark three times.
   [3] Then the lion disappears from stage, comes back with a pair of glasses and puts them on.
8. [1] A hare enters the stage and greets the public, followed by a fox.
   [2] The hare scratches the belly of the fox three times.
   [3] Then the hare disappears from stage, comes back with a paint brush and starts painting the wall of the theater.

II Screenshots illustrating the three scenes for item 1 (cow and giraffe)

Maria Voeikova and Sofia Krasnoshchekova
The use of pronouns as a developmental factor in early Russian language acquisition

Abstract: This chapter considers the earliest stages in children's acquisition of the Russian pronominal system. General tendencies in the acquisition of pronouns based on previous studies are compared to four detailed longitudinal corpora of children's spontaneous speech production to sketch common and individual features in their early use of pronouns and deictic adverbs. In all children, pronouns only occurred at a certain level of syntactic and lexical development based on the calculation of their mean length of utterance (henceforth — MLU) and vocabulary diversity (henceforth — VOCD). Children also exhibit different strategies in the acquisition of pronouns: two male children demonstrated a balanced pronoun usage, whereas one male and one female showed a clear preference for the early demonstratives followed by personal pronouns only several months later. Possible explanations and further research questions are proposed.

1 Introduction. Asymmetric features in the use of early pronouns by children: The state of the art

The acquisition of pronouns in any language presents a great challenge to small children, who are incapable of understanding the shifting nature of deictic pronouns and the language-specific rules of anaphora resolution (Jespersen 1923; Jakobson 1956, 1990; Fludernik 1989, 1990: 97). Over the last twenty years, pronoun acquisition has been carefully examined in experimental settings. The results, however, have been controversial. While some authors point to the fact that anaphoric pronouns are extremely difficult to comprehend by children between ages 4 and 6 (Avrutin 1999; Baauw and Cuetos 2003; Ruigendijk et al. 2011), others propose that children successfully and productively use these pronouns when provided with particular modeling. In a pilot study of Russian children between the

---

Maria Voeikova, Institute for Linguistic Studies, Russian Academy of Sciences, Tutschov per 9, 199004 St Petersburg, email: maria.voeikova@gmail.com
Sofia Krasnoshchekova, Institute for Linguistic Studies, Russian Academy of Sciences, Tutschov per 9, 199004 St Petersburg

ages of 2;5 and 3;1 who live in the United States, Kelly Dodson and Michael Tomasello (1998: 616–617) found that the children produced transitive constructions with novel verbs more easily if the latter had been presented to them in the so-called "Two-Participant Condition": namely, in a full sentence, wherein the subject and object are expressed first by nouns, and then by pronouns. Natalia Gagarina (2012: 111–112) points to the fact that bilingual children "overuse anaphoric personal pronouns in the two early groups and slowly approach the adult measures, while monolingual children already use the target number of pronouns by age three" (see Mann-Whitney-U+65.00; p<0.05); the latter finding for monolingual children has been discussed in detail in Gülzow and Gagarina (2007a).

Such findings show that pronouns have different natures, and are acquired in a piecemeal manner both in language comprehension and production. In general, these findings corroborate the conclusion that "children's early syntactic skills are much more concrete and lexically based than is widely believed" (Dodson and Tomasello 1998: 621). However, since most of the investigations cited above are based on experiments and involve artificial contexts, we find it necessary to describe the acquisition of different types of pronouns by Russian children younger than age 4 based on naturalistic longitudinal observations.

In general, children begin to use pronouns (and other deictic words) later than they begin to use labels such as nouns, verbs, and adjectives. Even then, children often choose false pronominal markers. These difficulties may be due to a deficit in the "theory of mind" that does not allow children to change the speaker's perspective. This suggests that, lacking a representational theory of belief, young children have a "conceptual deficit" that makes them incapable of passing the "false-belief test" (Goldman 2012). Two main cognitive operations are crucial for the correct use of pronouns: 1) the ability to choose the correct reference point, and 2) the capacity to generalize about people or objects that pronouns may refer to. The phenomenon may also be explained by an asymmetry between the comprehension and production of early pronouns (Hendricks and Spenader 2006). Children begin to produce personal pronouns and reflexives before they correctly understand the rules of their application (Avrutin 1999; Grolla 2010). As a result, full acquisition of the pronominal system is late.

For Roman Jakobson, first- and second-person pronouns were the prototypical shifters, changing their reference depending on the speaker's role in a given communication: "the sign *I* cannot represent its object without 'being in existential relation' with this object: the word *I* designating the utterer is existentially related to his utterance and hence functions as an index" (Jakobson 1956, 1990). This is a clear contrast to the third-person pronouns that may refer not only to people near to children's lives, but also to persons, creatures, or objects acting in the stories, picture stories, and fairy tales that children encounter. In the first case, we speak about the deictic functions of pronouns, whereas in the second case (while speaking about the past or fictional events), pronouns also fulfill the anaphoric function as one of the main means of text coherence (see Introduction, this volume). Thus, pronominal systems are not only cognitively complicated, but are also asymmetrical, since pronouns are not equally predestined for deictic or anaphoric functions.

Such cognitive difficulties are common for most children worldwide; however, there are also language-specific problems in early pronoun use. English children, for example, make case errors in pronouns in a late period, after the difference between subjects and objects has already been clearly manifested by the order of sentence constituents in nouns (Budwig 1989; Rispoli 1999). These errors also show asymmetry. Rispoli (1999) argues that *her* is more likely to occur instead of *she* than *his* or *him* instead of *he*. Rispoli attributes this observation to the fact that *her* is used in both possessive and beneficiary functions, and therefore it is more "loaded" and also more frequent. An earlier proposal by Rispoli (1991) concerns the "mosaic nature" of the acquisition of grammatical categories. In German, the nominative/accusative distinction is encoded in personal pronouns and definite articles before it is marked on indefinite articles (Mills 1985; Clahsen et al. 1994). Thus, the acquisition of pronouns, especially of their grammatical "package", is highly language-specific.

Caregivers often avoid using pronouns in child-directed speech (henceforth — CDS), calling their family members by names or by kinship terms (Gavrilova 2002). Compare a dialogue between a grandmother and a girl aged 2;7 in the low SES (social economic status) Russian family (1):

(1)
Violetta: *deda tam*
'granpa (is) there.'

Grandmother: *deduška devočku snimaet*
'Granpa-Dim is videotaping the girl.'

Grandmother uses noun forms to comment on their current situation, despite the fact that both Violetta and her grandfather are present. She takes an external point of view, telling them a story about them, but not involving them in the conversation. This strategy leads to a lack of pronominal input alongside an overuse of the third-person verb forms. The child-recipient of this kind of CDS may benefit from the clarity of the input, however, its pronominal deficit makes the child's acquisition of pronouns even more difficult.

Russian-speaking children acquire the deictic pronominal system gradually. According to Galina Dobrova (2003: 118), they begin by using the first-person pronoun *ja* in their speech production, and start with the second-person pronoun *ty* in their speech comprehension. The process of understanding personal pronouns is very complicated and includes several stages. Dobrova points to the fact that the earliest personal pronouns in children's speech (henceforth — CS) are often far from their conventional meanings. Her experiments with 39 children aged from 20 to 30 months show that the first occurrences of personal pronouns are used exclusively as labels, not as shifters (Dobrova 2003: 118–123). Children use them as secondary personal names that may not refer to other persons except themselves, demonstrating individual differences in choosing either personal names or deictic pronouns. The early use of pronouns is characteristic of so-called "expressive" children, whereas the overuse of personal names is common to "referential" children (Nelson 1978; Bates et al. 1988; Dobrova 2007: 186–194). Dobrova calls this period an "egocentric phase" and shows that children gradually proceed first to a more adult-like understanding the second-person, and later to the first-person pronouns. This period in most subjects is observed before 30 months. At this phase, most subjects even call their mirror image by name, such that personal pronouns occur only in dialogue. Also, according to Dobrova (2003: 140), for many children, second-person pronoun usage occurs in oblique case forms, whereas the first person is mostly used in the nominative. Our proposition is that the pronominal system in Russian (and in other languages) is highly heterogeneous and may only be acquired part-by-part. We suppose that main points in its development process coincide with significant moments in other spheres of language acquisition. To discover these possible points and to prove or disprove the principal prediction of this study we compare general indexes of language development (MLU, VOCD) with indexes of acquisition of pronominal systems.

The acquisition of pronouns is cognitively complicated, and is language- and subject-specific. In this chapter we address the earliest periods of this process, namely, the acquisition of personal and demonstrative pronouns mostly in the deictic function. The anaphoric function, which is acquired later, is based on the relevant deictic relations. Also, we presuppose that the early use of pronouns corresponds to other important developmental events.

2 Deictic and anaphoric pronouns in Russian

Deictic relations in Russian are expressed by several groups of pronouns and pronominal adverbs: personal, possessive, demonstrative, reflexive and relative. Personal pronouns *ja* 'I ' *ty* 'you-SG,' *my* 'we,' *vy* 'you-PL' and *on* 'he' (in forms *on* for masculine, *ona* for feminine, *ono* for neutral and *oni* for plural), and possessive pronouns *moj* 'my,' *tvoj* 'your-SG,' *naš* 'our,' *vaš* 'your-PL,' *ego* 'his, its,' *ee* 'her,' and *ih* 'their,' are related to the sphere of personal deixis. However, these pronouns do not have homogeneous functions. The first- and second-person personal and possessive pronouns refer to the interlocutors and serve as prototypical deictic markers. The third-person pronouns may refer either to persons not taking part in a dialogue or to the persons and objects mentioned in the earlier communication. The first function may be considered as pure deictic, whereas the second function is anaphoric.

Demonstrative pronouns *e~tot* 'this,' *tot* 'that,' *takoj* 'such,' and pronominal adverbs *tam* 'there,' *zdes'* and *tut* 'here,' and *tak* 'in a such way,' are usually connected with the area of locative deixis, though *takoj* and *tak* are qualitative rather than locative. Demonstrative adverb *togda* 'then' refers to the temporal deixis. Demonstrative adverbs and pronouns also may have either the pure deictic or the anaphoric function.

Reflexive pronouns *sebja* 'oneself' and *svoj* 'oneself's,' and relative pronouns and adverbs *kotoryj* 'which,' *čto* 'that,' *kto* 'who,' *gde* 'where,' *kogda* 'when,' and *kak* 'how,' are anaphoric like some of the third-person personal and possessive pronouns and like most demonstratives.

3 Data

This chapter is a case study based on corpus longitudinal data of four children: three boys (Vanja, Vitja and Filipp) and one girl (Liza). All children were recorded regularly. The recordings of Vanja and Liza include the period from 1;5 to 4 years of age. Recordings of Filipp range from when the child was aged 1;5 to 2;8 years, and recordings of Vitja are from when the child was aged 2;1 to 4 years. Recordings were made every month, though several months are missing from the corpora. In this study transcripts in CHILDES format are used, supported with morphological coding of both CS and CDS. The data is presented in layered cuts from almost each month, as shown in Table 1.

Tab. 1: Types/tokens

Age	Vanja	Liza	Vitja	Filipp
1;5	78 / 222	no data	no data	165 / 741
1;6	no data	49 / 94	no data	169 / 841
1;7	no data	37 / 71	no data	142 / 468
1;8	138 / 543	72 / 121	no data	560 / 1341
1;9	81 / 365	101 / 142	no data	486 / 1071
1;10	130 / 449	272 / 439	no data	184 / 305
1;11	97 / 371	153 / 177	no data	192 / 350
2;0	55 / 115	134 / 150	no data	358 / 632
2;1	139 / 306	371 / 482	139 / 221	651 / 1358
2;2	302 / 591	464 / 661	142 / 316	676 / 1535
2;3	884 / 1691	201 / 286	118 / 175	556 / 1239
2;4	225 / 320	409 / 609	157 / 211	558 / 1314
2;5	444 / 769	392 / 584	154 / 177	537 / 1403
2;6	425 / 706	340 / 536	274 / 378	346 / 797
2;7	514 / 993	128 / 199	452 / 784	547 / 1314
2;8	831 / 1793	240 / 392	569 / 1001	571 / 1615
2;9	357 / 545	880 / 1869	473 / 871	no data
2;10	664 / 1313	787 / 1777	222 / 426	no data
2;11	651 / 1345	440 / 1300	740 / 1921	no data
3;0	512 / 1030	282 / 534	666 / 1444	no data
3;1	673 / 1342	no data	no data	no data
3;2	788 / 1928	no data	no data	no data
3;3	941 / 2323	no data	no data	no data
3;4	1113 / 2645	no data	no data	no data
3;5	887 / 2018	252 / 532	no data	no data
3;6	665 / 1316	378 / 836	498 / 982	no data
3;7	no data	462 / 1095	no data	no data
3;8	no data	no data	no data	no data
3;9	no data	no data	no data	no data

Age	Vanja	Liza	Vitja	Filipp
3;10	no data	613 / 1693	no data	no data
3;11	no data	no data	no data	no data
4;0	372 / 715	no data	538 / 1232	no data
4;1	no data	139 / 208	no data	no data

All children are Russian monolinguals from educated, two-parent, middle-class families living in Saint Petersburg in the 1990s. The data present conversations between the children and their mothers, and with other family members. Vanja was mostly recorded with his grandmother, who was his main caregiver. None of the boys had siblings, whereas the girl, Liza, had an elder brother. In the cases of Liza and Vitja, we benefitted additionally from detailed parental diaries kept by the children's mothers. Liza and Vitja can be defined as "referential children," who definitely preferred nouns to pronouns, and grammatically correct morphological marking to syntactic richness and long utterances. Filipp and Vanja, on the contrary, demonstrated the "expressive" behavioral characteristic, using longer utterances and more pronouns from early on.

The records are part of the Collection of Data on Children's Speech, in the Laboratory of Children's Speech, at the Herzen State Pedagogical University and Institute of Linguistic Studies, Russian Academy of Sciences.

To show the development of pronominal systems, we measured the number of tokens of each pronoun in each analyzed transcript. According to this data, we built pronominal profiles presenting the individual combination for each group of pronouns, and one summary graph showing the dynamics of all groups for each child.

The language development profiles are based on those in the study done by Kira Ivanova in 2011, and use the developmental indexes MLU (mean length of utterance) and VOCD (vocabulary diversity).

4 General features in the acquisition of pronominal systems by Russian-speaking children

According to the normative scale of the Institute of Early Intervention in Saint Petersburg, Russian-speaking boys start to use at least one personal pronoun at the mean age of 25.7 months (SD = 7.7). 7% of the boys already utter pronouns at 15 months, and 89% of male children use pronouns at the age of 39 months. The corresponding mean age for girls is 23.5 months (SD= 7): 11% of them use pronouns starting from 15 months and 91% use them at 39 months. For both boys and girls, the acquisition of pronouns is closely related in time to the acquisition of the negative particle. In this same period, they utter sentences consisting of two to three words and more, use verbs in the past and present tenses, and start to use possessive pronouns (Shapiro, Chistovich 2000). The questionnaire, however, does not give any information on whether children use personal pronouns correctly, nor whether they only use them to refer to persons in their nearest surroundings, or whether they use them to tell stories. Anaphoric pronouns occur much later: boys start to use them describing consequent events at 38 months and girls at 36 months (SD = 8). The ability to use anaphora coincides with the acquisition of modality, at approximately the same time that children begin using epistemic modal markers and speaking about possible events.

Our longitudinal data shows the relevance of these observations for all our subjects. Age frames in the acquisition of deictic pronouns can differ significantly from individual to individual, both concerning the first occurrence of pronouns and their further development. First pronominal deictic words in our data are found at the age of 1;3 in the speech production of three children; at the same time, some children may produce their first pronouns at the age of 2;0 or even later. Similar age differences can be seen in the occurrence of certain pronouns, emergence of anaphora etc. Nevertheless, some generalizations can be drawn, and the process of acquisition of pronouns can be divided into three stage.[1]

The first stage, or the stage of the occurrence of early frozen pronominal forms, includes mostly adverbs and demonstratives, such as *tam* 'there,' *tut, zdes'* 'here,' *e~to* 'this.SG.NEUT.' Some rare personal pronouns also occur at this stage, such as *ja* 'I,' *moj* 'my,' and *on* 'he.' These short and frequent forms are easy to remember and produce, but there is no evidence that children understand their meaning outside of their frequently used constructions. The initial function of the first pronouns is demonstrative (2).

(2)   *E~t-im* (Liza, 1;11.22, shows a shovel)
        this-INSTR

---

[1] These stages do not completely coincide with the stages of acquisition of personal deixis, as described by G. Dobrova in (2003): the non-deictic stage, the egocentric stage and the deictic stage. Same stages are found in the acquisition of locative and temporal deixis in (Korolev 2011).

'(Take it) with this.'

The first forms of demonstratives, according to our data, are usually repeated, for children rarely make mistakes in their inflectional endings, in spite of the fact that the pronominal paradigm differs from both the substantive and adjective paradigms. It is known, too, that children rarely make errors in the forms of pronouns (Gvozdev 1949: 172), or in the choice of pronominal lexemes (Golovenkina 1996). First anaphoric expressions also appear at the end of this stage, usually with the occurrence of a third-person pronoun agreeing with its antecedent (3).

(3) *Kengurenok... mama u nego* (Liza, 2;0.11)
 kangaroo.baby mother at he-MASC:GEN
 'Baby-kangaroo, he has its mother.'

The second stage features a growth of diversity of pronominal functions and meanings, and an increasing frequency of pronominal tokens. This usually happens with three pronouns: *ja* 'I,' *on* 'he' (third-person pronoun that has gender and number forms) and *e~tot* 'this' in the middle of the third year. This stage is also characterized by the occurrence of demonstratives *takoj* 'such' and *tot* 'that,' first- and second-person personal and possessive pronouns that have not appeared earlier (*my* 'we,' *tvoj* 'your-SG' etc.), and sometimes reflexive and relative pronouns. At this stage, pronouns achieve new meanings. For example, *e~tot* 'this' receives its proper locative meaning when the child starts distinguishing between distal and proximal demonstrative pronouns (Elivanova 2007). The first-person plural pronoun *my* 'we' develops an exclusive meaning next to the already-present inclusive one (Lepskaja 1987). Utterances with demonstrative pronouns begin to be used to express searching for objects (4), approximation (5), focusing (6), and emphatic stress (7).

(4) **Tak-oj** *dom* (Vanja, 2;3.19)
 such-SG.MASC.NOM house-SG.MASC.NOM
 ***tak-oj** *bašnj-a*
 such-SG.MASC.NOM tower-SG.FEM.NOM
 'Such a house...such a tower.'
(5) *Ujdet* *takuju* (Vanja, 2;8.15)
 go.away-FUT.3.SG in such-ACC.FEM
 babuškinu *komnatu*
 grandmother's- ACC.FEM room-ACC
 'He will go away to such a grandmother's room.'

(6) Kolgotk-i.   Netu   kolgotok. (Sonya, 2;2.14)
    tights-NOM   No   tights-GEN
    Vot   oni,   kolgotki
    Here   they,   tights
    'Tights. No tights. Here they are, the tights.'
(7) Malen'kij,   malen'kij   **takoj** (Vanja, 2;5.23)
    small   small   such
    'Small, small, so (small) (speaking with a special "sweet" voice).'

At this second stage, correct grammatical forms co-exist with slightly incorrect semantic and pragmatic functions. Example (4), above, is thus egocentric, in the sense that the boy is commenting on his own actions, while example (5) shows that children may combine demonstrative pronouns with possessive adjectives in an unusual manner. The children's use of grammatical forms is also not yet adult-like, as the incorrect agreement in (4) demonstrates.

The final stage is marked by the development of syntactic and narrative competence. In order to produce long narratives, children start regularly using anaphoric binding, such that progress in the acquisition of the pronominal system is manifested through the increasing frequency of anaphoric reflexive (8) and relative (9) pronouns, and demonstratives in anaphoric function (10). The narrative competence that reveals itself in anaphoric binding is already developed in three-year-old children, and they use *on* 'he' and *e~tot* 'this' as default anaphoric pronouns up to the age of five years (Gagarina 2004, 2009). Children almost never have any difficulty in anaphoric binding with reflexives (Avrutin 2010: 272).

(8) Vot   krolik   našel (Vanja, 2;9.4)
     here   rabbit-NOM   find-PRET.SG.MASC
     sebe   stul
     oneself-DAT   chair-ACC
     'Here the rabbit found himself a chair.'
(9) Čin-ju   mašinu, (Filipp, 2;8)
     fix-1.SG Vot   car-ACC
     kotoruju   slomal
     which-ACC.FEM   break-PRET.SG.MASC
     'I'm fixing a car that I've broken.'
(10) Ja   mušku   ubila,   mušku
     I-NOM   fly-ACC   kill-PRET.SG.FEM   fly-ACC
     Muška   uže   ne letaet   **eta**
     fly-NOM   already not fly-PRES.3.SG   this-NOM.SG.FEM

'I've killed a fly. This fly does not fly any more.' (Liza, 3;0)

As for the relations between children's syntactic progress and their acquisition of pronouns, one-word and two-word utterances usually correspond to the stage of early frozen pronominal forms. The earliest one-word utterances with pronouns and deictic adverbs are always supported by a demonstrative gesture (11) and are usually produced as a response to an adult's utterance (12).

(11) Child: *Danja, tam Danja!*
Danja there Danja
'Danja is there.' (Sveta, 1;3.21, points to the door)
(12) Mother: *Gde kiska? Gde sobačka?*
where kitty where doggy
'Where is kitty? Where is doggy?
Child: *Tam* (Borja, 1;3.15, points to the picture)
There
'There (they are).'

At the stage of two-word utterances, pronouns and pronominal adverbs often occur in the pivot-word in pivot-constructions.[2] Standard pivot-pronominals are *e~to* 'this' (neutral form of *e~tot* 'this'), *tam* 'there,' and *vot* 'here, look!' Nevertheless, there are also cases where children start using pronouns only at the multi-word stage, paying more attention to nouns and verbs. These different strategies likely correspond to the distinction between referential (rather nominal) and expressive (rather pronominal) children (Nelson 1978; Bates et al. 1988).

The most significant points in the acquisition of pronouns at the multi-word stage are the appearance of anaphora and the acquisition of relative constructions. In the following section, we use the MLU index to get a more detailed picture of syntactic development, while the VOCD index shows lexical proficiency.

In the acquisition of morphology, finite forms of verbs usually occur earlier than the corresponding personal pronouns; case oppositions in nouns are also usually acquired earlier than in pronouns.

The acquisition of deictic systems is closely related to the child's psychological development. Very young children go through an egocentric stage (Piaget 1923), when they pay most attention to objects, actions and situations that are

---

[2] A pivot-construction consists of two positions, one of which is filled by a constant word and the other is filled by variable words from an open list (Braine 1963).

close to them and ignore distant situations. According to Galina Dobrova, a specific egocentric stage also takes place in the process of acquisition of personal deixis (Dobrova 2003).

The general scheme of pronominal development is given in Table 2. It presents general milestones in the acquisition of pronouns by Russian children, taking into consideration their psychological, syntactic, and lexical development.

Tab. 2: Main stages in the acquisition of pronouns and related skills

Psychological development	Egocentric phase	Reference to the speech situation: here and there	Describing distant and invisible situations	Establishing other reference points
Syntax	1-word stage	3–5-word stage	3–5-word stage	Complex sentences
Lexicon	50–100 words	Lexical spurt	Adjectives, adverbs	Conjunctions
Deictic adverbs	Occur with pointing gesture	Pivot grammar	Close vs. distant objects	Distant and invisible reference points
Personal pronouns first-/second-person	Lables	Shifters: deictic function	Deictic function	Deictic function
Personal pronouns third-person	Lables	Shifters: deictic function	Deictic and anaphoric functions	Deictic and anaphoric functions
Possessive pronouns	Frozen forms, moj 'my'	Agreement, predicative use, second-person	Predicative vs. attributive use, third-person	Reflexive-possessive: svoj 'his own' referring to S
Demonstrative pronouns	Frozen form (Sg: Neut)	Pivot word, agreement, deictic function	Close vs. distant objects, anaphoric function	Introducing relative clause
Reflective pronouns	-	Frozen forms: sam/sama 'myself, by my own'	Deictic function	Deictic and anaphoric functions
Relative pronouns	-	-	Repetitive (poems, fairy tales)	Anaphoric

Our children, however, show individual (or group) differences regarding the correspondences between these milestones, especially regarding the relation between syntactic and lexical development, on the one side, and in the acquisition of different elements of pronominal system, on the other. In paragraph 5, we shall address these differences.

5 Individual differences in the acquisition of pronouns: pronominal profiles

5.1 Vanja

Compared to the norms developed by the Institute of Early Intervention in Saint Peterburg, Vanja is a late-talker, however, he is otherwise still a normally developing child, and his comprehension in some regards is even higher than the mean norms. It is possible that his rich input influenced the simultaneous emergence of a large number of lemmas, though some unexplored mechanisms prevented the child from starting his speech production earlier. As for his grammatical development, one can see with Figure 1 and 2 that his MLU is constantly rising, significant age points being 2;3 and 2;8. These observations correspond to phase 1-3 in Table 2.

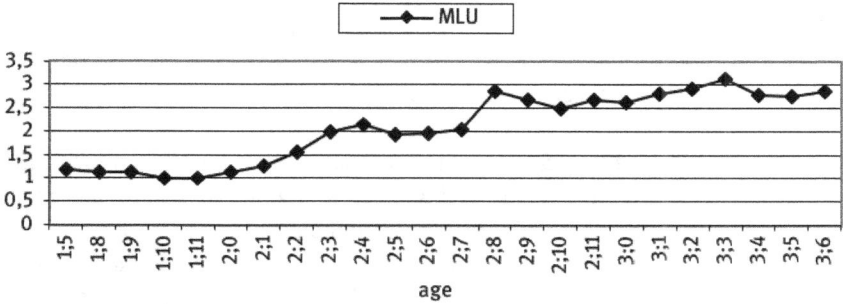

Fig. 1: Vanja's MLU

The real index of lexical development (VOCD) suggests the age of 2;3 as the beginning of the lexical spurt. After this age, the pattern also shows several rises and falls, but the oscillations are not as great as the first rise (see Figure 2).

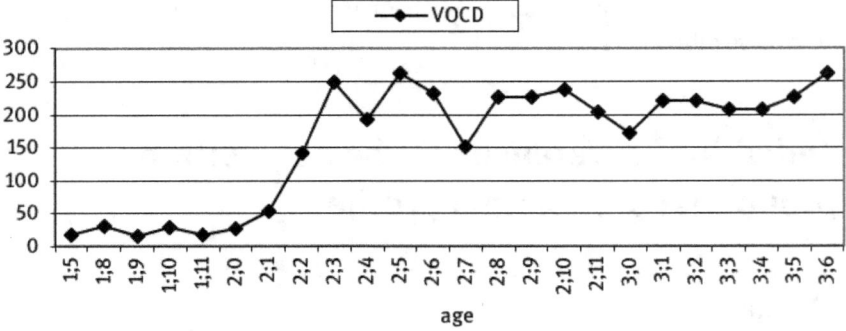

Fig. 2: Vanja's VOCD

The pronominal system in Vanja develops as follows: demonstrative pronouns are the first to appear, and, surprisingly, not only as pivot or frozen forms but also agreeing with the head noun. Compare Vanja's dialogue (13) with his grandmother at 2;3:

(13) Grandmother: *Kak-aja*   *tjotj-a?*
                           Which-SG:FEM:NOM   aunt&FEM-SG:NOM
                           'Which aunt (was it)?
       Vanja: *vot*   *e~t-a,*   *E~llen.*
                           Here   this-SG:FEM:NOM   Helen
                           'This one, aunt Helen'

The early agreement pattern definitely shows that Vanja uses the demonstrative *e~ta* 'this' in the deictic function, referring to the imaginary female protagonist of a fairy tale. Thus, the first frequency peak of demonstratives corresponds to the lexical spurt (compare to Figure 2). At the same time, Vanja's MLU exceeds 3 (see Figure 1). Personal pronouns are introduced at the transition from the one- to two-word stage. Pronouns feature several spurt points (Figure 3[3]): a spurt of demonstratives at 2;4; a spurt of personal pronouns at 2;9; and two peaks at 3;0–3;1 and at 3,6. This last rise corresponds to the period of intensive anaphoric use of personal and demonstrative pronouns.

---

[3] The pronominal profiles (Figures 3-5, 8-10, 13-15, 18–20) show the ratio between the number of tokens of each pronoun or a group of pronouns and the overall number of tokens recorded in the corresponding month (see Table 1).

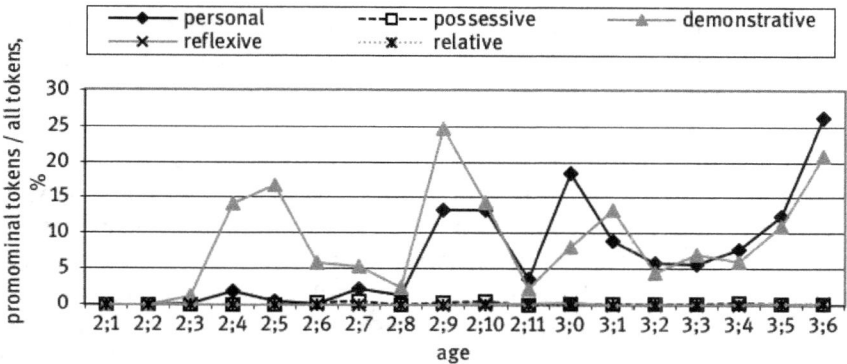

Fig. 3: Most frequent subclasses of pronouns at Vanja

Figure 4 shows different personal pronouns occurring in Vanja's speech.

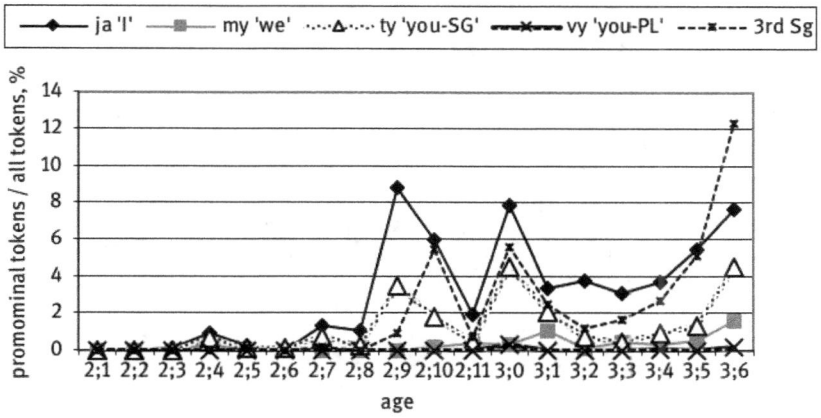

Fig. 4: Vanja's personal pronouns

The first pronouns to appear are *ja* 'I' and *ty* 'you-SG,' which are used sporadically as labels for several months till 2;9–2;10, when abruptly three pronominal lemmas (*ja* 'I,' *ty* 'you-SG,' *on* 'he') begin to be used very frequently. The growing frequency of the first- and second-person pronouns marks their deictic use. Beginning at this point, Vanja seems to understand their nature as shifters. Vanja uses *ja* 'I' in a regular deictic sense at 2;7. At first he exclusively refers to himself: compare *e~to ja teležku (sdelal)* 'it's me who has made this trolley,' to *oj, čut' ja ne upal* 'oh, I'm almost fallen down!' (Vanja, 2;7). Starting from 2;8 he also uses *ty* when referring to his interlocutors, like in *smotri, teper' ty ešče delaj* 'look, now you make another one' (when he wants his grandmother to build one more door in a construction game).

The most frequent pronouns are *ja* and *on*, then *ty*, less frequent is *my* 'we,' and rarest is *vy* 'you-PL.' The peaks of frequency of *ja*, *ty* and *on* coincide, while *my* follows its own pattern with a slight rise at about three years, and maintains a steady position from that time on. *Vy* 'you-PL' is found only eleven times in all data. It is also significant that *on* takes the first position instead of *ja* at 3;4, revealing the development of narrative competence and the rise of anaphoric binding.

Figure 5 shows the use of demonstrative pronouns by Vanja, which clearly begin to occur earlier compared to personal pronouns.

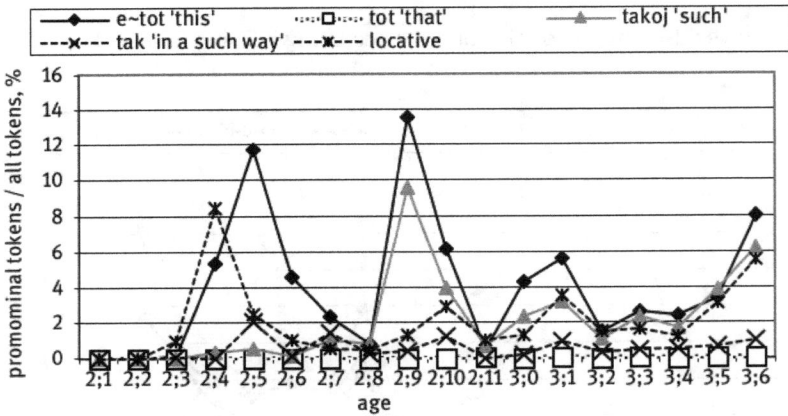

Fig. 5: Vanja's demonstrative pronouns

The first demonstratives are locative adverbs, closely followed by *e~tot* 'this.' *Takoj* 'such' appears and starts being used rather regularly only one month after *e~tot*. This makes Vanja's pattern slightly different from the general one, as *takoj* 'such' usually appears two or three months later than *e~tot* 'this,' and sometimes marks the beginning of the second stage. Vanja can be called an early *e~tot* child, and the emergence of *e~tot* is remarkable because *tot* 'that' is as marginal as personal *vy* and does not even occur at the late "anaphoric" stage.

Two groups of pronouns are expanded most, while the three next groups (possessive, reflexive, and relative pronouns) are too small to observe separately. Nevertheless, one can spot certain tendencies. The possessive first- and second-person pronouns follow the patterns of their personal counterparts; while third-person pronouns are not found in the examined data of Vanja's spontaneous speech. Only ten third-person possessive tokens are found in the diary of Vanja's grandmother starting from 2;9. Vanja is a child who develops possessive pronouns much later than personal pronouns. The age frames are the same for reflexive and relative pronouns, appearing at the high point of pronominal spurt at 2,9–2,10 and getting regular later on.

To conclude, Vanja's acquisition of deictic pronouns has several special features. Vanja develops pronouns relatively late, after 2 years, and maybe for this reason, most basic pronouns appear in his speech production almost simultaneously (*ja*, *ty* and *on*; *e~tot* and *takoj*). Vanja starts with demonstratives (at 2;3–2;4), whereas personal pronouns gain frequency only five to six months later. His first peak age point in the acquisition of pronouns is 2;9–2;10; it can be seen as the start of a pronominal spurt. Anaphoric pronouns rise later than pure demonstratives; this is an almost universal feature. The final peak of 3;6 corresponds to the apogee of anaphora.

Finally, the age of Vanja's lexical spurt coincides with the age of the spurt of demonstratives; the spurt and development of personal pronouns is delayed with respect to the lexical development by several months. The rise in Vanja's syntactic development relate to the demonstrative and personal pronominal peaks.

5.2 Liza

Liza's data show that her grammar develops gradually with a significant increase at 2;1-2;4 and 2;11. Compared to Vanja, Liza is an early talker. Her syntax develops simultaneously with the lexical spurt: from 1;11 to 2;1, Liza's MLU increases from 2 to 4 (see Figure 6).

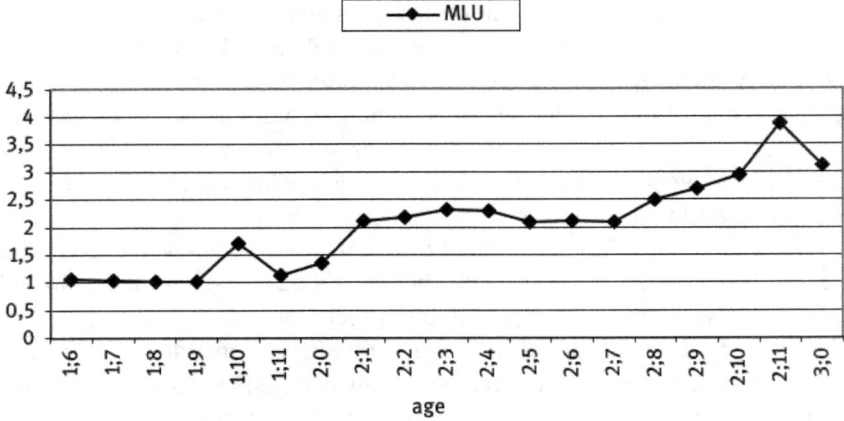

Fig. 6: Lisa's MLU

The lexical spurt happens at 2;0, but after that, lexical diversity slows down (see Figure 7).

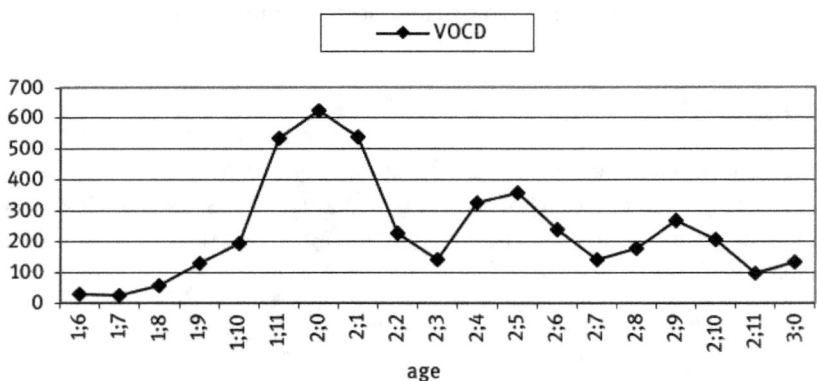

Fig. 7: Lisa's VOCD

Figure 8 shows the development of different classes of pronouns. The data shows a correspondence between VOCD and the development of demonstrative pronouns.

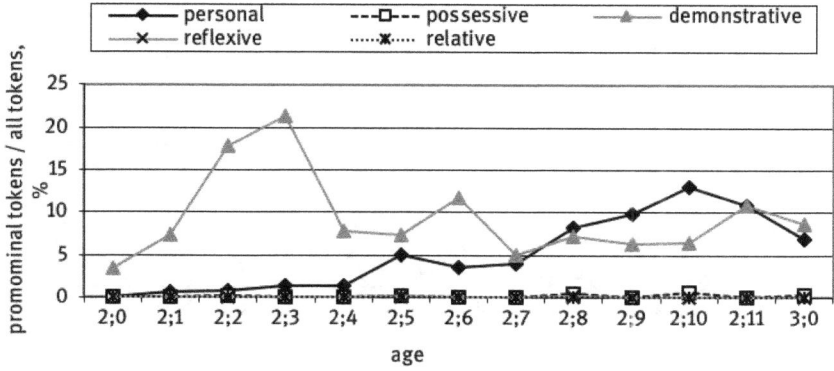

Fig. 8: Most frequent subclasses of pronouns with Liza

Demonstratives and some frozen forms of personal pronouns are the first to appear, and for a long time remain the most frequent pronouns in Liza's speech (Eliseeva 2008: 72). She starts to produce a lot of personal pronouns two months earlier than Vanja does (Liza at 2;5 vs. Vanja at 2,7), which corresponds to her earlier lexical spurt. Another characteristic of Liza's speech is a large temporal delay between the first frozen forms of pronouns at 2;0 and their most frequent use in both deictic and anaphoric functions starting from 2;9–2;11. Pronouns feature two main spurts, the first one at the peak of demonstratives at 2;2 and the second at the spurt of both demonstrative and personal pronouns at 2;8–2;10. After this age, their frequency remains stable. The first peak of demonstratives is, in fact, determined by frequent use of the construction *e~to x* 'this is x' including the neuter form of the demonstrative *e~tot* 'this.' According to Tomasello (2003: 114–117), such constructions are unanalyzed pivot schemata in which one can hardly distinguish their components. However, in Russian where the verb *byt'* 'to be' is omitted in the present tense, this pivot schema consists only of the demonstrative pronoun that is easily defined.

Personal pronouns (first-and second-person) occur already at 2;3, but their use rises only at the age of 2;8 and from this age they develop in close relation to the demonstratives (see Figure 9).

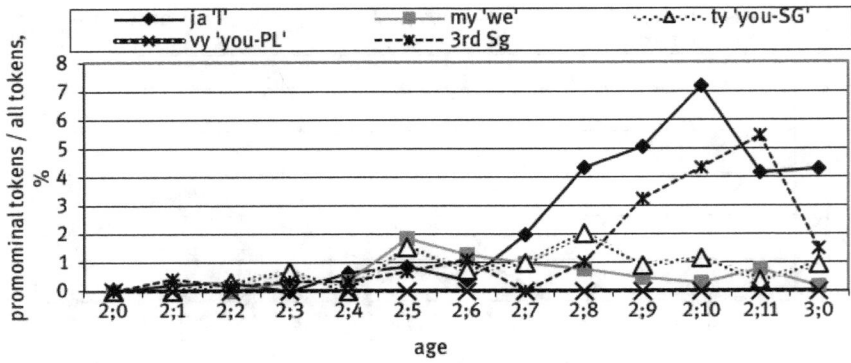

Fig. 9: Liza's personal pronouns

The first personal pronoun to appear is *ja* 'I,' though it doesn't take the leading position until the age of 2;7. Before this age pronouns *my* 'we' and *ty* 'you-SG' are used more frequently than the others. The diary data from Liza's mother reports a particular feature in Liza's early use of pronouns: she refers to herself using the second-person pronoun *ty* 'you.' The unexpected frequency of *my* 'we' can be explained by the speech input from the mother, who uses *my* when addressing a child. Most personal pronouns but *vy* 'you-PL' already appear by 2;3. Anaphoric *on* 'he' becomes frequent at 2;9 and becomes more frequent than *ja* 'I' at 2;11. As in Vanja's case, this depends on the anaphoric binding of phrases and the construction of long monologic narratives. On the whole, personal pronouns are present in Liza's data sporadically until 2;8 and, as with Vanja, develop rather quickly after this age. One can say that at the early stages Liza, like Vanja, is not a "personal-pronominal" child. This may be explained by her general referential style: she prefers to refer to objects and persons with nouns and not with personal pronouns. Demonstratives, on the other hand, play an important role in Liza's deictic system from the very beginning. Her first demonstrative adverb *tam* 'there' is recorded at 1;8. Locative adverbs are used steadily and regularly throughout, though not so often as the demonstrative pronoun *e~tot* 'this.' *E~tot* 'this' builds the pattern of Liza's pronominal spurts. The first spurt happens at 2;2, the second at 2;6, and the last at 2;11. The pronoun *takoj* 'such' is not as widespread as in Vanja's data; *tot* is also rare and appears at the age when all other demonstratives have already been acquired (see Figure 10).

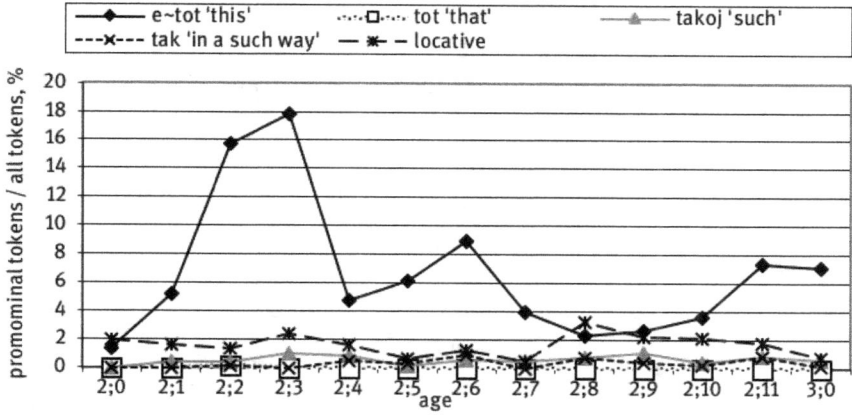

Fig. 10: Liza's demonstratives

Possessive pronouns appear rather early, alongside personal and demonstrative pronouns. The number of possessive pronouns is too small to allow any conclusions. Liza uses only two possessive tokens: *moj* 'my' and *tvoj* 'your-SG,' which follow the paths of their personal counterparts. Reflexive and relative pronouns do not occur until 2;5. Reflexives are also rather rare and become regular only by the age of 3;7. The first relative pronouns are noticed at 2;11, with the anaphoric *on* 'he.' This is a significant point in the acquisition of anaphora.

To conclude, Liza's strategy of acquisition of pronouns is demonstrative-oriented, not personal-oriented. Liza is a referential (nominal) child and pays more attention to nouns and adjectives than to pronouns, with her only pronominal replacer being *e~tot* 'this.' It is possible that pronominal features are acquired on the base of *e~tot*, while personal deixis develops mostly in verbal morphology. The acquisition of pronouns here shows two significant points: the first at 2;2 and is related to the rapid development of *e~tot*; the second at 2;9–2;11 and is related to her anaphoric development. Between the first and the second stage there is a transitional period that includes several months between 2;2 and 2;5, while the third "anaphoric" stage starts after 2;11.

While an early talker, Liza is a rather late pronoun user. Generally, this coincides neither with the lexical nor the grammatical indexes. The pronouns start developing at the stage of a high MLU index, but after the age of an abrupt grammatical rise. The lexical spurt coincides with the spurt of demonstratives.

5.3 Vitja

Vitja's MLU index steadily rises up to the age of 2;11, with an insignificant decrease later on (Figure 11).

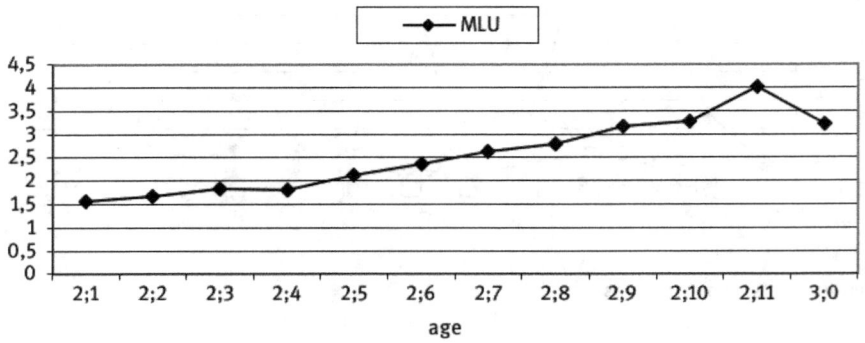

Fig. 11: Vitja's MLU

The VOCD index shows that Vitja's lexical spurt occurs at 2;5. Later, after a decrease in lexical diversity, it increases though not to the same high level, at 3;0 (Figure 12).

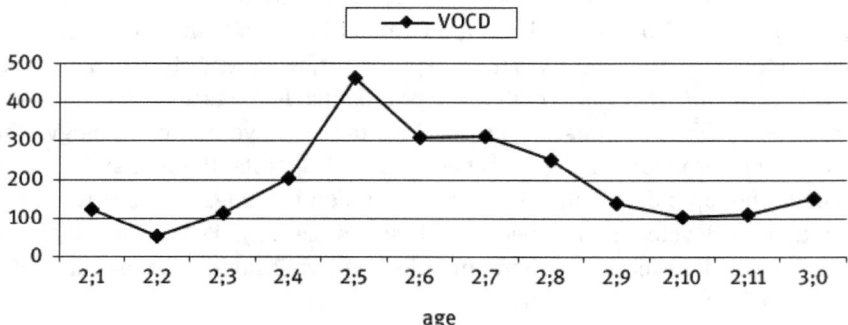

Fig. 12: Vitja's VOCD

The development of Vitja's pronominal system proceeds differently, in some aspects, than in the two previous children's cases. Personal and demonstrative pronouns both appear and develop almost simultaneously; however, their number is relatively small before reaching 2;5 (see Figure 13).

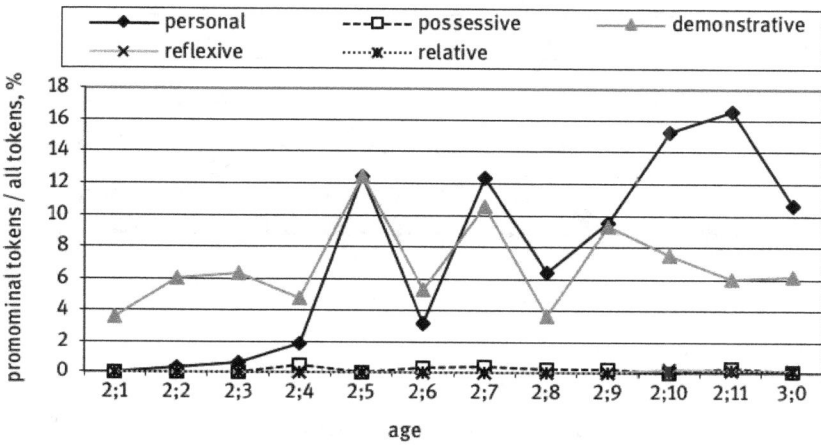

Fig. 13: Most frequent subclasses of pronouns at Vitja

Though the order of occurrence is the same in the data of all three children, Vitja's speech production differs in the number of contexts with pronouns. Several pronominal tokens are found at the first half of the third year of life (2;1–2;4), but the first significant rise happens only at 2;5; another one occurs at 2;7, and the abrupt spurt takes place at 2;10.

Figure 14 shows the frequency of personal pronouns in Vitja's speech.

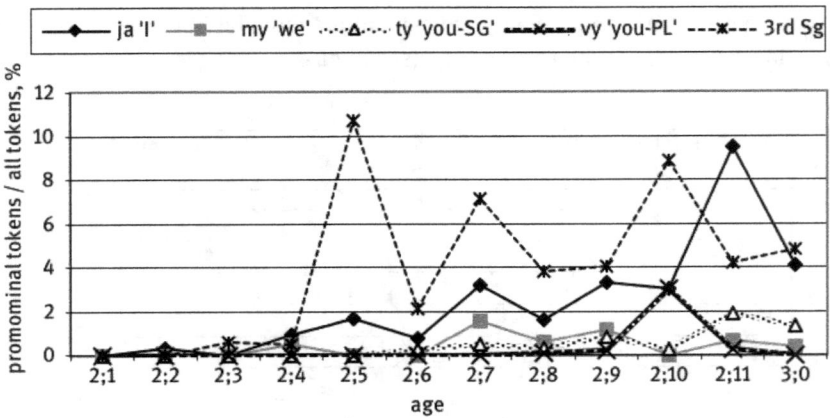

Fig. 14: Vitja's personal pronouns

In the group of personal pronouns, the third-person *on* 'he' is unexpectedly frequent and regular from the first instances and prevails over *ja* 'I' all but at the age of 2;11, see Figure 14. The first utterances with *on* are not anaphoric, but demonstrative, and are supported by a demonstrative gesture and by the repetition of the corresponding noun (e.g. *vot on, zontik* 'here it is, an umbrella'; *vot ona, mashinka* 'here it is, a car' etc.). Sometimes the child also points toward himself using the same phrase with *on* (14), but at the same time uses *ja* 'I' regularly (see example 15). Usually, a child that names himself or herself in the third person doesn't use personal pronouns, but only a proper name. This third-person deictic stage usually ends before the emergence of necessary pronouns.

(14) *Vot on!* (Vitja, 2;5.14, points to himself)
 here he
 'Here he is'
(15) *Ja otkroju sam* (Vitja, 2;2.7)
 I open-FUT.1.SG self
 'I'll open myself'

Second-person pronouns are late to appear: Vitja doesn't use *ty* 'you-SG' before 2;6, which suggests he has problems with shifters. At the same time, Vitja is the only child in our corpus who produces the second-person plural pronoun *vy* 'you-SG' regularly and relatively frequently after 2;9 (see Figure 14). *Vy* does not have a plural meaning but a social, deictic one, used as regular polite *you* in game situations (for example, when Vitja pretends he is a shop assistant and his mother is a client, they address each other with polite *vy*).

Demonstratives in Vitja's speech are presented in Figure 15. The main demonstrative word in Vitja's data is *tam* 'there.' It is his first demonstrative, and in some months, also the most frequent one. The ratio between *tam* and *e~tot* 'this' (generally two main demonstratives in children's speech) is uneven in Vitja's speech and differs from month to month.

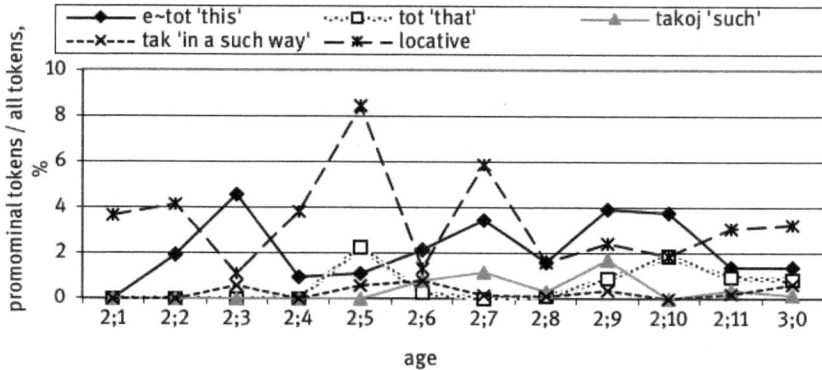

Fig. 15: Vitja's demonstratives

Considering that *e~tot* 'this' is used first as a pivot word and later on in deictic contexts, we can explain its peak at 2;7 by the development of its deictic function. Later the amount of *e~tot* tokens rises and the amount of *tam* falls. Vitja prefers personal *on* 'he' to *e~tot* 'this' in most contexts. *Takoj* 'such' occurs at 2;6 and follows the pattern of *e~tot*. An interesting feature of Vitja's strategy is a regular use of the demonstrative *tot* 'that,' which is usually marginal among children. It functions in regular demonstrative situations in its core meaning of referring to a distant object. This is the second infrequent pronoun that appears regularly in Vitja's data after the personal *vy* 'you-PL.' Most notably, both pronouns are not more frequent in Vitja's input than in the input of other children.

Possessives occur a month later, after demonstratives and personal pronouns. The first-person items *moj* 'my' and *naš* 'our' present early possessive pronouns in Vitja's speech. The amount of second-person possessives is insignificant (six tokens for singular and two for plural), and the third-person possessives are missing from the data. Anaphoric pronouns (reflexive and relative) appear at 2;10 and are used rarely.

In Vitja's case, it is not difficult to discriminate between the stages of the acquisition of pronouns. The most significant period is the age of 2;9–2;11 with the second pronominal spurt and that of the acquisition of late anaphors. This period marks the transition between the second and third stage. The first stage of early pronouns features a very small number of tokens – mostly demonstrative adverbials – and ends at the age of 2;5–2;7 with the rise of both personal and demonstrative pronouns. Vitja's strategy in acquisition is supposedly a strategy of diversification. The child uses a wide number of pronominal lemmas, including those that are rare or absent in other children's data. However, most pronouns are not very frequent.

As for the relation to general developmental indexes, Vitja's pronominal development coincides with his grammatical development. Like in Vanja's case, the late anaphoric pronouns begin to be used in the period of an MLU rise. The lexical spurt, however, happens one month before the first pronominal rise, which means that no specific coincidence between the lexical and pronominal development is found.

5.4 Filipp

Filipp developed the ability to speak earlier than the other children in our data did. According to the general profile, he begins acquiring both grammar and lexicon early: at the beginning of the recordings his MLU is already rather high (2,6), and it continues to rise slowly with time. No definite increase in MLU is attested, though there are two rises at 2;2 and at 2;8. The lexical spurt happens at 2;1, and after that, as in the data of the two previous children, the lexical diversity decreases. There is also a slighter lexical rise at the age of 1;8 (see Figures 16 and 17).

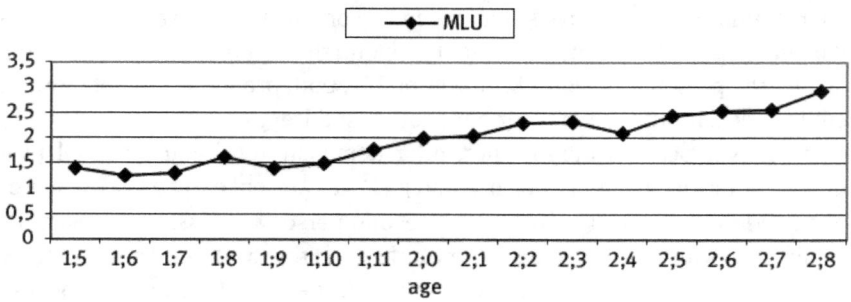

Fig. 16: Filipp's MLU

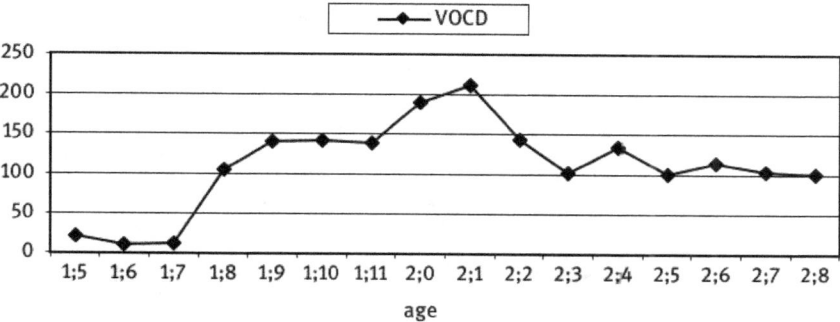

Fig. 17: Filipp's VOCD

The first pronouns are also acquired by Filipp rather early. The first pronominal items are recorded in the very beginning of the transcribed data, at 1;5, though their amount is close to zero and they are mostly used in repetitive contexts.

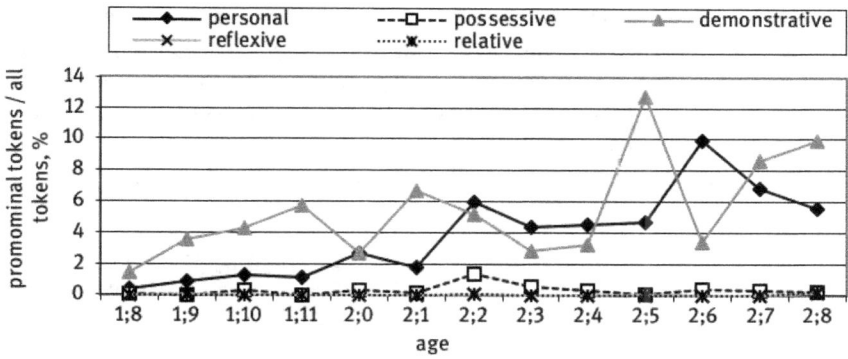

Fig. 18: Most frequent subclasses of pronouns at Filipp

Pronominal development shows one gradual rise, up to the age of 2;2, and one spurt at 2;5. The first deictic words are demonstratives closely followed by first-person pronouns, both personal and possessive. There are two significant age points: the age of 2;2 is important for personal, possessive (and reflexive) pronouns, whereas at the age of 2;5, the peak of demonstratives is attested (see Figure 18). This is due to a particular situation: Filipp and his mother are looking through a picture book while they indicate what they see. Personal pronouns in Filipp's speech are presented in Figure 19.

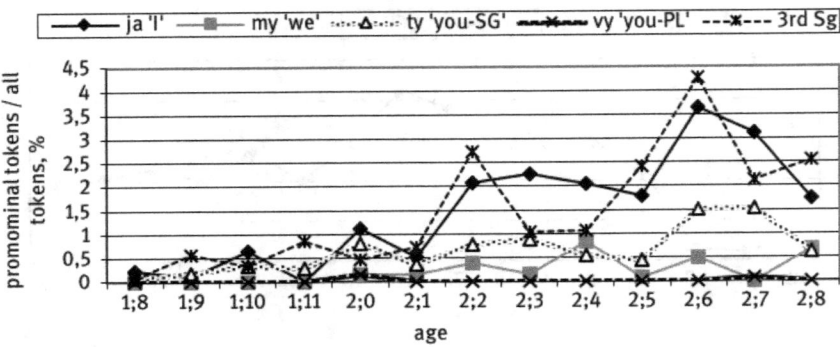

Fig. 19: Filipp's personal pronouns

Personal pronouns show two obvious spurts at 2;2 and 2;6, and a steady rise of frequencies during the following months. Before the first spurt, the number of personal pronouns is limited, and the most used lemma is *ja* 'I.' *On* 'he' and *ty* 'you-SG' are added two months after the occurrence of *ja*. *My* 'we' appears at 2;0, and *vy* 'you-PL' is almost absent from the data. The overall percentage of personal pronouns remains rather low. One cannot trace here any significantly rapid rise of anaphoric *on* 'he'. Though its usage grows gradually, it always stays almost on the same level as *ja* 'I.' It is possible that anaphoric rise happens later, at an age that is not covered by the data.

Figure 20 presents the demonstrative pronouns in Filipp's speech.

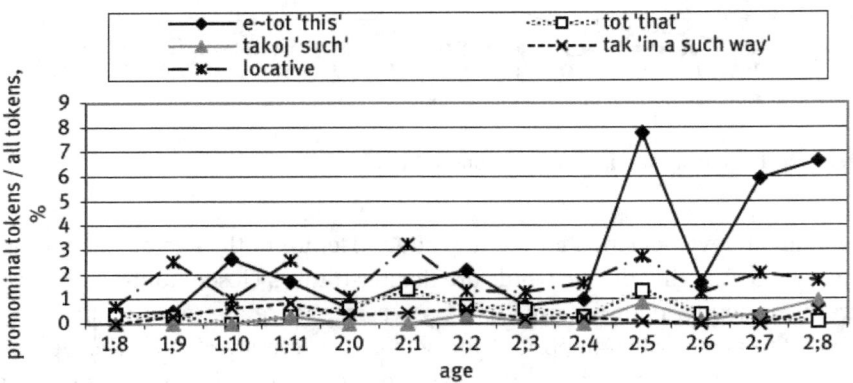

Fig. 20: Filipp's demonstratives

Demonstratives show a definite spurt at 2;5. The most frequent demonstrative is *e~tot* 'this.' It occurs at 1;8 alongside other demonstratives: *tot* 'that,' *tam* 'there,' and *tut* 'here.' While most children ignore *tot* until late age and use only *e~tot* 'this,' Filipp doesn't have problems in acquiring and producing *tot* in obligatory contexts so that is interpreted as correct. However, the early tokens of *tot* and *e~tot* are not strictly opposed at the early stage, so it is possible that Filipp at first does not distinguish between the two demonstratives and chooses the phonetically easier option. *Takoj* 'such' appears when Filipp's pronominal production is rather low: at 1;11, and shows no specific development after that (see Figure 20). In general, Filipp acquires demonstratives in two clusters, the first consisting mostly of *e~tot* and the second including all other demonstrative words.

Though his number of possessives is small, Filipp is the only child in our data who produces a relatively high number of tokens of the pronoun *moj* 'my.' This starts at an age of 2;2 which is also significant for personal pronouns. Thus, unlike other children, Filipp starts to use pronouns early, paying almost as much attention to the personal sphere as to the demonstrative one.

In Filipp's data it is not possible to clearly discriminate developmental stages in the acquisition of pronouns. There is definitely a period of transition between the stage of low pronominal production and the stage of high pronominal production at 2;2–2;5. Like in Liza's case, we can assume that for Filipp this period lasts several months. At the age of 2;6 there is a peak in the pronominal spurt. However, no definite event marks the end of the second and the beginning of the third stage. The data also doesn't show any particular change in anaphoric production. It is possible that the third stage of late anaphoric pronouns starts after the end of the recorded data, that is after 2;8, closer to 3 years. Filipp starts building a pronominal system with first-person pronouns *ja* 'I' and *moj* 'my.' As far as personal and demonstrative pronouns are concerned, Filipp has no particular preferences with respect to either proximal (first-person, *e~tot* 'this,' *tut* 'here') or distal (third-person, *tot* 'that,' *tam* 'there'). This proves that some parts of Filipp's pronominal system are acquired earlier than in other children. This may be due to his general repetitive strategy (Voeikova 2015: 55-57).

Comparing pronominal and lexical data, one can see that Filipp's MLU rise at 2;2 corresponds to the age that is significant also for personal pronouns, while his lexical pattern partly repeats the development of demonstratives. The most important rises, however, do not coincide: while corresponding lexical and demonstrative rises happen at the age of 2;1, the pronominal peak point at 2;5–2;6 meets no specific changes in the lexical development pattern.

6 Discussion and Conclusion

The children under investigation go through similar phases in the acquisition of pronominal systems but differ in the set of pronouns they use at the early stage, as well as in the speed of their acquisition. Demonstrative and personal pronouns are of utmost importance for the early phases of language acquisition. All four children began with demonstrative pronouns and/or adverbs that exhibited no deictic function at that time and were part of pivot constructions. In all four subjects, the spurt in demonstrative pronouns took place simultaneously alongside or a bit after the lexical spurt. Table 3 gives an overview of the correspondence between the maximal percentages of demonstrative and personal pronoun tokens and children's top MLU and VOCD values.

Tab. 3: Coincidence of peaks and spurts in acquisition of pronouns and the syntactic and lexical development

	MLU	VOCD	Demonstrative Pronouns	Personal Pronouns
	Age (Value)	Age (Value)	Age (Percentage to all tokens)	Age (Percentage to all tokens)
Vanja	2;3 (4)	2;3 (250)	2;5 (15%)	2;9 (13%)
	2;8 (5)	2;5 (260)	2;9 (25%)	3;0 (18%)
	3;4 (5.5)	3;6 (260)		3;6 (26%)
Liza	2;1 (4)	2;0 (600)	2;3 (20%)	2;5 (5%)
	2;11 (6.5)	2;6	2;6 (13%)	2;10 (13%)
	3;6 (7)	(350)	2;11 (10%)	3;5 (12%)
		2;10 (250)	3;5 (12%)	
Vitja	2;6 (4)	2;5 (460)	2;5 (12%)	2;5 (12%)
	2;11 (6)		2;7 (11%)	2;7 (13%)
			2;9 (9%)	2;11 (16%)
Filipp	2;8 (3)	1;8 (100)	1;11 (5%)	2;2 (6%)
		2;1 (210)	2;1 (7%)	2;6 (10%)
		2;4 (100)	2;5 (12%)	
			2;8 (10%)	

Our assumption that the main points in pronominal development relate to the significant moments in the acquisition of syntax and lexicon has not received enough direct evidence, as all four children showed different patterns of coincidence.

Two tendencies, however, can be observed. First, syntactic development affects the acquisition of both pronominal types: this happens in all of the children's data except Liza's (the peak of frequency in personal pronouns in her speech precedes the MLU peak value). Second, the acquisition of demonstratives is related to the lexical spurt: strict month-to-month coincidence takes place in all children's data. The effect of personal pronouns being more "grammatical" and demonstratives more "lexical" may be linked to the fact that personal pronouns are more "pronominal" or more shifting than demonstratives (Krasnoshchekova 2016: 214). However, as we discussed, this might have been an effect of special activities during the recording.

Several parameters seem to play a role in the acquisition of the pronominal system. First, the age when pronominal words first appear and, correspondingly, the age when the production of pronouns becomes plentiful. In our data, Filipp and Liza are definitely early pronominal producers. Vanja develops the regular pronominal system rather early, though later than the two previous children, and while Vitja acquires pronouns later, however, he nonetheless manages to reach comparable percentages very soon. The early-talking Filipp and Liza do not use many pronouns at the beginning of their observation, whereas in the speech of late-talkers Vanja and Vitja, the share of personal pronouns exceeds 10% in the first period.

Though no two children showed similar development in all parts of the pronominal system, several common features may be found. First, all four children at the early age show a preference for the central deictic sphere: proximal pronouns prevail over distal pronouns, in particular, first-person over third-person and *e~tot* 'this' over *tot* 'that.' Second-person plural *vy* is also very rare. This fact is related to the psychological reality of early egocentrism. Second, all groups of pronouns with the exception of personal and demonstrative pronouns, are very rare: possessive pronouns are infrequent, and late anaphoric groups of reflexive and relative pronouns are marginal. A similar pattern occurs in the general order of appearance: personal, demonstrative, and possessive pronouns appear earlier than the reflexive and relative ones. The behavior of anaphoric pronouns does not contradict the well-known fact that in English, Russian, Italian, etc., regular production of anaphoric third-person and reflexive pronouns develops from four years on, and comprehension is acquired even later (Chien and Wexler 1990; Conroy et al. 2009; Matthews et al. 2009). However, this does not greatly influence children's speaking capacity.

The second distinction is in the clusters of pronouns that appear together, and in the order in which these pronouns occur. Vanja and Liza are "demonstrative-pronoun children": the use of pronouns in their speech production starts with the spurt of demonstratives, and is followed by personal pronouns in a later period of time. Liza uses more demonstrative pronouns, and doesn't produce a large number of personal ones.

In Vitja's speech, demonstratives and personal pronouns occur simultaneously and develop gradually without any significant increase. Moreover, during the first months of pronominal development, his main demonstrative is not *e~tot* 'this,' but locative *tam* 'there.' His pronominal system is balanced from the very beginning, though he copes with it rather late: it is only at 2;7 that he develops an opposition of *on* 'he' and *ja* 'I' simultaneously with the opposed demonstratives *e~tot* 'this,' *tam* 'there' and *takoj* 'such.'

Filipp combines two strategies. He is an early pronoun user, although his first demonstrative pronouns are repetitions with unclear deictic functions, occurring at 1;8. At 2;2 he already uses the opposition of *on* 'he' and *ja* 'I.' From this moment on there is no evident preference for demonstratives in his speech. Being an early talker, he easily begins to distinguish the opposed forms of pronouns and demonstrative adverbs.

Thus, the "demonstrative-oriented children" (Liza and Vanja) seem to have problems with the opposition of shifters, whereas the "balanced pronoun-users" (Vitja and Filipp) use pronominal oppositions from the very beginning. However, there is not sufficient evidence that they completely understand the difference between the members of pronominal oppositions and that they are not simply repeating different pronouns based on their caregivers' examples. Different strategies in the acquisition of pronouns do not correlate with an early or late start of speech production. More data is needed to prove whether "balanced pronoun-users" develop anaphora earlier or more quickly than "demonstrative-pronoun children," and whether there is such a category as "personal-pronoun children". Any future investigation should be based on longer longitudinal studies and on experiments wherein the subjects are investigated from the onset of their speech production.

7 Notes

The longitudinal corpora analyzed here were collected for different purposes but in the same manner at the Chair of Child language, Herzen State Pedagogical University and at the Institute for Linguistic Studies, Russian Academy of Sciences.

We are grateful to the mothers and caregivers of the children in this study—T. V. Pranova, M. B. Eliseeva, E.K. Limbach and E.A. Oficerova—as well as to the coders (E.K.Limbach and M.I. Akkuzina) and supervisors of this collection (M.B. Eliseeva, N.V. Gagarina, E.A. Oficerova) for the opportunity to use the data. Most of it is already described in (Eliseeva 2008; Gagarina 2008; Voeikova 2015; Oficerova 2005).

We are grateful to Ms. Anne Wheeler for proof-reading and correcting our English. Of course, the remaining errors are our fault.

References

Avrutin, S. 2010. Usvoenie jazyka [Language Acquisition (in Russiar)]. In Andrej, A., Kibrik, I., M. Kobozeva and Sekerina, I. A. (eds.), *Fundamental'nye napravlenija sovremennoj amerikanskoj lingvistiki*. Moscow: URSS, 261–276.
Avrutin, S. 1999. *Development of the Syntax-Discourse Interface*. Springer Science and Business Media.
Bates, E., Bretherton, I. and Snyder L. 1988. *From first words to grammar: Individual differences and dissociable mechanisms*. Cambridge, MA: Cambridge University Press.
Baauw, S. and Cuetos, F. 2003. The interpretation of pronouns in Spanish language acquisition and breakdown: Evidence for the "Principle B Delay" as a non-unitary phenomenon. *Language Acquisition* 11, 219–275.
Braine, M. 1963. The ontogeny of English phrase structure. *Language* 39 (1), 1–13.
Budwig, N. 1989. The linguistic marking of agentivity and control in child language. *Journal of Child Language* 16 (2), 263–284.
Clahsen, H., Eisenbeiss, S. and Vainikka, A. 1994. The seeds of structure. A syntactic analysis of the acquisition of case marking. In Teun, H., Schwartz, B. D. (eds.), *Language Acquisition Studies in Generative Grammar*. Amsterdam: Benjamins, 85–118.
Ceytlin, S.N. 2000. Jazyk i rebenok Lingvistika detskoj reči [*Language and child. Linguistics of child's speech* (In Russian)]. Moscow: VLADOS.
Ceytlin, S.N. 2009. Očerki po slovoobrazovaniju i formoobrazovaniju v detskoj reči [*Essays on word and form derivation in children's speech* (In Russian)]. Moscow: Znak.
Chien, Y. and Wexler, K. 1990. Children's knowledge of locality conditions in binding as evidence for the modularity of syntax and pragmatics. *Language Acquisition* 1 (3), 225–295.
Conroy, A., Takahashi, E., Lidz, J. and Phillips, C. 2009. Equal treatment for all antecedents: How children succeed with Principle B, *Linguistic Inquiry* 40 (3), 446–486.
Dobrova, G. R. 2003. Ontogenez personal'nogo dejksisa (Lichnye mestoimenija i terminy rodstva) [*The ontogeny of personal deixis (personal pronouns and kinship terminology)* (In Russ-ian)]. Saint Petersburg: Izdatel'stvo RGPU im. A.I. Gerzena.
Dobrova, G. R. 2007. Osvoenie det'mi funkcional'no-semanticheskoj kategorii personal'nosti [Acquisition of the functional semantic category of personality (In Russian)]. In *Semanticheskie kategorii v detskoj rechi*. Saint Petersburg: Nestor-Istorija, 181–200.
Dodson, K. and Tomasello, M. 1998. Acquiring the transitive construction in English: the role of animacy and pronouns. *Journal of Child Language* 25, 605–622.

Eliseeva, M.B. 2008. Foneticheskoe I leksicheskoe razvitie rebenka rannego vozrasta [*Phonetical and lexical development of a child at the early stages* (In Russian)]. Saint Petersburg: Izdat-el'stvo RGPU im. A.I. Gerzena.

Elivanova, M.A. (2007). Kategorija lokativnosti i ee vyrazhenie v detskoj rechi [Category of locativity and its expression in the speech of children (In Russian)]. In Ceytlin, S.N. (eds.). *Semanticheskie kategorii v detskoj rechi*. Saint Petersburg: Nestor-Istorija, 317–339.

Fludernik, M. 1989/90. Jespersen's Shifters: Reflections on Deixis and Subjectivity in Language. *Klagenfurter Beiträge zur Sprachwissenschaft* 15/16, 97–116.

Gagarina, N. 2004. The hare hugs the rabbit. He is white ... Who is white? Pronominal anaphora in Russian. *ZAS papers in linguistic 35*. Berlin, 139–170.

Gagarina, N. 2008. Stanovlenie grammaticheskih kategorij russkogo glagola v detskoj rechi [*First language acquisition of verbal categories in Russian* (in Russian)]. Saint Petersburg: Nauka.

Gagarina, N. 2009. Parallelism as an anaphora resolution factor in Russian. In Tatiana, A. Tripol'skaja (eds.), *Diskretnost' i kontinual'n'st' v jazyke i v tekste: Materialy Mezdunarodnoj konferencii*. Novosibirsk: Izdatel'stvo NGPU, 31–37.

Gagarina, N. 2012. Elicited narratives of early Russian-German sequential bilinguals. In Braunmüller, K., Gabriel, C. (eds.), *Hamburg studies on multilingualism. — Vol. 13: Multilingual individuals — Multilingual Societies*. Amsterdam: Benjamins Publishing Company, 101–119.

Gavrilova, T.O. 2002. Registr obshchenija s det'mi: strukturnyj I sociolinvističeskij aspekty (na materiale russkogo jazyka) [*Baby-talk mode in Russian: structure and sociolinguistic aspects* (in Russian)]. PhD dissertation. Saint Petersburg.

Gibson, E. and Perlmutter, N.J. (eds.) 2011. *The Processing and Acquisition of Reference*. Cambridge, MA – London: MIT Press, 133–156.

Goldman, A. I. 2012. Theory of Mind. In: Margolis, E., Samuels, R.and Stich, S. (eds.), *Oxford Handbook of Philosophy and Cognitive Science*. Oxford: OUP.

Golovenkina, L.H. 1996. Mestoimenija v rechi detej [Pronouns in the speech of children (in Russian)]. In Ceytlin, S.N. (eds.), *Problemy detskoj rechi-1996. Materialy mežvuzovskoj konferencii*. Saint Petersburg.

Grolla, E. 2010. *Pronouns as Elsewhere Elements: Implications for Language Acquisition*. Newcastle upon Tyne: Cambridge Scholars Publishing.

Gvozdev, A. N. 1949. Formirovanie u rebenka grammaticheskogo stroja russkogo jazyka [*Acquisition of Russian grammar system* (in Russian)]. Moscow: Izdatel'stvo Akademii Pedagogicheskih Nauk RSFSR.

Gülzow, I. and Gagarina, N. 2007. Introduction. In Gülzow, I. and Gagarina, N. (eds.), *Frequency Effects in Language Acquisition, 1–11*. Berlin: Mouton de Gruyter, 1–20.

Hendriks, P. and Spenader, J. 2006. When production precedes comprehension: An optimization approach to the acquisition of pronouns. *Language Acquisition* 13, 319–348.

Ivanova, K. 2011. Otsenka individualnykh strategij usvoenija russkogo jazyka detmi s pomoshchju avtomatizirovannogo analiza dannykh spontannoj rechi (rannie etapy) [*Estimate of individ-ual strategies of children's acquisition of Russian language by means of the automated analysis of spontaneous speech data (early age)* (In Russian)]. Master paper. Saint Petersburg. [Manuscript].

Jakobson, R. 1956/1990. Shifters and Verbal Categories. In Waugh, L. R. and Monville-Spurton, M. (eds.), *On Language*. Cambridge, MA: Harvard UP, 386–392.

Jespersen, O. 1923/1959. *Language: Its Nature, Development and Origin*. London: Allen and Unwin, 123–124.

Korolev, V D. 2011. Stadii osvoenija det'mi sredstv vyrazhenija lokat'vnogo i temporal'nogo deiksisa [Stages of children's acquisition of means of expression of locative and temporal deixis (in Russian)]. *Izvestija RGPU im. A.I. Gerzena* 131, 222–226.

Krasnoshchekova, S.V. 2016. Mestoimennyj deiksis v russkoj detskoj rechi [*Pronominal deixis in Russian children's speech* (in Russian)]. PhD dissertation. Saint Petersburg.

Lepskaja, N.I. 1984. Lichnye mestoimenija v jazyke detej (stanovlen e, funkcii, semantika) [Personal pronouns in the children's language (acquisition, functions, semantics) (in Russian)]. *Vestnik MGU*.

Matthews, D., Lieven, E., Theakston, A. and Tomasello, M. 2009. Pronoun co-referencing errors: Challenges for generativist and usage-based accounts, *Cognitive Linguistics* 20 (3), 599–626.

Mills, A.E. 1985. The acquisition of German. In: Slobin, D.I. (eds.), *The Crosslinguistic Study of Language Acquisition*. Vol. 1. Hillsdale, NJ: Erlbaum, 141–254.

Nelson, K. 1973. Structure and Strategy in Learning to Talk. *Monographs of the Society for Research in Child Development* 38 (1–2, Serial No. 149).

Oficerova, E.A. 2005. Vyraženie modal'nyx značenij vozmožnosti I neobxodimosti v russkoj detskoj reči [The expression of modal meanings of possibility and necessity in Russian child language]. Unpublished PhD dissertation. Saint Petersburg: Institute for linguistic studies, RAS.

Piaget, J. 1923. *Le langage et la pensée chez l'enfant*. Neuchâtel: Delachaux 8r Niestlé.

Rispoli, M. 1991. The mosaic acquisition of grammatical relations. *JCL* 18, 517–51.

Rispoli, M. 1999. Case and agreement in English language development. *JCL* 26, 357–372.

Ruigendijk, E., Baauw, S., Zuckerman, S., Vasić, N., de Lange, J., and Avrutin, S. 2011. A crosslinguistic study of the interpretation of pronouns by children and agram–matic speakers: evidence from Dutch, Spanish, and Italian. In: Gibson, E. and Perlmutter, N.J. (eds.) *The Processing and Acquisition of Reference*. Cambridge, MA – London: MIT Press, 133–156.

Shapiro, J. N. and Chistovich, I. A. 2000. Rukovodstvo po ocenke urovnja razvitija detej ot 1 goda 2 mesjacev do 3 let 6 mesjacev po rusificirovannoj škale RCDI-2000. [Guidlines for the evaluation of children's developmental level from 1;2 to 3;6 accorcing to RCDI-2000 scale adopted to Russian (in Russian)]. Saint Petersburg: Institute of Early Intervention.

Voeikova, M. D. 2015. Stanovlenie imeni: Rannie ètapy usvoenija det'mi imennoj morfologii [Establishment of Noun: Early Stages in the Acquisition of Nominal Morphology (in Russian)]. Moscow: Znak.

Index

aber 13, 60, 62
aber/dagegen 21
Accessibility Theory 109
acquisition of connectives 58, 70
acquisition of deictic systems 181
acquisition of morphology 181
acquisition of pronouns 171, 178–182
acquisition order of specific connectives 58
additive relations 13, 28
adpositions 63
adverbial connectives 63
adversative coherence relations 60
adversative relations 13, 29
after 15, 31
also 62
alternative coherence relations 60
although 61
anaphora resolution by mono- and bilinguals 132
and 13, 21, 28, 57, 62, 64
and then 15
and vs. *und* 77
antecedent type 107, 109, 122–134
anteriority 14
articles 143
attractiveness 48
auch 62

backward-looking processes 109
because 14, 21, 45, 58, 60–62
because of 63
before 15, 21, 31
bevor 15, 31
bevor/zuvor 21
but 13, 21, 45, 63
but rather 62

causal coherence relations 60
causal relations 12, 27
causality 14
CDS 173

child-directed speech 173
children's speech 174
cognitive complexity of coherence relations 12, 28, 29, 36, 62
coherence 1
coherence relations 1, 11
coherence relations expressed by "and" 73, 75
coherence relations, comparison of 25
coherence relations, complexity of 12
coherence relations, development of 23, 36, 41
coherence relations, processing of 15
comparison of coherence relations 25
concessive 60
conditional coherence relations 60
conditional relationships 13
consecutive coherence relations 60
contrast 13
contrastive relations 13
coordinating conjunctions 62
CS 174
cue reliability 106

da 14
daarom 45
dann 60
deep text comprehension 14
definite noun phrases 139
definiteness 143
denn 14
deshalb 58, 63
development of coherence relations 15, 23, 41, 51, 58, 71–73
development of oral narrative skills 3
developmental language disorder (DLD) 85
developmental language disorders 3
developmental stages 18, 29
diagnosis 3
DLD 3, 87–90

Expectancy Hypothesis 109

https://doi.org/10.1515/9781501510151-009

explicit relation 1, 12
explicit vs. implicit coherence relations 19, 36, 42–57
externally reliable 107

forward-looking processes 108
fragmented layout 42, 48, 50–53

gender 105, 110, 124–133
gender agreement 110–112
gender information 107
given 139
Givenness Theory 109

iconic sequences 12
if 60
implicit relation 1
in order to 60
indefinite noun phrases 140
indem 60
independence/dependence of narrative macrostructure from language proficiency 100
individual differences in the acquisition of pronouns 200, 201
information status 140
information status of referents 164
instrumental coherence relations 60
integrated layout 43, 48–53
internal state terms (IST) 90
internally reliable 107
introduction of discourse referents 139–141

lean form 140
level of difficulty 17
literacy, predictors of 3
LITMUS 88

maar 45
macrostructure 86
MAIN 88
maintained reference 146, 153–159
mapping between connectives and coherence relations 58
microstructure 86

milestones in the acquisition of pronouns 182
MLU 171
morphological markings of the noun phrase 139
multiple cues relevant to anaphoric pronoun resolution 107

narrative ability 3
natural order 31
negative relation 12
new 139
non-iconic sequence 12, 31
number 106
number of connectives 69

obwohl 60
oder 60, 62
off-line 16
OLA 111
on-line 16
or 60, 62
oral narrative skills, development of 3
overuse of definiteness 166

perceived difficulty 48
personal pronouns 143
position in the previous sentence 106
position of the referring noun phrase 139
positive relation 12
possible way of encoding 141
post-posed clauses 51
post-pronominal 107, 108
pragmatic relation 12
pre- and postverbal positions 164
pre- vs. postverbal position 143
predictors of literacy 3
preferred way of encoding 141
pre-knowledge 17
pre-posed clauses 51
pre-pronominal 107, 108
presentational constructions 149
principle of chronological order 31
principle of natural 31
processing of coherence relations 15
pronominal profiles 183
pronouns 140

purpose coherence relations 60

referent introduction 148–152
referential coherence 2, 6
reintroduction 146
relational and referential coherence 2
relational coherence 1, 5
resolution of anaphoric pronouns 106
return sweep 43, 51, 52

salience 140
saliency 109
school texts 42
semantic relation 12
sequence coherence relations 60
SES 173
SLI 3
slope 118
so that 60, 62
social economic status 173
sodass 60, 62
sondern 62
specific language impairment 3
story complexity (SC) 91
story structure (SS) 90
strongly connective 12
subject-verb inversion 142
subordinating conjunctions 62
syntactic behaviour of connectives 62
syntactic classes of connectives 69, 70
syntactic functions of potential antecedents 106
syntactic role 106

temporal anteriority relations 30
temporal connectives 166
temporal relations 12
text genre 16
text organization and language (in)dependence 91
text topic 47
texts in school 3
that's why 45
then 60
theory of mind 172
therefore 58, 63
typically developing (TD) 85

um 60
und 13, 21, 28, 57, 62, 63

V2-constraint 142
VOCD 171

Wackernagel position 143
want 45
weakly connective 12
wegen 63
weil 14, 58, 60, 62
weil/denn 21
wenn 60, 62
when, if 62
whereas 60
word order in French 142
word order in German 142

zero pronouns 143
zuvor 15, 32

www.ingramcontent.com/pod-product-compliance
Lightning Source LLC
Chambersburg PA
CBHW071819230426
43670CB00013B/2500